Ecotourism: Impacts, Potentials and Possibilities?

Second Edition

Stephen Wearing & John Neil

University of Technology School of Leisure, Sport and Tourism Sydney, New South Wales, AUSTRALIA

ELSEVIER

AMSTERDAM · BOSTON · HEIDELBERG · LONDON · NEW YORK · OXFORD · PARIS · SAN DIEGO · SAN FRANCISCO · SINGAPORE ·SYDNEY · TOKYO
Butterworth-Heinemann is an imprint of Elsevier

Butterworth-Heinemann is an imprint of Elsevier

Linacre House, Jordan Hill, Oxford OX2 8DP, UK

The Boulevard, Langford Lane, Kidlington, Oxford OX5 1GB, UK

Second Edition 2009

Copyright © 2009 Elsevier Ltd. All rights reserved

Notice
No responsibility is assumed by the publisher for any injury and/or damage to persons or property as a matter of products liability, negligence or otherwise, or from any use or operation of any methods, products, instructions or ideas contained in the material herein.

British Library Cataloguing in Publication Data

A catalogue record for this book is available from the British Library

Library of Congress Cataloguing in Publication Data

A catalogue record for this book is available from the Library of Congress

ISBN 978-0-7506-6249-9

For information on all Butterworth-Heinemann publications visit our website at www.elsevierdirect.com

Printed and bound in Hungary

Working together to grow
libraries in developing countries

www.elsevier.com | www.bookaid.org | www.sabre.org

ELSEVIER   BOOK AID International   Sabre Foundation

**Ec otouri
an d Pos**

Table of Contents

PREFACE TO THE SECOND EDITION ix
INTRODUCTION xi

CHAPTER 1   Departure: surveying the ground
The ecotourism alternative 2
The nature of ecotourism 6
Sustainable tourism: conserving nature's base 8
Moving towards a definition 11
Further reading 14

CHAPTER 2   If ecotourism is not just an activity but a philosophy, which philosophy
Human nature 15
Exchanging value(s) 17
Toward ecocentrism: modern roots 20
Whose sustainability? 24
Ethics and (of) resource management... 28
Further reading 31

CHAPTER 3   Tourism development: government, industry, policy and planning
Sustainable tourism development 36
Planning and policy frameworks – who is involved
and how? 38
Government-led planning and policy initiatives 38
Integrated policy and planning.. 42
Industry-led planning and policy 46
Codes of practice.. 46
Compliance.. 51
Accreditation 52
Cooperative government and industry initiatives:
community involvement and cooperative approaches 54
Using policy to achieve best practice 56
Zoning... 59
Further reading 60

CHAPTER 4 Ecotourism and protected areas: visitor management for sustainability

Tourism and protected areas 65

Protected areas and capitalist realism 67

Tourism as a key 70

Sustainable management techniques 74

A short history of protected areas and sustainable management strategies 76

Carrying capacity.. 77

The recreation opportunity spectrum (ROS) 79

Limits of acceptable change (LAC)... 80

Visitor impact management (VIM) 82

Visitor activity management process (VAMP)................................ 83

Tourism optimisation management model (TOMM) 84

Managing visitor use.. 84

Use limitation 86

Zoning.. 88

Trial system design.. 89

Education 90

User fees and charges.. 92

Further reading 93

CHAPTER 5 The role of interpretation in achieving a sustainable future

Defining interpretation 96

Changing understanding, attitudes and behaviour........................ 98

Interpretation techniques 99

Visitor centres 99

Education centres.. 100

Displays and exhibits 100

Publications, websites and DVDs 101

Self-guided trails... 102

Guided tours 102

Principles for successful interpretation.. 103

The benefits of interpretation.. 104

Promotional benefits... 104

Recreational benefits 106

Educational benefits.. 107

Interpretation as a conservation management tool 108

Economic benefits... 109

Problems limiting interpretation.. 111

Further reading 114

CHAPTER 6 Linking conservation and communities: community benefits
and social costs

Ecotourism and local communities: conflict,
compromise or cooperation? 118

Ecotourism and local communities... 119

The issues and problems.. 121

Employment 126

Local planning and development.. 130

Further reading 135

CHAPTER 7 Ecotourism case studies

Case study 1. trekking on the Kokoda Track,
Papua New Guinea: enhancing decision-making
capacity for Kokoda communities. 137

Introduction.. 137

History 139

Tourism and Papua New Guinea (PNG) 140

Trekking and host community involvement.................................. 141

Trekking strategy 142

Planning for trekking development 144

Case study 2. porters and the trekking
industry of Nepal.. 146

Introduction.. 146

Nepalese porters 147

Porter representations in tourism marketing.............................. 148

Implications for ecotourism 150

Complexities of development.. 151

Complexities of local economies 152

Gaining the community's perspective 153

Discussion and conclusion 154

Case study 3. surfing tourism in Indonesia's
Mentawai Islands by Jess Ponting.. 156

Introduction.. 156

The Mentawai Islands and people 157

Tourism in the Mentawai Islands 158

Surfing tourism 158

Why are the Mentawai Islands so good for surfing? 159

Swell... 160

Wind 160

Reef.. 161

Surfing tourism in the mentawai 161
Recreational carrying capacity management............................. 164
The land issue... 167
Solutions?... 168
Further reading 169

CHAPTER 8 Marketing ecotourism: meeting and shaping expectations and demands

Ecotourism's place in the tourism industry 171
Marketing ecotourism: supplying demand or demanding supply? . 173
Marketing ecotourism 174
Ecological and social marketing... 176
The 'greening' market 177
Strengths in marketing ecotourism.. 181
Threats in marketing ecotourism 181
Opportunities in marketing ecotourism 183
Weaknesses in marketing ecotourism 184
Further reading 194

CHAPTER 9 Could the 'real' ecotourist please stand up!

Building a profile of the ecotourist 196
Tourist motivations 200
Tourism interactions 203
Economic differences 209
Further reading 211

CHAPTER 10 Ecotourism: a model for sustainable development?

Developing tourism partnerships.. 218
Sustainable models and ecotourism 222
Climate change and ecotourism 223
Volunteering and ecotourism 225
Impacts, potentials and possibilities 227
Further reading 228

GLOSSARY.. 229

A GUIDE TO ECOTOURISM AGENCIES AND OTHER SUSTAINABLE TOURISM RESOURCES.. 239

REFERENCES 241

INDEX.. 283

Preface to the Second Edition

It has now been 10 years since the first edition of *Ecotourism: Impacts, potentials and possibilities* was published. In that time ecotourism has been transformed both within tourism studies and more widely in the tourism industry. In the academic realm there has been an exponential growth in the publication of books on the topic of ecotourism, and in 2002 the first edition of the *Journal of Ecotourism* was published; 2002 was also proclaimed the International Year of Ecotourism by the United Nations. In his opening address marking the occasion, the World Tourism Organization (WTO) Secretary-General Francesco Frangialli noted the increasing growth of the ecotourism industry, and the prominent role ecotourism will play around the world in securing the future of the tourism industry.

There have also been significant developments in international environmental policy and international political agreement on a range of environmental issues. The most prominent being climate change, which has now become the single biggest issue on the international political agenda. In February 2007, the Intergovernmental Panel on Climate Change released its findings indicating that there is a 90% chance that global warming is caused by human-induced factors and that it is the biggest environmental catastrophe to ever face the planet. Also in 2007, Al Gore (the former United States Vice President and climate change documentary filmmaker) and Rajendra Prachandra (representing the Intergovernmental Panel on Climate Change) were co-recipients of the Nobel Peace Prize.

Confronted with these and other challenges ecotourism has gone from fringe to significant player within the tourism industry. The second edition of *Ecotourism: Impacts, potentials and possibilities* comes at an important time as ecotourism seeks to cement its place within the industry as a viable alternative to more mainstream approaches.

The second edition keeps its original structure with Chapter 7 containing three new major case studies, the first on the Kokoda Track, Papua New Guinea, the second on porters in Nepal and the third by Jess Ponting on surfing tourism in Indonesia's Mentawai Islands. This edition has added seven new mini case studies (which are found throughout the text) as well as a revision and update of those that were retained from the first edition. Given the breadth and depth of new knowledge published in ecotourism since the first edition, the new edition contains references from over 300 new sources.

Readers will also note an added 'Further readings' section at the end of each chapter for those wishing to pursue more in-depth and specific reading on the topics presented. There is also an updated glossary and another new section at the end of the book that provides web links to ecotourism organizations and other sustainable tourism resources.

Introduction

Ecotourism? A simple enough word but a complex and often contradictory concept: A fashion, a fad? – *Ecological travel is the 'next big thing'; the hippest way to travel is to backpack off the beaten track to experience 'nature' up close and personal (with all the luxuries of home included).*

Or a way for tourism to market itself in the twenty-first century where environmental issues now top the international political agenda? – *Conservation issues are now at the forefront of public opinion. Global warming, the decline of rainforests, loss of endangered species, and land degradation have galvanized public support for conservation worldwide.*

Whatever the origins, nature is calling and we are responding in droves. And ecotourists are leading the charge. But getting 'off the beaten track' often means that the track soon becomes a road, even a highway. And the beautiful wild spaces sought after by ecotourists are often fragile and sensitive to human impact, however 'lightly we tread'. One thing, however, is certain, the increasing global interest and exponential growth in ecotourism cannot simply be explained as another in a long line of recreational trends. Instead it reflects a fundamental shift in the way human beings view and engage with nature. We have begun with a lot of questions and no easy answers yet in sight. Where would you dare start? Well why not the word itself – *Ecotourism*: Within this word exists two seemingly contradictory meanings. Let us take the most obvious: *Tourism*. Tourism is currently the world's largest industry. For example, the number of international arrivals shows an evolution from a mere 25 million in 1950 to an estimated 806 million in 2005, corresponding to an average annual growth rate of 6.5% (WTO, 2007).

Travel and tourism consumption, investment, government spending, and exports are expected to grow by 4.6% (in real terms) and total US$6.5 trillion in 2006. The 10-year annualized growth (2007–2016) forecast is 4.2% per annum illustrating the outlook for strong long-term growth. The travel and tourism industry (direct and indirect) is expected to create nearly 10 million new jobs for the world in 2005, for a total of 234.3 million jobs dependent on travel and tourism worldwide (WTTC, 2006: 4).

For these reasons alone tourism is valued highly by many countries and in many cases holds a very prominent position in development strategies.

It is actively promoted and industry bodies are courted by governments due to its potential to significantly bolster foreign exchange and domestic employment.

Increases in leisure time, the growth in real income, mobility, technological improvements in communications and international transportation, and demographic changes in the West have led to the strong global demand for tourism (Godbey and Robinson, 1997). This growth has significant implications for developing countries, which are attracting an increasing share of global international tourist arrivals from 20.8% in 1973 to 42% in 2000 (WTO, 2002). This represents an important source of foreign exchange, as tourism has become the principle export earner for 83% of developing countries. For the world's 40 poorest countries, tourism is the second most important source of foreign exchange after oil (Mastny, 2001).

Travel to developing countries has been greatly stimulated by deregulation in the airline industry, leading to increased competition and cheaper air travel, which puts the world within easier reach of the modern-day tourist. Over one-third of the people who now holiday abroad do so in the developing world because it offers a cheaper alternative to domestic holidays or holidays in other developed countries. Moreover the majority of the world's developing nations tend to be situated in climates which attract 'sun-lust' tourists wanting to escape the northern hemisphere winter.

And somewhere in this tourism 'explosion' lies ecotourism. 'Ecotourism' has evolved into a type of specialty travel, incorporating a diverse (and often bewildering) array of activities and tourism types, from bird watching, scientific study, photography, diving, trekking, to regeneration of damaged ecosystems. It is a broad and loose garment this word 'ecotourism'. For some it is a subset of 'nature-based' tourism activities; for others it is a 'niche' market, a specific type of 'special interest tourism'. In a relatively short period of time it has caught the imagination of many local communities, governments, and international environmental organizations. Ecotourism has also been able to capitalize on the increased motivations to experience and preserve natural environments, which stem in part from more fundamental changes in societal values (Blamey, 1995; Diamantis, 2004). Research indicates that 60–90% of USA, Australian, and British tourists consider active protection of the environment, including support of local communities, to be a part of a tourist destination responsibilities (Chafe, 2005). The continuation of these fundamental changes, particularly in developing countries, should lead to continued growth in demand for ecotourism (Jenner and Smith, 1992; Higgins, 1996).

Estimates of ecotourism's growth are extremely variable at the present time, but range anywhere between 10 and 30%[1] (Kallen, 1990; Vickland, 1989). Despite this variability, the tourism industry has wholly embraced ecotourism, even to the extent of the United Nations designating 2002 'The Year of Ecotourism'.

In a multifaceted world something can mean anything depending on how the light strikes it. So let us narrow the prism and focus on the prefix – *eco* – from the word 'ecology' which itself is derived from the Greek word *oikos* meaning house or habitat. The environment that we humans inhabit is, at its most fundamental, our home, our dwelling, or our life support. And despite the relative newness of the term, ecotourism's origins are deeply rooted in a form of environmental experience, as both a philosophy and an experience, and its philosophical heritage is embraced by conservationists and environmentalists alike. The environmental movement was born from the nature conservation movement, which recognized that nature is essential to human well-being. In recent years this conviction has been strengthened by the scientific understanding that biodiversity is essential to not only well-being, but to human survival also. Many have also articulated the need for nature to be conserved regardless of any utility or value to humans but because nature has a right to exist and conversely the human species does not have the right to determine the fate of all other species (Nash, 1989).

But tourism involves travel away from our origin, from our individual homes, into dwellings that are not our own, but that may be constructed specifically for tourists; to places that we tread upon which are a life support for 'others' both human and non-human. The world is a stage across which wealthy people stride, relentlessly striving to satisfy our desire, traveling across the globe to experience these 'others' – cultures, nature, sights, sounds and smells – to see sights that are unusual, to explore the unknown, the alien, the 'magical'. The not-here.

This book embarks on a journey of our own, a journey in understanding that will, through the following pages, take us across the globe. We will be making stops along the way: visiting countries such as Australia, Laos, Nepal, the Arctic, Indonesia, Papua New Guinea and Africa. The initial part of this journey takes place in Chapter 1 where we will discuss ecotourism's key principles. Fundamentally ecotourism involves travel to relatively undisturbed or protected natural areas, fostering understanding, appreciation and conservation of the flora, fauna, geology and ecosystems of an area. The

---

[1] As we shall see, the diversity of tourism forms and controversies in classification partly explain the difficulties and variability in estimating the size of the ecotourism market.

fauna, geology and ecosystems of an area highlight the nature-based element of ecotourism. But ecotourism is not defined by this relationship alone. Biological and physical features are central to ecotourism therefore the conservation of natural areas and sustainable resource management are therefore essential for planning, development and management of ecotourism. However, it also involves the notion that the activity of ecotourism must positively contribute to conservation in the destination area or host community. The understanding that ecotourism has the potential to create support for conservation objectives in both the host community and in the visitor alike, through establishing and sustaining links between the tourism industry, local communities and protected areas will provide the basis for our journey and leads us into understanding the central issues of conservation and sustainability of natural and social environments.

Chapter 2 places ecotourism within its historical context to connect it to the major philosophic and social currents that have contributed to its development. We focus here specifically on the human–nature relationship and the interaction between them as this will help us to understand the shift in the way nature is valued, both historically and philosophically, and how ecotourism fits into this change in values.

In the dominant free market economies of the developed world policy implications are heavily influenced by the interplay of government regulation and market forces. Chapter 3 examines why tourism is attractive for governments particularly in its potential for providing an alternative to traditional industry such as forestry, mining, fishing and agriculture. However, in many cases tourism has not lived up to its high expectations as its benefits are often circumscribed by the significant impacts tourism engenders upon ecosystems and local communities. Tourism is often promoted by government or industry without an overall strategy, without adequate attention to legislative frameworks, without consultation or inclusion of local communities and without effective protected area management plans. We will examine the key policy issues related to ecotourism including a discussion of mechanisms to ensure that it does not exceed its sustainable base, in moving toward understanding the provision of infrastructure for development and the policy and institutional prerequisites for planning and managing ecotourism.

Nowhere are the conflicting views over ecotourism more evident than the current debate over the function and purpose of protected areas. It is a conflict over two primary orientations; 'preservation' versus 'use' and tourism in protected areas embodies precisely this dilemma. Such an opposition is illustrated and reinforced through accepted institutional arrangements in which tourism and conservation goals are pursued by independent organizations. The current focus of the debate on tourism in parks is the extension of a long controversy, a controversy that has existed since the conception of protected areas and equivalent reserves. The imperative for conservation advocates becomes *how* to conserve rather than whether or not to conserve. In this way ecotourism, as a sustainable development strategy, is increasingly being turned to as part of a political philosophy for protected area managers and conservation agencies as a means of providing practical outcomes in the struggle to provide a basis for continued protection for these areas.

Chapter 5 introduces the key elements of interpretation and education which help us to differentiate ecotourism from other forms of nature-based tourism. A focus on the dimensions of visitor experience reveals that the visitor is concerned not with simply looking at a setting or object, but with feeling and realizing some of its *value*. In this way, interpretation is oriented toward a visitor's cognitive and emotional state in order to raise awareness, enhance understanding, lead to positive environmental behaviors and hopefully, clarify or enlarge each participant's perspective and attitude. In this way, interpretation is essential to conservation goals and therefore central to ecotourism.

The tourism industry makes extensive use of natural assets such as forests, reefs, beaches, mountains and parks, but what does it contribute to the management of these assets? The provision of tourism infrastructure, and the costs of managing the impact of tourism on host communities, is often borne by the environment, the community itself and the government. Local communities are particularly vulnerable to the deleterious impacts of tourism development – especially indigenous or traditional custodians – as they directly experience the socio-cultural impacts of tourism. In many cases indigenous cultures are used extensively to promote destinations to overseas markets yet many indigenous people rightly feel that the tourism industry has a poor track record, in disregarding their legitimate interests and rights, and profiting from their cultural knowledge and heritage.

Chapter 6 explores ecotourism's relationship to local communities, particularly as an alternative form of development that is able to satisfy conservation and sustainability objectives. Features of the natural and cultural environments and supportive host communities are the foundations of a successful industry. Neglect of conservation and quality of life issues threatens the very basis of local populations and a viable and sustainable tourism industry.

Chapter 7 presents three new case studies to give an operational context to what has been presented in the previous chapters of the book. The first case study investigates trekking on the Kokoda Track in Papua New Guinea. Trekking and tourism in this part of the world is a wholly new phenomenon, having only begun 10 years ago. The case study follows the drafting and implementation of the Ecotrekking Strategy for the area which emphasizes the involvement and ownership of the venture by local communities along the track and the conservation of the areas unique environmental and cultural conditions. The second case study like the first investigates trekking, albeit in the much more developed context of Nepal. It is argued that an important issue of sustainability for tourism in Nepal is the safety and treatment of the local porters who are integral to the industry as they ferry loads of food, water, fuel, tents and trekkers' personal belongings over some of the most rugged terrain in the world. The third case study by Jess Ponting explores surfing tourism in the Mentawai Islands of Indonesia. Surfing tourism has grown rapidly in this part of the world due to the significant attentions the islands have received in the surf media over the last 15 years. Living conditions in the Mentawai Islands are highly impoverished; however, local communities have been largely excluded from participating in the industry in any meaningful way despite legislation by the provincial government. Ponting outlines an alternative vision for how local Mentawai Islander's could be involved by developing linkages between surfing tourism and local transport, retail and agricultural industries.

The global political agenda is increasingly being dominated by economic principles which serve to actively promote the ever increasing consumption of resources in the West, even at a time of growing environmental consciousness. Chapter 8 explores the relationship between ecotourism and one of the fundamental tools to enhance consumption and marketing. We examine the structure and nature of marketing in the tourism industry, focusing particularly on understanding and evaluating the connection between ecotourism and marketing – the issue of supply versus demand-driven marketing. Pivotal to understanding the marketing relationship to ecotourism are the implications for protected areas, conservation and local communities. Ecotourism marketing has been surrounded by much confusion and controversy as it attempts to take into account the dual objectives of protected areas and local communities on the one hand and those of the tourism industry on the other.

By analyzing the market of ecotourism we find a new group of tourism clients, the ecotourists. In Chapter 9 we examine who they are and what they are demanding. We will explore the characteristics that differentiate ecotourists through an analysis of tourist motivation, demographic and psychographic characteristics, the needs of ecotourists, the images and attitudes ecotourists ascribe to a destination, and the influence of social, cultural and physical environments.

Ecotourism is argued as a catalyst for change and this book will explore broad issues such as ecology, biodiversity, bioregionalism, economic rationalism, equity of access, approaches to management of protected areas, social policy, directions of the tourism industry and local communities. Central to all of these areas is the question of sustainability and its centrality to development. Sustainable development underpins questions of resource use, not only in providing income benefits to a region but also for the preservation of social infrastructure and biosphere conservation. Chapter 10 discusses these issues in relation to ecotourism as a model for sustainable development.

But what of the future? Despite ecotourism's potential as a model for sustainable development we need to be aware of ecotourism's future direction. Frameworks are needed in which to evaluate ecotourism, mindful that economic benefits from tourism often create insufficient incentives for local communities to support conservation. Benefits are often offset in the eyes of the local communities by the intrusion of tourists, greater income inequality within and between local communities, increased pollution, sequestering of profits from outsiders and rising local prices.

Without continual questioning and evaluation of alternative evaluative frameworks we risk losing the impetus of change that ecotourism offers. Traditional approaches are often resistant to new approaches to operational and institutional arrangements. Without adequate regulation of private sector activities and sound protected area management, ecotourism development may have adverse impacts on the resource base upon which it depends. However, a viable tourism practice needs to address the imperatives of the market. Alternative approaches in areas like research, management, marketing and planning can provide new answers to perennial questions that may keep ecotourism at the cutting edge of change in society.

In spite of the complexities of these issues, ecotourism is one of the few areas where the link between economic development and conservation of natural areas is clear and direct and we need to keep this at the forefront of our minds as we undertake our learning journey.

CHAPTER 1

Departure:
Surveying the Ground

Despite the conflicting interpretations and convenient deployment of the term 'ecotourism' within the tourism industry, one thing is certain, the increasing global interest and growth in ecotourism cannot simply be explained as another in a long line of recreational trends. Instead it reflects a fundamental shift in the way human beings view and engage with nature and tourism (Chafe, 2005, 2007).

This chapter will briefly trace the evolution of the ecotourism phenomenon and some of the definitional debates which have marked its evolution. Originally conceived as an alternative to the increasing threat posed to both the culture and the environment of destination areas by mass tourism, the original emphasis of ecotourism was on low key, unobtrusive tourism which has minimal impacts on natural ecosystems. However, the term 'alternative tourism' is interpreted by various authors in widely differing and sometimes openly contradictory ways. For some it is up-market package tours of rich people to exotic destinations, mostly wilderness areas, young people carrying rucksacks wandering the globe with limited financial means, or travel that gives emphasis to contact and understanding between locals and tourists, as well as the environment (e.g., Butler, 1990; Cohen, 1972; Newsome et al., 2002; Priporas and Kamenidou, 2003; Richards and Wilson, 2004).

For these reasons a definition of ecotourism, particularly as alternative tourism, is both contentious and difficult to determine with precision and it has been debated contentiously for a number of years (e.g., Donohoe and Needham, 2006; Fennell, 2001). For clarity, let us begin by unpacking the many elements that belong under the term 'ecotourism.' The term itself encompasses a wide range of elements and we will be covering each in detail throughout this book:

- a form of 'alternative tourism' opposed to mass tourism

- a particular philosophical orientation toward nature

CONTENTS

The Ecotourism Alternative

The Nature of Ecotourism

Sustainable Tourism: Conserving Nature's Base

Moving Toward a Definition

Further Reading

1

- tourists characterized by particular motivations
- touristic practices
- a touristic product
- levels of technology
- solutions to planning
- an approach to local, regional, national, and international politics
- a strategy for sustainable development

THE ECOTOURISM ALTERNATIVE

The word 'alternative' logically implies its opposite. 'Alternative tourism' then is contrary to that which is seen as negative or detrimental about conventional tourism: it is characterized by its attempt at minimizing the perceived negative environmental and socio-cultural impacts of people at leisure in the promotion of radically different approaches to conventional tourism.[1] Therefore the terminology of alternative and mass tourism is mutually interdependent, each relying on a series of value laden judgments that themselves structure the definitional content of the terms. In this way the concept of alternative tourism can itself be as broad and vague as its diametrical opposite with many divergent leisure types being classified as alternative tourism, including adventure holidays, hiking holidays, or the solitary journeys undertaken by globe trotters. Some authors even going so far as to suggest that anything other than mass tourism classifies as alternative tourism (Newsome et al., 2002).

Dernoi (1988: 253) initially defined alternative tourism by accommodation type: 'In alternative tourism the client receives accommodation directly in, or at the home of, the host with, eventually, other services and facilities offered there.' However, he then went on to list a number of other features by which alternative tourism might be distinguished from 'mass tourism': 'Simply stated, AT (alternative tourism)/CBT (community-based tourism) is a privately offered set of hospitality services (and features), extended to visitors, by individuals, families, or a local community. A prime aim of AT/

---

[1] Like 'alternative tourism,' 'conventional tourism' itself has been designated by varying terms, the most prominent being conventional mass tourism (CMT – Mieczkowski, 1995) and mass tourism (MT – Butler, 1990).

CBT is to establish direct personal/cultural intercommunication and understanding between host and guest' (Dernoi, 1988: 89). Similarly, for the ECTWT (Ecumenical Coalition of Third World Tourism): 'alternative tourism is a process which promotes a just form of travel between members of different communities. It seeks to achieve mutual understanding, solidarity, and equality amongst participants' (Holden, 1984: 15). The stress here is on the facilitation and improvement of contacts between hosts and guests, especially through the organization of well-prepared special interest tours, rather than on actual development of facilities.

Another body of literature dealing with tourism typologies gives greater attention to particular variations in terms of tourism classifications, often with a particular tourism form being placed in three or more categories. However, 'alternative tourism' rarely occurs specifically as one of the classes in the typology literature, which reflects the often disparate and very broad characteristics that it may encompass. Mieczkowski (1995) does identify 'alternative tourism' as a tourism type but only in its relation as one of the two broad categories along a spectrum of tourism types. The first is Conventional Mass Tourism (CMT), which has prevailed on the market for some time. The second broad category is that of Alternative Tourism (AT), a flexible generic category that contains a multiplicity of various forms that have one feature in common – they are alternatives to CMT. That is, they are not associated with mass large-scale tourism but are essentially small scale, low-density, dispersed in non-urban areas, and they cater to special interest groups of people with mainly above average education and with relatively high-disposable incomes.

As to the specific forms of AT, Mieczkowski (1995) distinguishes such forms as cultural, educational, scientific, adventure, and agri-tourism with rural, ranch, and farm subsets *(see Fig. 1.1)*. Significantly, there is some overlap with CMT but the main criteria of distinction are the scale and character of the impacts. Another overlap occurs between the various types of AT themselves. Cultural tourism, for example, is to a large extent educational and ecotourism is aligned with nature-based tourism. Thus Mieczkowski (1995) finds it difficult to place ecotourism in the context of AT because, while not coinciding directly with cultural tourism, it overlaps with the educational, scientific, adventure, and agri-tourism forms; and more recently this would include pro-poor tourism and volunteer tourism.

Rather than entering into an increasingly complex debate over classifications of particular tourism forms as alternative, specific features are common to alternative tourism and we have identified several of the key characteristics below *(see Table 1.1)*. Although not considered to be

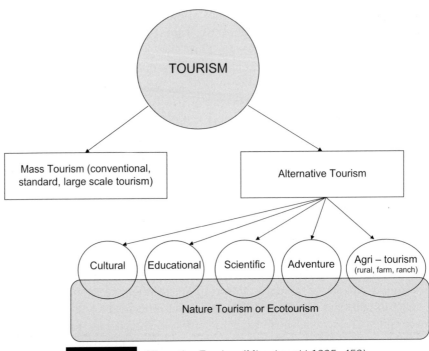

FIGURE 1.1 *Alternative Tourism (Mieczkowski 1995: 459).*

exhaustive, they are included here to provide the conceptual ideas and specific practices of forms of tourism that are in opposition to 'mass tourism.'

Thus, in its most general sense, alternative tourism can be broadly defined as a form of tourism that sets out to be consistent with natural, social, and community values and which allows both hosts and guests to enjoy positive and worthwhile interaction and shared experiences.

Against the above broad characteristics we can begin to see ecotourism as a form of alternative tourism. In its simplest terms, ecotourism can be generally described as a low key, minimal impact; interpretative tourism where conservation, understanding, and appreciation of the environment and cultures visited are sought. It is a specialized area of tourism, involving travel to natural areas, or areas where human presence is minimal, with the ecotourist involved in the ecotourism experience expressing an explicit motivation to satisfy the need for environmental, social and/or cultural education and awareness through visiting and experiencing the natural area.

Table 1.1	Features of Alternative Tourism

- The attempted preservation, protection, and enhancement of the quality of the resource base which is fundamental to tourism itself
- The fostering and active promotion of development, in relation to additional visitor attractions and infrastructure, with roots in the specific locale and developed in ways which complement local attributes
- The endorsement of infrastructure, hence economic growth, when and where it improves local conditions and not where it is destructive or exceeds the carrying capacity of the natural environment or the limits of the social environment whereby the quality of community life is adversely affected (e.g., Bıcak et al., 2006; Cox, 1985: 6–7; Yum, 1984)
- Tourism which attempts to minimize its impact upon the environment, is ecologically sound, and avoids the negative impacts of many large-scale tourism developments undertaken in the areas which have not previously been developed (e.g., Bilsen, 1987; Gonsalves, 1984; Howard, 1999; Saglio, 1979; Travis, 1985)
- An emphasis on, not only ecological sustainability, but also cultural sustainability. That is, tourism which does not damage the culture of the host community, encouraging a respect for the cultural realities experienced by the tourists through education and organized 'encounters' (e.g., Holden, 2007; Semple, 2005)

Hector Ceballos-Lascurain is widely acknowledged as having coined the term ecotourism. In 1981, Ceballos-Lascurain began using the Spanish term *turisimo ecologico* to designate forms of ecological tourism. This term then became shortened to *ecoturisimo* in 1983 and he used the word in discussions in his capacity as President of PRONATURA, conservation Non-Government Organization (NGO), and Director General of SEDUE, the Mexican Ministry of Urban Development and Ecology. At the time he was lobbying for the conservation of rainforest areas in the Mexican state of Chiapas and a primary strategy for maintaining the integrity of forest ecosystems involved the promotion of ecological tourism in the region. He emphasized that ecotourism could become a very important tool for conservation.

The first appearance of the word in the written form was in the March–April 1984 edition of *'American Birds'* as an advertisement for a tourist operation run by Ceballos-Lascurain. His definition as we now know it first appeared in the literature in 1987 in a paper entitled *'The future of ecotourismo'* which was reprinted in the *Mexico Journal* of 27 January 1988 (Ceballos-Lascurain, n.d: 2).

Ceballos-Lascurain identified ecotourism as a form of travel in which the natural environment is the primary focus and it is this element which provides us with a simple, yet core, starting point in understanding the ecotourism phenomenon; particularly as a specific form of alternative tourism. The centrality of the natural environment to ecotourism comprises two main facets:

- It involves travel to unspoilt natural environments.

- This travel is predominantly for experiencing the natural environment.

Ecotourism's focus on the natural environment has, in recent years, facilitated its evolution into a catchphrase that encompasses numerous tourism forms including 'nature tourism,' 'wilderness tourism,' 'low impact tourism,' and 'sustainable tourism' to name a few.[2] These diverse forms of tourism all focus on the natural environment to some extent and, although closely aligned and related to ecotourism, need to be distinguished from ecotourism as there are a number of dimensions to nature-based tourism. Those two main paradigms have emerged here, ecotourism, which is a demand-driven concept limited to nature-based tourism; and sustainable tourism, which is a supply-sided view characterized by industry regulations. Nevertheless our concern here is to what degree the tourist experience depends upon nature.

THE NATURE OF ECOTOURISM

Tourism activity is expected to grow by 4.3% per annum in real terms between 2008 and 2017 (WTO, 2007). Ecotourism/nature-based tourism has become the fastest growing sector of the tourism industry growing 3 times faster than the industry as a whole (Huybers and Bennett, 2002; International Ecotourism Society, 2008). There can be no doubting of the increasing trends in environmental concern allied with the historically prevalent trend of travel as a form of escape to nature, driven by 'the pressures of urban living [which] encourage people to seek solitude with nature' therefore increasing 'the numbers of visitors to national parks and other protected areas' (Ceballos-Lascurain, 1990: 1).

There are a number of dimensions to nature-based tourism. All forms of travel to natural areas are not necessarily ecotourism, but this provides a useful step in differentiating nature-based tourism from ecotourism and

---

[2] Other examples include green tourism (Jones, 1987), 'nature-oriented tourism' (Durst and Ingram, 1989), 'soft tourism' (Mader, 1999), and 'defensive tourism' (Krippendorf, 1982, 1987).

gives us a number of levels at which to distinguish the relationship between specific tourism activities and nature:

- those activities (experiences) that are dependent on nature

- those activities (experiences) that are enhanced by nature

- those activities (experiences) for which the natural setting is incidental

There are several classes of nature-based tourism, each utilizing a combination of these dimensions. Bird watching, for example, can provide a 'pleasant and relaxing holiday based around a general interest in nature and the environment' (Curtin and Wilkes, 2005: 455). So that without the natural environment it would be difficult to carry out the activity. Similarly, camping is an activity/experience which is often enhanced by nature. Most people would prefer to camp in some type of natural setting rather than on the side of a busy road. Therefore nature is an integral part of these experiences but not the fundamental motivation for them.

This is in contrast to non-specialist nature tourists whose interests may fundamentally lie in a desire to experience 'somewhere different from home.' These tourists may also have an interest in nature and a sense that a part of improving the quality of life is related to interaction with nature (Tonnini et al., 2006). However, fundamental concerns of ecotourism include environmental degradation, impact on local communities, and the need for high-quality tourism management for achievable sustainability (Ioannides et al., 2001). Clearly the overall definition of nature-based tourism is not totally appropriate for defining ecotourism.

Within this auspice we find 'Low Impact Tourism' (LIT) which is a specific form of tourism that enhances our understanding of ecotourism's nature base. Low Impact Tourism focuses on establishing indigenous natural resource management through private sector incentives and investment in rural village-based tourism business infrastructure and on training villagers and rural area dwellers to take part in the tourism business. LIT is supply-driven (see Chapter 8), that is, it only takes on as many visitors as the cultural and physical environment can cope with. It is concerned explicitly with 'social impact, economic development, and natural management of the supplier country and destination sites' (Lillywhite and Lillywhite, 1990: 90). Being supply-driven, LIT places control and regulation of tourism development into the hands of the destination country, rather than the travel and tour operators who are reliant on a demand-driven rationale (e.g., Speelman, 1996). Thus, it is a fundamental consideration that LIT should not degrade the cultures they are involved with. Control by a destination country of tourism development requires a full and broad commitment. It requires the need for regulations to protect the environment and the quality and integrity of the tourism experience, the establishment of carrying capacities, a large percentage of small operators as suppliers, value-added tourism, and a sensitively developed infrastructure (e.g., Brunet et al., 2001).

The goals of LIT then are to establish, coordinate, and mutually support conservation and tourism policy, to fund park's development and management and foster indigenous involvement of protected areas, and to improve village standards in tour destination areas (Lillywhite and Lillywhite, 1990: 92). The characteristics of LIT include

- local management
- the provision of a quality travel product and tourism experience
- active valuation of culture
- a training emphasis
- a dependency on natural and cultural resources
- the integration of development and conservation (Lillywhite and Lillywhite, 1990)

The principles of LIT are aligned strongly with ecotourism but significantly, LIT has no specification location. Whether it is a remote rainforest village or a specialized chocolate making plant, its main focus is on the impact on the location of travel experiences. The important point to make here is that LIT does not necessarily take place in relatively undisturbed natural areas, while ecotourism generally does.

SUSTAINABLE TOURISM: CONSERVING NATURE'S BASE

The natural environment is central to ecotourism which has a focus on biological and physical features. The conservation of natural areas and sustainable resource management are therefore essential for planning, development, and management of ecotourism. Valentine (1993) draws attention to the 'two-way interaction' between ecotourism and the environment upon which it depends, by suggesting that one characteristic of ecotourism is that it is both contributory to conservation as well as enjoyment of nature, thus merging these two dimensions. That is, ecotourism involves a focus on nature as the primary motivation for travel with the activities undertaken by tourists on the ecotour being based on furthering knowledge and awareness of nature. However, it also involves the notion that the activity of ecotourism must positively contribute to conservation in the destination area or host community. Planning for ecotourism is based on resource limitations as ecotourism opportunities will be lost if the resilience of an area and the ability of its communities to absorb impacts are exceeded, or if its biodiversity and physical appearance are altered significantly. Achieving this balance is a difficult challenge requiring ongoing monitoring of the resource base and a continued community interest in seeing such projects succeed (Cusack and Dixon, 2006).

Therefore an essential feature of ecotourism is sustainability – and sustainable development by implication – and we shall be dealing with these issues in detail in Chapters 3 and 4. Suffice it here to say that, despite the ambiguity surrounding it, the concept of sustainability is fundamental to the positioning of any tourist experience as alternative. The Bruntland Report introduced the concept of sustainable development, defining it as 'development that meets the needs of the present without compromising the ability of future generations to meet their own needs' (Mieczkowski, 1995: 457). Sustainability requires the establishment of baseline data from which change and rates of change can be measured (Jennings, 2004; World Wide Fund for Nature, 1992). Environmentally sustainable tourism has come to be fundamentally identified with alternative tourism. Butler defines environmentally sustainable tourism as follows:

> *tourism which is developed and maintained in an area (community, environment) in such a manner and at such a scale that it remains viable over an infinite period and does not degrade or alter the environment (human and physical) in which it exists to such a degree that it prohibits the successful development and well being of other activities and processes. (1991: 29)*

In a later article Butler (1999) suggested that sustainable 'tourism' is just one component of development in general and that it needs to be thought of as one element that is a part of a larger mix. Taking a single sectoral approach Butler notes

> *is something that is at odds with the concept of sustainable development, which by its very nature is holistic and multisectoral. Thus sustainable tourism is not automatically the same as tourism developed in line with the principles of sustainable development. As long as it is taken to be so, then ambiguity and confusion will continue. The need to define the type of tourism being studied or developed*

beyond the catch-all of 'sustainable' is therefore crucial, if knowledge about the sustainability of tourism is to be expanded. (1999: 12)

According to The World Tourism Organization (WTO, 2004) sustainable tourism should

1. Make optimal use of environmental resources that constitute a key element in tourism development, maintaining essential ecological processes and helping to conserve natural heritage and biodiversity.

2. Respect the socio-cultural authenticity of host communities, conserve their built and living cultural heritage and traditional values, and contribute to inter-cultural understanding and tolerance.

3. Ensure viable, long-term economic operations, providing socio-economic benefits to all stakeholders that are fairly distributed, including stable employment and income-earning opportunities and social services to host communities, and contributing to poverty alleviation.

Sustainable tourism development requires the informed participation of all relevant stakeholders, as well as strong political leadership to ensure wide participation and consensus building. Achieving sustainable tourism is a continuous process and it requires constant monitoring of impacts, introducing the necessary preventive and/or corrective measures whenever necessary. It should also maintain a high level of tourist satisfaction and ensure a meaningful experience for the tourists, raising their awareness about sustainability issues and promoting sustainable tourism practices amongst them (WTO, 2004).

Having minimal impacts implies that ecotours operate on a small scale thus requiring little specialized infrastructure and therefore not contributing to damaging the environment on which ecotourism (and all forms of tourism) depends. For as Butler puts it if ecotourism damages the natural resource then it is not ecotourism (Butler, 1992). Similarly Bragg (1990) states that ecotourism has by definition minimal environmental impact, since unspoiled natural environments are the attraction of this type of tourism. Fortunately, after much discussion at international conferences[3] conservationists and responsible tourism operators now believe that conservation is an essential part of any definition of ecotourism. As we saw in

---

[3] Chief among these were held in 1992: United Nations Earth Summit; International Union for Conservation of Nature and Natural Resources (IUCN); IV World Congress on National Parks and Protected Areas.

Introduction, the 'eco' prefix is derived from the word 'ecology.' Thus, to be considered as ecotourism, an activity or experience must positively contribute to the environment: The naive assumption that tourism which is nature-focused will automatically be sustainable is often incorrect and also harmful, if the environment has not at least achieved a net benefit toward its sustainability and ecological integrity, then the activity is not ecotourism (Butler, 1992). However, the 'environment' here refers not only to the natural environment – flora, fauna, landforms, and atmospheric considerations – but also to the social, economic, scientific, managerial, and political elements. The International Ecotourism Society (2007) concurs with this principle, stating that 'ecotourism must raise sensitivity to host countries' political, environmental, and social climate.' Furthermore ecotourists must contribute to a sustainable future for the destinations they visit (O'Neill, 1991).

MOVING TOWARD A DEFINITION

Ecotourism then includes four fundamental elements: Firstly, the notion of movement or travel from one location to another. This travel should be restricted to relatively undisturbed or protected natural areas as ecotourism's focus is fundamentally on experiencing natural areas. Protected areas are a critical ingredient in ecotourism because of their natural, historical, and cultural richness (Cengiz, 2007). Ceballos-Lascurain (1990: 2) adds that protected or undisturbed natural areas offer the 'best guarantee for encountering sustained natural features and attractions.' This leads to the second component which must be included in a definition of ecotourism that ecotourism is nature-based. Activities such as business travel, travel to cities, conventional beach holidays, and sporting holidays cannot be considered as ecotourism as their focus is not primarily on an experience based on the natural environment of the area visited. As Cater (2006) notes, despite the plethora of definitions as to what actually constitutes ecotourism, the most common denominator is that it is nature-based. Swanson adds

> Ecotourism is travel, often to developing countries, to relatively undisturbed natural areas for study, enjoyment or volunteer assistance that concerns itself with the flora, fauna, geology and ecosystems of an area – as well as the people (caretakers) who live nearby, their needs, their culture and the relationship to the land. (1992: 2)

This definition encompasses the fundamental components of ecotourism, with only one query: 'relatively undisturbed natural areas.' Ecotourism can rejuvenate nature as well. Rehabilitating degraded areas as a result of human activity can be classified as ecotourism as in this case there is a definite contribution to the environment and a direct benefit to the local community. There is an ethical impetus for tourists traveling to these areas in volunteering their services to the environment. Common examples include protecting endangered animal habitats with a range of measures, removing litter from protected areas, planting native species, eradicating noxious weeds, and carrying out flora and fauna surveys (e.g., Buckley, 2003; Davies, 2002).

Thirdly, ecotourism is conservation-led. As a segment of the tourism industry ecotourism has emerged as a result of 'increasing global concern for disappearing cultures and ecosystems' (Kutay, 1990: 34) and as a repudiation of 'inappropriate tourism development' which 'can degrade a protected area and have unanticipated economic, social, or environmental effects on the surrounding lands' (Ceballos-Lascurain, 1990: 1). Ecotourism then includes cultural and environmental awareness, environmental conservation, and empowerment of local people upon whose resources ecotourism depends (Chafe, 2007). Ecotourism aims to take small groups of people to natural or protected areas with a minimum impact on the physical, social, and cultural environments. Further to the notion of conservation is the idea that ecotourism will 'contribute to a sustainable future' (O'Neill, 1991: 25) and that ecotourism strategies play a supporting role in wider development strategies (Butler, 1999) in the form of economic returns or volunteer assistance. In this way, 'ecotourism has the potential to foster conservation of natural resources by increasing the awareness of people in the importance of the natural resources' (Swanson, 1992: 2) and for this reason, the notion of conservation must be included in a definition of ecotourism (Merino, 2006). Ecotourists are, as a general rule, more concerned with environmental impacts than mass tourists and as such ecotourism 'promotes a greater understanding and respect of cultures, heritage, and the natural environment – and people usually protect what they respect' (Richardson, 1991: 244). In essence, ecotourism experiences are sustainable in respect to both the environment and local populations, their culture, needs, and desires.

The fourth idea that must be included in a definition of ecotourism is that it has an educative role. The ecotourist generally has an awareness of nature-related issues and a desire to learn more about the environment (Galley and Clifton, 2004). Tisdell and Wilson (2005) have similarly identified the importance of learning and the interaction of tourists with wildlife as contributors to their pro-conservation sentiments and actions. Therefore, a great emphasis is placed on nature appreciation, education, and interpretation through the explanation of 'concepts, meaning, and inter-relationships of natural phenomena' (McNeely and Thorsell, 1989: 37).[4]

Ecotourism's dependency on nature, as opposed to other forms of tourism where nature is incidental to the experience, includes the touristic motivation of satisfying an educational need which is derived from interactions with the natural environment.[5] Ecotourism operators may therefore be expected to provide an appropriate level of environmental and cultural interpretation, usually through the employment of appropriately qualified guides and the provision of environmental information both prior to and during the trip. This educative role refers not only to the tourists themselves but also to industry operators and local communities: 'The need to disseminate information to tourists on appropriate behavior in fragile social and ecologic settings is increasingly being recognized as the responsibility of industry operators' (Blangy and Epler-Wood, 1992: 1). By their active participation, ecotourists are educated to appreciate the importance of natural and cultural conservation. Ecotourism attracts people who wish to interact with the environment and, in varying degrees, develop their knowledge, awareness, and appreciation of it. Ecotourism can also provide local people the opportunity to learn about and use the area and attractions that tourists come to visit (Wallace, 1992). Ecotourism sustainability is more likely to occur if 'community leaders develop and support programs for families and children to learn more about environmental conservation and preservation' (Vincent and Thompson, 2002: 153). For the host community, ecotourism may also stimulate renewed appreciation of the unique value of their own cultural traditions as a result of the interest shown by tourists (Cole, 2007: 955; Kutay, 1990: 40).

Ecotourism then has the potential to be a vehicle for the enhancement of an understanding of environmental values, supportive of local communities' economies, and sense of cultural identity, as well as an activity which has arisen due to a fundamental shift in the way nature is viewed by the society.

---

[4] Grossberg et al. (2003) argue that some tourists may become incidental ecotourists if some attempt is made to provide environmental education at tourism destinations, which has been found to motivate them to become advocates for conservation of endangered species.

[5] Consider, for example, a family on holiday to a resort in Hawaii. They each use the foreshore for leisure, pleasure, and recreation such as swimming, running, reading and so on. Had a component of their visit been for purpose of learning about the sand dune ecosystem, then they would be considered as ecotourists.

FURTHER READING

Fennell, D.A. (2001). A content analysis of ecotourism definitions. *Current Issues in Tourism*, 4(5), 403–421.

Donohoe, H.M. & Needham, R.D. (2006). Ecotourism: the evolving contemporary definition. *Journal of Ecotourism*, 5(3), 192–210.

Both of these journal articles explore various definitions of ecotourism by reviewing classic and recent literature.

Ceballos-Lascurain, H. (1993). Ecotourism as a worldwide phenomenon. In *Ecotourism: A Guide for Planners and Managers* (K. Lindberg, & D.E. Hawkins, Eds.). Ecotourism Society, North Bennington, VT, pp. 12–14.

Hector Ceballos-Lascurain is a pioneer of the ecotourism movement. In this chapter he outlines the emergence of ecotourism, its potential benefits and impacts, and his views on how sustainable development using tourism can be best achieved.

CHAPTER 2

If Ecotourism is Not Just an Activity But a Philosophy, Which Philosophy?

This chapter places ecotourism within its broadly historical context, in order to chart the major philosophic and social currents that have contributed to its development. We approach this chapter's question by looking closely at the human–nature relationship and the interaction between them for, as we have seen in Chapter 1, ecotourism by definition relies on the natural environment as its basic resource. This, however, tells us little for the logging, mining, pastoral and fishing industries all rely on the environment in fundamental ways. However, differentiating specific activities is crucial in determining the relationship between human activity and the environment, especially in understanding the specific values that such activities embody and this will help us to understand the shift in value of nature that ecotourism embodies.

CONTENTS

Human Nature

Exchanging Value(s)

Toward Ecocentrism: Modern Roots

Whose Sustainability?

Ethics and (of) Resource Management

Further Reading

HUMAN NATURE

Throughout human history it has been nature that has provided both the raw material and inspiration for human existence. Nature sustains our very existence, from the most basic of needs – water, food, air – to the materials from which we fashion our distinct ways of life – our symbols, meanings and behaviors which constitute the diversity of our cultures; even our very conception of self is mediated by and through nature. Poets and artists, from our earliest beginnings, from the cave paintings at Lascaux in France, from traditional and contemporary indigenous art, to the Romantic poets, have turned to nature in expressing all that is human (Scott, 1974). However, it was the Scottish empiricist philosopher, John Locke (1632–1704) who expresses most succinctly our modern inheritance of the natural world in claiming that everything in nature is waste until people transform it into useable things of value (Locke, 1841). It is an ethos that western societies have embraced with unrestrained enthusiasm. All over the world vital ecosystems are being replaced with infrastructure – houses, towns, industry, roads – all for the exclusive benefit and utility of the human species alone.

The environmental devastation that has resulted from this impetus to 'develop' and use nature for our own material ends has now been recognized as the most significant political issue of the twenty-first century. It is indeed a grim harvest to reap and is a product of our own making, a result of our historical and contemporary human relations for our social customs, institutions and economy are the embodiment of specific systems of value, many of which have a long historical lineage: What we do about ecology depends on our ideas of the human–nature relationship (Newsome et al., 2002; White, 1967). However, Holden (2005) laments that although the presence of a conservation ethic is resulting in a move to resource-conserving behavior; there is still a lack of recognition of the intrinsic value of nature. Indeed, many have argued that the remedy for our environmental predicament lies precisely here, in a change of values. However, it is of little real import to identify a certain set of values and to claim that we need simply to change them. Only by understanding the complexity of relations and the historical ideas that have contributed to our current position can we begin to make sense of the 'ethic' or behaviors that these values underpin.

Facts, figures and scientific data in themselves do not seem to have been enough to challenge the global trends of environmental decline. Instead:

> *Numerous theoretical frameworks have been developed to explain the gap between the possession of environmental knowledge and environmental awareness, and displaying pro-environmental behaviour. Although many hundreds of studies have been undertaken, no definitive explanation has yet been found.* (Kollmuss and Agyeman, 2002: 239)

In December 1987, the Nobel Prize for Economics was awarded to Robert Solow of the United States for his theory of economic growth, not surprising in itself, but of particular interest was Solow's overt premise: the dispensability of nature. In his own words: '[t]he world can, in effect, get along without natural resources, so exhaustion is just an event, not a catastrophe' (Shiva, 1989: 219). Equally noteworthy was the former United States President Bush's address in 1992 before departure to the UN Earth Summit in Brazil. He made his position and that of the United States clear in refusing to sign any treaty or document involving environmental controls that would inhibit US economic growth. More recently in 2007 at the United Nations Climate Change Conference in Bali the United States used obstructive tactics to avoid having to meet binding targets in the reduction of CO_2 gas emissions. Officials representing the US government at the conference argued that binding targets would catastrophically slow the growth of the US economy.

This is the heart of the problem faced by not only ecotourism but also by all forms of activities that involve resource use: the question of *how* we use resources. Peng notes

> *If northern politicians are afraid to advise their public to buy fewer cars and use less oil, can a southern government really be expected to tell its people to tighten their belts further and make room for two structural adjustments: one forced on us by external debt, the other by new ecological imperatives? The legacy and inequality of anthropocentric policies followed by the industrial North is now being inflicted on the South. (1992: 25)*

EXCHANGING VALUE(S)

Questions of value are central to the considerations of the (often competing) conceptions of, and practices, toward the natural world (e.g. Belshaw, 2001). If we want to respect nature, if we consider that the way we relate to nature is not morally neutral, we must stop seeing it as simply a set of instrumental values (resources) and be willing to recognize that nature has intrinsic values (Larrère and Larrère, 2007). Godfrey-Smith (1980) identifies two primary ways in which value is assessed in western society. If the value that something is said to hold is a means to a valued end then it is designated as being of 'instrumental' value. 'Intrinsic value' on the other hand is value that exists in its own right, for its own sake.

What is central here is the ethic that such ideas and values underpin.

- An ethic of 'use' – this is the normative or dominant mode of how human beings relate to nature: where nature is viewed predominantly as a set of resources which humanity is free to employ for its own distinct ends. It is an instrumental and anthropocentric view.

- An ethic 'of' nature – holds that non-human entities are of equal value with the human species. It is broadly intrinsic and ecocentric.

An ethic of use begins from a human locus and it is this univocal perspective that is often described as anthropocentrism. The ultimate grounding of value in the western world is intrinsic as human beings are placed as the source of all value and, by extension, the measure of all things. Such a view allows nature no intrinsic value in itself and for itself as its value lies only in satisfying human needs and desires. However, it is unfair to make Locke the villain of this piece of anthropocentrism which has a very long and deeply entrenched history. It has, to all intents and purposes, been the single deepest and most persistent assumption of (at least) all the dominant Western philosophical, social and political traditions since the time of the classical Greeks and the rise of the Judeo-Christian religions (Fox, 1990; Nash, 2001; White, 1967).

For the ancient Greeks it was the mind that set humanity apart from nature. As the exclusive repositories of mind we humans became the exclusive locus of meaning. Similarly, the Judeo-Christian tradition set the soul apart from, and above, a merely physical natural world and in doing so devalued nature and transformed it into an object. Its biblical injunction to subdue the earth, and its destruction of pagan animism created a fear and loathing of nature, especially wild nature in the minds of all God fearing men (Donagan, 1977; Nash, 2001; White, 1967). Matter, all that is not soul or mind, became the inert and dead and raw material which is possessed only by the value that we chose to project upon it (Mathews, 1987: 38).

The 'anthropocentric morality' and its ethic of use are difficult for us to argue against. The notion that a wilderness or natural areas might have intrinsic value in itself is often dismissed as a transparent example of wishful thinking (Messer and Mosley, 1980). For in the great majority of cases it is an instrumental justification that is used to argue for the preservation and conservation of nature. Godfrey-Smith (1980: 56–71) places such justifications in four main categories:

- the aesthetic/spiritual (the 'cathedral' argument) – where nature is valued for providing spiritual revival and aesthetic delight

- the biological/biodiversity (the 'silo' argument) – where nature is valued for its stockpile of genetic diversity

- the scientific (the 'laboratory' argument) – where nature is valued for scientific inquiry

- and the athletic (the 'gymnasium' argument) – where nature is valued for tourism and recreation

Within the last few decades, however, an ecocentric philosophy has (re)emerged,[7] one which fundamentally challenges intrinsic and anthropocentric value

---

[7] Re-emerged in the sense that such a view is not particularly new, its origins can be traced back to at least the pre-Socratics – Pythagoras for example – or many indigenous and non-Western cultures throughout the world.

systems. It is a broad philosophy that encompasses many elements and often includes:

- a belief in humanities harmony with nature
- attempts to alleviate (or eliminate) negative human impacts on the environment – atmospheric pollution, land degradation, etc.
- the argument for all life having its own specific intrinsic value
- arguments against economic growth and consumerism
- embracing of alternative technology – such as solar power, passive energy systems, recycling
- the devolution of political and institutional structures
- the promotion of minority oppressed and marginalized groups into the political process

It is a broad philosophical position which attempts to give validity to intrinsic value and which is holistic, strongly grounded in the biology and ecology of nature and rejects the view that the world is divided into mutually exclusive parts. Therefore it affirms the intrinsic interconnectedness of all things, both living and inert. It is a belief that the world is a shared web of life. A view:

> *shared by most indigenous peoples and environmentalists…that nature is the fabric of all life – a vast interconnected web that sustains life on earth, that humans are but one species among the millions and have no intrinsic right to dominion over all other life forms. Nor do humans have the exclusive right to decide whether other life forms have the right to survive. In this philosophy nature has the right to exist and thrive regardless of whether it delivers commodities or dollar benefits or in any way meets human needs and demands. (Nash 1989: 149)*

In an attempt to balance anthropocentrism and ecocentrism O'Riordan suggests that 'environmentalism seeks to embrace both worldviews' (O'Riordan, 1989: 85–6). Gough et al. (2000) suggest a blurring of these extremes between the ecocentric/anthropocentric polarities which is rendered necessary partly by an acceptance that all human worldviews are in some sense anthropocentric. Aspects of environmentalism – can be organized along the single dimension of ecocentricity/anthropocentricity *(see Table 2.1)*.

Table 2.1 Ecocentric–Anthropocentric Spectrum (Gough et al., 2000)			
Ecocentric	**Anthropocentric**		
Gaianism	**Accommodation**	**Communalism**	**Intervention**
Trust 'GAIA' above all	Value 'life' above all	Value 'fairness' above all	Value 'progress'above all

TOWARD ECOCENTRISM: MODERN ROOTS

In, *'Modern Environmentalism: An Introduction'* David Pepper (1996) cites four eras in recent history where deep felt concerns of the public for the quality of the environment have been voiced – the 1890s, 1920s, late 1950s, the early 1970s. To these dates we could also add Chernobyl (1985), the Exxon Valdez disaster (1989), the systematic land clearing practices that reached their apotheosis in the late 1980s and 1990s, and most recently the findings of the Intergovernmental Panel on Climate Change (2007).

The serious questioning of anthropocentrism, however, was not taken up significantly until the early 1960s and 1970s, provoked in large part by the influence of Rachel Carson's (1962) seminal book *'Silent Spring'* and Lynn White's (1967) *'The Historical Roots of Our Ecologic Crisis'*. This shift, once begun, posed a fundamental challenge to the priority of a human-centered value system in a reorientation toward identification with a more impartial, ecosphere centered view of the world and of advocating behaviors appropriate to such a view (e.g. Capra, 1988; Fox, 1990).

The type of behaviors, or ethic, appropriate to such a view, as we shall see below, can be interpreted in varied ways. However, those who dismiss that nature has an intrinsic value in itself argue that such a position is essentially not rational, or logically founded (often rhetorically characterized as overly 'emotional') with no biological or economic justification (scientific basis) and would therefore define an ethic of nature, or ecocentrism, on more pragmatic and rational grounds. Such a perspective is often referred to as technocentrism, or technological environmentalism (Pepper, 1996).

For the technocentric, it is the function of economic growth and technological advancement to provide material well-being for humanity. Conservation, when advocated, is seen as the domain of efficient environmental management – the utilization of scientific and technological knowledge to provide responses to the environmental effects of industrial processes. Technology is then deployed to make the world a better place for all its peoples by converting a hostile nature into a benign productivity. Such a philosophy satisfies most people who are concerned about global environmental issues as it lends comfort to the uneasiness felt in the face of the all too evident damage of humanity's impact on the earth by providing a justification for not relinquishing any of the privileges and comforts currently enjoyed.

This idea can be extended to ecotourist's level of commitment to environmentalism so that some ecotourists would be considered to be 'light green' while others would be 'dark green'. Most ecotourists could be classed as light green in so far as they are interested in sustainability and may undertake some efforts to behave in an environmentally responsible manner, however, in the end they will put comfort over conservation. At the other end of the spectrum are dark green ecotourists who make a significant commitment to environmentally responsible behavior and who put conservation before comfort.

Beneath the technocentric facade, however, is a raw and sometimes irrational faith – a faith in the idea of progress (Pepper, 1996). For technocentrism's underlying principles are

- an overt belief in the ability and efficiency of management

- that problems can (indeed should) be solved by the use of objective analysis and recourse to the laws of physical science (and technology)

- that the 'natural' authority of the above is legitimated with recourse to economic laws (Pepper, 1996)

An ecocentrist perspective on the other hand would argue that reform is fundamentally necessary at all levels – a re-evaluation of our social, economic and educational institutions; indeed a complete reorientation of society as we currently know it (Capra, 1988). A major element of this shift in values would be the recognition of nature's right to exist in its own right, apart from the benefits humankind can derive from it. In these terms maintaining biodiversity or the web of life on earth is clearly in the interest of not only the human species but all species. Charles Birch speaks of the importance of a biocentric ethic:

Our way of life is tied to an anthropocentric ethic that sees the non-human world as simply the stage on which the drama of life is performed. All other creatures have no more than instrumental value to us. What is now urgently called for is a biocentric ethic that sees in all life some intrinsic value as well as instrumental value. Sentience, the capacity for feeling, gives life intrinsic value. A great achievement of our time could be to extend the concepts of compassion, rights and justice to all living creatures, not only in theory but in the practice of a biocentric ethic. (Birch, 1991: 82)

James Lovelock's (1988) GAIA hypothesis can be seen as the ultimate expression of this ecocentric view. For Lovelock, the earth is a living organism where its species and their environment are coupled together evolving as a single system, the largest living organism. As humans we are simply a part of this interdependent organism, but have a disproportionate effect on its life cycle. This organism, through its planetary feedback mechanisms, will optimize the necessary conditions needed to maintain life but not necessarily human life.

This line of thought moves us into the ideas surrounding 'deep ecology',[8] which is one of the most widely discussed ecocentric streams of thinking (Newsome et al., 2002; Pepper, 1996). Deep ecology is a comprehensive philosophical worldview that believes a harmonious relationship with nature can be made available, through extending care from the human to the non-human world (de Jonge, 2004). Deep ecology takes a holistic view of nature in which the human being, through the 'self', is intrinsically connected to all life. No absolute boundaries exist between humanity and nature (a single ontology); therefore there is no point at which 'I', the individual or self, ends and other life-forms begin. The self encompasses the entire earth around us; nature becomes an extension of ourselves (e.g. Capra, 1997; Mathews, 1993). Thus it becomes incumbent on us to respect and serve cross-species common interests. Recognition of our interrelatedness with life and the intrinsic value of other things, deep ecologists argue, indicates that we need to reduce our impact on the earth, taking only what satisfies our vital needs. Actions which follow from this philosophical position include not only 'treading lightly on the earth' but also actions that respectfully attempt to alter the views and behavior of those who persist in the delusion that self-realization lies in dominating nature and transforming it to satisfy our own needs (Young, 1990).

According to de Jonge (2004) deep ecology represents four main principles:

1. A deep questioning of the relationship between human beings and nature.

2. A metaphysics of ethics rather than an environmental ethics.

3. A political movement whose premises are both descriptive and normative.

4. An activist approach for dealing with the ongoing destruction of natural entities.

---

[8] Deep ecology begins primarily with the Norwegian philosopher Arne Naess (1912–2004) who was strongly influenced by the science of ecology and the philosophy of Benedict Spinoza (1632–1677).

Aldo Leopold (1886–1948) can be considered one of the first modern deep ecologists. Deep ecology's concern with addressing a 'transpersonal sense of ecological self' that embraces other beings (human and non-human) and ecological processes, would, in Leopold's terms be an 'ecological conscience', which reaches its fullest expression in a 'land ethic'. For Leopold our relation to the land, or earth, should not be governed solely by economics: 'our basic weakness in a conservation system based wholly on economic motives is that most members of the land community have no economic value' (1966: 20). In Antarctica, for example, some treaty countries are weighing up the economic value of oil and mineral exploration against the preservation of the existing unique ecosystem. But can the ecosystem be valued solely (or adequately) in economic terms? It is inextricably bound to existing (and future) relationships of species dependency, relationships between species and communities that are often intangible to our human dimension. As Leopold stated: 'these creatures are members of the biotic community, and its stability depends on its integrity, they are entitled to continuance' (1966: 21). The stability of an ecosystem depends on all of its members. For example, overharvesting the krill in Antarctica is having major impacts on the bird life, seals, whales and other members of the community, in fact the whole Antarctic marine ecosystem.

A land ethic according to Leopold is based on the principle that each individual organism is a member of a complex community of interrelated parts. This community exhibits values such as diversity, connectivity and stability/change and for Leopold, processes that preserved the integrity, stability and beauty of the biotic community are ethically the ones to pursue. Leopold argued that contemporary land economics does not achieve this for economics places a 'value' on land that rests on 'ownership' and property rights.

Leopold advocated a drastic revision of society, a profound change in intellectual emphasis, human loyalties, affections and convictions. This change is based on an ethical relation to the land which requires care, respect and admiration for land and a high regard for its intrinsic value (e.g. Leopold, 1966; Lutz Newton, 2006; Mathews, 1993; Young, 1990; Lovelock, 1988). Our relation to land, or the 'earth', or 'environment' should be determined by ethics in the social world, an ethic which 'reflects the existence of an ecological conscience and this in turn reflects a conviction of individual responsibility for the health of the land' (Leopold, 1966: 20).

Perhaps the most serious obstacle impeding the evolution of a land ethic, or ethic of nature, is that western societies are headed away from an intimate connection to land – a 'stewardship' of nature – through the dominance of a predominantly individualistic and economic value system. The pre-eminence of technology (backed up by enormous advances in scientific understanding) allied with a growing secularization of social institutions has led to an alienation of humans from the land and hence to the demise of an 'environmental ethos' or ethic of nature (Capra, 1988; White, 1967). And this loss of a sense of stewardship has become institutionalized through the growth of private property and all of its associations of legal exclusivity, ownership and profit maxims (e.g. Eckersley, 1992).

Most significant here is that Leopold's ideas reflect a concern for conservation based solely on economic terms. He maintains the basic weakness in a conservation system based wholly on economic motives which is that most members of the land community (i.e. animals, plants, etc.) have no economic values. 'Ecosystems' cannot be valued in economic terms for they are communities made up of inextricably linked elements. Removing one member or link, by valuing only one dimension, will damage the whole community.

However, resource conservation, resource preservation and alternative approaches to development do not necessarily challenge anthropocentricity or economic value as they are usually advocated on the grounds of nature's instrumental value to society (as we have seen above) be it for the cathedral, laboratory, silo, or gymnasium value.

WHOSE SUSTAINABILITY?

The concept of sustainability has become a mediating term in bridging the ideological and political differences between the environmental and development lobbies, a bridge between the fundamentally opposed paradigms of eco and anthropocentrism. Hore-Lacy notes

> *Perhaps it arises from the Federal Governments boundless ability to be gulfed by some greenies, in this case by sticking the adjectives 'ecological' on the front of the Brundtland term sustainable development. A sleight of hand unique in the world I believe. The choice of adjective has severely distorted the whole process and made any economic perspective a defensive one. (1991: 375)*

However, this sleight of hand is not particularly a unique one to greenies. Often the interests aligned with conventional development (growth in the production of commodities for profitable sale) have recourse to sustainability in justifying the present conditions of production against the environmental advocates who use it to promote alternatives. This is advanced through the magical transmutation of the term 'ecological sustainable development' into 'economically sustainable development' through the substitution of the letter E in the acronym 'ESD'. It is an indication of the latitude with which the concept of sustainability can be interpreted. Thus the concept of sustainability is both contested and deployed, often for profoundly different reasons. As Butler (1999) notes sustainable tourism is not automatically the same as tourism developed in line with the principles of sustainable development.

For the technocentrist the concept of what heritage we leave for our children is not phrased in terms of clean air, water and biodiversity but in terms of 'intergenerational equity'; that is, their inheritance should include an accumulation of community wealth generated by environmentally acceptable economic growth (Hore-Lacy, 1991). Apparently we are all entitled to a thriving economy.

Sustainability is inherently linked to conservation as it relies on the ability of the environment to renew itself without impairing or damaging its ability to do so (Swarbrooke, 1999). Definitions of conservation are numerous but most often include ideas such as 'to keep from harm, decay or loss especially for future use'; 'protection, preservation and careful management of natural resources and of the environment'. Certain environmental groups, for example, believe that natural areas should be conserved by non-intervention which means little or no human involvement (thus impacts) whatsoever. This is the 'hard' deep ecology orientation.

But is the 'preservation' or non-intervention position excessively utopian? As Eckersley (1992) suggests, it is self-defeating to focus solely on setting up small areas of pristine wilderness while ignoring the growing global population and pollution, since these problems sooner or later impact upon those remaining areas of 'wild' nature. Therefore deep ecology and non-intervention approaches must at least consider the influence of human beings. 'Soft technologists' exhibit one such approach in embracing the ideals of deep or transpersonal ecology in the conservation of nature but suggest that the human species play a necessarily evaluative role, one that recognizes the diversity of interrelationships between humanity and nature but not solely premised on an economic value. Such approaches realize the importance of the biotic community and are opposed to the technological optimism of the technocentrics. The 'soft technologist' approach[9] would also consider the welfare of humans as equally, as significant as the biotic community because of their essential interdependence. This position advocates a 'stewardship'

---

[9] This approach is related to 'human welfare ecology' that also realizes that humans are necessary parts of the natural process.

ethic that is premised on the belief that we must protect and nurture the biological systems on which our survival depends on. Human beings role as stewards of nature is a necessary one in order for both the human and non-human species to survive. The continued study of nature in order to monitor human impacts on nature is central to such a position and underpins most approaches to resource management.

Resource conservation is thus a form of 'restrained development' in that, at a minimum, development must be sustainable in not endangering the natural systems that support life on earth – the atmosphere, the waters, the soils and all living beings. An early advocate of resource conservation was the first head of the US Forest Service, Gifford Pinchot. In his book '*The Fight for Conservation*' (1910), Pinchot's three principles of conservation were development, prevention of waste and development for the benefit of the many and not merely the profit of the few. Such an approach is evident today in many public resource management bodies. It considers natural resources as factors of production and as such, the term 'resource development' would be more appropriate.

However, the use of the terms conservation and development may seem incompatible. It could be argued, however, that resource conservation and alternative approaches to development, such as resource development or restrained development, while acknowledging the need for a change from the practices of unrestrained exploitation and economic growth, merely change the temporal framework of exploitation by forestalling it. A technocentric frame is built into such a view in the belief that any impediments to the system, resource depletion and pollution, for example, can be remedied by a technical solution. However, a technical solution may be defined as the 'one that requires a change only in the technique of the natural sciences, demanding little or nothing in the way of change in human values or ideas of morality' (Hardin, 1968: 124). Moreover, it in no way guarantees its own success. For if humans continue to search for technical solutions to the world's economic, social and ecological problems, they will fall far short of producing an adequate solution. For example, the US government has urged scientists to develop technologies to block the sunlight in a last ditch effort to halt global warming. It says research into techniques such as giant mirrors in space or reflective dust pumped into the atmosphere would be 'important insurance' against rising emissions, and lobbied for such a strategy to be one of the recommendations in a major UN report on climate change published in 2007 (Adam, 2007).

According to Garrett Hardin's (1968) article that introduces the '*Tragedy of the Commons*', all resources owned in common – air, oceans, fish, bushland, etc. – are or eventually will be overexploited. The rational individual has the incentive to take as much as possible before someone else does. No one is motivated to take responsibility for the resource. Because they belong to everyone, no one protects it. Applying these ideas to tourism suggests that each tour company would seek to maximize their own gain, and become locked into a system that compels them to 'increase his herd' (maximize their profit by increasing the number of tourists) without limit, in a tourism system which is finite. Hardin (1968) proposes that to control this kind of undisciplined exploitation, an attitude of temperance rather than prohibition is required, through mediation of administrative law and 'coercion' (via taxes, incentives and other biased options). These are fundamental implications for policy and management regimes and will be discussed in more detail in Chapter 3.

The commons argument has significant implications for ecotourism. The commons or destination area can only be justifiably used under low-population (visitor) densities. As visitor numbers increase, the destination area has to be controlled or even abandoned. The only way to preserve and nurture other more precious freedoms (such as host populations) is by relinquishing the freedom to visit or the number of visitors. Freedom in these terms is the recognition of necessity, the necessity of relinquishing the personal or individual (human) freedom in placing restrictions on visitor numbers and experiences.

Hardin's answer to the ruin of the commons is mutual coercion. This is not prohibiting certain acts, but having in place carefully biased options which make these acts uneconomic for example. These options would coerce companies to not act in certain ways and the options would be mutually agreed upon by the majority. The end result would be less freedom for individual companies but more long-term sustainability which could be seen as freedom in other ways. As Hardin suggests individuals are locked into the logic of the commons as free only to bring on universal ruin, once they see the necessity of mutual coercion they become free to pursue other goals.

'Freedom' in these terms is the freedom that comes with the necessity of mutual coercion, in other words, individuals are only free to pursue their own goals when abiding by laws mutually agreed upon by the majority of the people affected. Those who oppose any restrictions on their 'rights' – the rights to do as they please – will only bring on universal ruin.

These issues are at the heart of ecotourism and environmental management – the rights of individuals and their duty to others, to how far any person can understand the effects of their individual actions on the well-being of the ecosystem and the enjoyment of others, what the cumulative consequences are when many abuse an area (each in small ways) and how society should regulate individual use so that freedom of access is not unfairly restricted and maintains environmental quality (Hardin, 1998).

Any form of government intervention requires the exercise of Hardin's (1968, 1998) dictum of 'mutual coercion' mutually agreed upon, because without public acceptance of authority regulation cannot be enforced. If tourists are made more aware of the consequences of their acts, will they become more morally concerned about the effects of these consequences on others and on future generations, and will they accept and respect the fact that some kind of governmentally imposed regulation of use is necessary in the public interest?

Ecocentrically informed resource management recognizes that modern science and technology cannot prevent environmental degradation if current economic growth and resource use trends continue. What is required is a change in philosophy, politics and economics to ensure that a sustainable human population can exist in balance with its environment, and where we must not be afraid to carry out forceful solutions in order to better our world in the future (Hardin, 1993). This 'preservationist' position (which we shall discuss in more detail in Chapter 4) emphasizes the need for prior macro-environmental constraints, such as government legislation, scientific monitoring and use restrictions.[10]

Therefore conservation involves the management or control of human use of resources (biotic and abiotic) in an attempt to restore, enhance, protect and sustain the quality and quantity of a desired mix of species, ecosystem conditions and processes for present and future generations (Dunster and Dunster, 1996: 69).

It is becoming increasingly apparent that, at least for the immediate future, natural areas can only be defended for their instrumental value. But we should not dismiss the efforts to create new modes of ecological understanding simply as 'wishful thinking'. Even within the fields of economics, mathematics and analytic philosophy much work has been done on equating the value of non-measurable and non-comparable value dimensions.[11]

ETHICS AND (OF) RESOURCE MANAGEMENT

It can be argued that management itself is an anthropocentric concept for if we accept that natural areas have intrinsic worth then why do they have to be managed? Further, if a localized ecosystem is protected as a wilderness area,

---

[10] Deep ecology can be viewed as an extreme preservation position as it argues for the recognition of an intuitive acceptance of the notion of intrinsic (as apposed to instrumental) value in nature and thus the recognition of 'rights' for non-human species.

[11] E.g Peterson et al. (1988) in specific relation to natural resources.

'management' itself can be seen to be an intrusion into the system. Similarly, in enclosing nature within certain boundaries, who is it we are trying to protect? Where do we draw the boundary line – are resource managers deciding what is natural? More pragmatically still management requires expenditure – whose responsibility is it to finance the management of protected areas?

For environmental ethics to be of significance they must be able to be acted upon, that is, made operationally relevant:

> *The imposition of regulation reduces freedom, and by definition, reduces the need for individuals to exercise moral judgement...ethical behaviour willingly takes the rights, the needs and welfare of others into account. It is not behaviour that simply responds to the pressure of the law, regulation or code. (Mackay, 1992: 3)*

However, sustainable tourism development can only be achieved through international cooperation and agreed regimes for surveillance, development and management in the common interest (e.g. Brundtland Commission,

CASE STUDY: The Nepalese Himalayas, A Protected Ecosystem?

In May of 2007 some 43 expeditions totalling 470 climbers summitted Mount Everest from both the Nepalese and Tibetan sides of the mountain. At one stage over 60 climbers were on or near the summit waiting (in some cases up to 1–2 hours) in order to get their chance to stand on the highest point in the world. If those 470 climbers had been asked why they chose to climb Mt Everest, somewhere in their answers would have been sentiments expressing a desire to experience one of the wildest places on earth (Edward, 1992). Technological innovations in mountaineering equipment, such as advanced clothing, bottled oxygen and the growth in the popularity of commercialized expeditions where clients are charged between US$40,000 and US$50,000 to be guided up the mountain will continue to attract hundreds of climbers as they attempt to fulfill a desire to experience one of the wildest places on earth.

Research carried out in Sagarmatha (Mt Everest) National Park indicates that ecosystems above 4000 metres have been significantly impacted by tourism in the past 30 years. Impacts include the overharvesting of fragile alpine shrubs and plants for expedition and tourist lodge fuel, overgrazing, accelerated erosion, and uncontrolled lodge building (Byers, 2005).

The present Nepalese government will continue to encourage tourism, as it is the country's highest income earner. International groups, such as the Mountain Protection Commission, advocate a drastic reduction in expedition numbers and call for the complete banning, for 1 year, of climbing on all peaks over 8000 metres high.

This then is the tragedy of the Nepalese Himalayas. It is a salutary lesson for any management body in trying to mediate a compromise between the conflicting needs of access, availability and presentability of an environmental or ecological product – wilderness – with those of the local population and the regenerative capacity of the ecosystem **(see Fig. 2.1)**.

FIGURE 2.1 *Trekkers walking past the imposing Cho Oyu (8201 m) in the Nepalese Himalayas.*

1987). But at stake is not just the sustainable development of shared ecosystems, our 'commons', but of all nations whose tourism development depends to a greater or lesser extent on their rational management. Without equitable rules future generations will be impoverished by the loss of these places to visit, and the people who suffer the most will be those who live in developing countries that can least impose regulation in the global market economy that tourism operates in.

Ecocentric management, in the case of tourism, would recognize that modern science and technology cannot prevent environmental degradation if the current economic growth and resource use trends continue, and that a change in human philosophy, politics and economics is needed to ensure that a sustainable tourism population (guest) can exist in balance with its social and physical environment (host). Further to this, ecocentrism can be viewed as 'communalist' – a preservationist position, which re-emphasizes the need for prior macro-environmental constraints on economic growth and favors a decentralized socio-economic system or 'deep ecology' underpinned by the notion of intrinsic (as opposed to instrumental) value in nature for non-human species (e.g. Pepper, 1996).

Mistakenly, ecocentrism is often criticized as a hands off, only in theory, 'wishful thinking', put it on the agenda for future discussion approach which is ideal yet impractical to implement on any real level. However, it is important here to express ecocentrism's centrality for ecotourism clearly and purposefully in relation to the management question. Ecocentrism as an approach to management would argue that protected areas are not being conserved or preserved or protected for anyone but can exist because they have a value in and for themselves (e.g. Page and Dowling, 2002). This approach is a challenge to a more dominant worldview which has been basically adopted by resource economists who support the idea that the non-human world is valuable only in as far as it is valuable to humans.

These are the radical views of a continuum of perceptions, yet they deal with the same biosphere. What place and role does the market have in a finite natural world? Conversely, what is the place of the natural environment in an economically rationalist world? How do we begin, and is it possible to reconcile or move from an economically based mass tourism system to a more eco orientated system?

An economist sees tourism as a part of a US$733 billion economy looking to expand five times over the next few decades. To do this our tourism systems will raid the ecosystems of the biosphere for resources as raw materials for this growth. In order to achieve and justify such growth natural systems must be viewed through ecological rather than economic eyes. These natural systems will be valued for their resource utility rather than for their ecological value.

As demonstrated through this discussion, numerous philosophical and political ideologies have contributed to the present form of ecological thought and the formation of the nature travel known today as ecotourism. Various other forms of tourism including 'nature tourism', 'low impact tourism' and 'sustainable tourism' have formed the basis of the definitions' debate surrounding the ecotourism phenomenon. Common themes are evident in the numerous descriptions of ecotourism and can be linked to a number of underlying philosophical approaches which help to define it as an activity.

As ecotourism has the potential to impact on such a variety of sectors, intervention by various bodies including governments, the tourism industry, the community and conservation groups is widespread and quite intense. These agencies play a major role in promoting, planning and implementing sustainable ecotourism practices as a means of satisfying the tourist, the economy and the environment. The next chapter will examine this exchange in an attempt to investigate how regulation might work for ecotourism.

FURTHER READING

Carson, R. (1962) *Silent Spring*. Penguin, London.

Caron's book has become one of the most influential environmental texts of the twentieth century as it succeeded in raising environmental awareness which led to the changes in government policy and inspired the rise of the ecological movement.

Leopold, A. (1966) *A Sand Country Almanac*. Ballantine, New York.

Hardin, G. (1968) Tragedy of the commons. *Science*, 162, 1243–8.

Like Carson's work both Leopold and Hardin's writings have become classics in environmental thinking.

Belshaw, C. (2001) *Environmental Philosophy*. Acumen, Stocksfield, UK.

Belshaw's text provides a good introduction to the various strands of environmental philosophy.

CHAPTER 3

Tourism Development: Government, Industry, Policy and Planning

Ecotourism has become a central platform in many countries' development strategies. It is particularly attractive for governments in its potential in providing an alternative to other forms of economic development: through employment generation, for its ability to generate foreign exchange, and its ability to generate sustainable regional growth (Weaver, 1998). Chok et al. (2007) state that forecasts of high-tourism growth in developing nations, where widespread poverty exists, have led to considerable interest in tourism as a tool for poverty alleviation.

However, in many cases tourism has not lived up to these high expectations. Although tourism is highly regarded in its ability to generate significant levels of revenue in the form of Gross Domestic Product (GDP) – in many cases tourism's potential in generating foreign exchange has surpassed that of traditional commodity exports – thus allowing for flow-on benefits in the form of local infrastructure such as roads and electricity. Yet, these benefits are often circumscribed by the significant impacts on local communities, such as increased pollution and rising local prices and the export of profits from tourism out of the community itself. Even without considering the physical impacts, the flow of revenues out of the country or local region significantly challenges tourism's status as a foreign exchange generator. Many local communities and economies where tourism development takes place lack the infrastructure and necessary skills required in establishing tourism operations – chief of which is capital – along with the range of goods and services desired by tourists. As a result leakages are usually high. Leakages are the flows of money out of a country or specific area as a result of the necessity to import certain skills, infrastructure, technologies and commodities along with the flow of revenue in the form of profits taken out of a locale by operators (e.g. Hjerpe and Kim, 2007; Lindberg, 2000; Mazibuko, 2007). This is significant for tourism development for in many cases the necessary infrastructure required for tourism is provided by foreign owned corporations, particularly airlines, hotels, car rental agencies and

CONTENTS

Sustainable Tourism Development

Planning and Policy Frameworks – Who is Involved and How?

Industry-Led Planning and Policy

Cooperative Government and Industry Initiatives: Community Involvement and Cooperative Approaches

Using Policy to Achieve Best Practice

Further Reading

package tours. In many cases[12] leakages have been estimated at up to 80–90% in developing countries that do not have a significant share of the necessary tourism services such as airlines, hotels and transportation companies (Mathieson and Wall, 1982). Zheng (2000) adds that for developing countries in Indo-China, for example, embarking on tourism for economic growth hinges on minimizing three types of tourism leakages, namely financial, structural and operational.

Tourism expenditure is considered to have significant flow-on effects throughout all levels and sectors of a local economy. This is the 'multiplier' effect whereby initial expenditure of tourist dollars is calculated to initiate expenditure on local goods and services. That is, for every dollar spent an additional amount of dollar is further spent throughout the economy. Despite the multiplier effect, however, in many cases the negative economic, environmental and social effects of tourism build over time and are often not felt directly and are only experienced after the initial positive economic impacts. These problems are further exacerbated through the political imperatives to realize the short-term gains of tourism which often offset government intervention in planning or managing tourism. The result is that the immediate economic benefits are valued highly and accrue to national accounts while the often significant social and environmental costs have to be borne by local communities.

Similarly, tourism is often promoted by government or industry without an overall strategy, without adequate attention to legislative frameworks, such as determining if the planning and nature protection laws are adequate, without consultation or inclusion of local communities and without effective protected area management plans. This raises significant policy questions for government.

Against these effects we shall discuss ecotourism's potential to generate significant benefits to local communities as an alternative form of development, through employment, increased revenues for infrastructure and for community projects. Importantly, if the potential for these benefits is to be realized they need to avoid compromising conservation or sustainability objectives. Indeed, ecotourism is a significant alternative development strategy due to its ability to link local income generation directly through conservation initiatives.

---

[12] Lindberg (1991: 24) estimates that only 10% of tourism spending remains in Zimbabwe, similarly Church (1994) estimated that only 10–20% of tourism spending is retained in Jamaica.

During the 1970s and 1980s, integrated rural development projects were used to raise rural living standards in developing countries, and focused primarily on irrigation, roads and social services. However, the World Bank (1992: 86) found that the results were often disappointing, with low success rates because of over-emphasis in appraisals on outcomes, a tendency to select large and complex projects and overly optimistic projections of project outcomes. The development of ecotourism and its infrastructure in providing for tourism experiences in the new millennium may suffer the same fate (Harrison, 2001).

In order to ensure that tourism does not exceed its sustainable base, an understanding of the mechanisms that lead to the provision of infrastructure for development and the policy and institutional prerequisites for planning and managing ecotourism is fundamental. Through an examination of the principles of sustainable development, the nature of ecotourism and its potential environmental effects we will discuss the role of government and industry policy in facilitating ecotourism. We will discuss a range of sustainable approaches, from the role of government- and industry-led policy and planning initiatives along with the relative strengths and weaknesses of self-regulation. There are many advocates for effective control measures developed through integrated programs that incorporate federal, state and local legislation and policy (e.g. McKercher, 1991a: 69), while others present a case for industry-based 'best practice' (e.g. Richardson, 1995). Regardless, the development of strategic plans and control mechanisms are only as effective as the will to implement them.

CASE STUDY: 'Carrying Capacity', Galapagos Islands, Ecuador

The Galapagos Islands are located 1000 kilometers east from the South American coast and form a unique ecotourism attraction based on native species endemic to the region. Conservationists involved in sustaining the resources of the islands have increasingly attempted to control the expanding tourism industry. In 1986, the island's second airport opened, with arrivals escalating to 108,436 in 2004 – almost four times the recommended carrying capacity of 12,000 visitors. A third airport on Isabella Island has raised tourist numbers to an extra 50,000 per annum (Galapagos Conservation Trust, 2008).

Despite the fact that the Galapagos Islands have had excellent controls on environmental damage per tourist, it has had few controls on the total number of tourists. Strict government regulatory policies include the control of zoning, the stipulation that tourists be accommodated on boats, the registration of naturalist guides and strict regulations for onshore visits. However, the focus on controlling damage per tourist often neglects the fact that most impacts are due to the volume of tourist arrivals.

A steady growth in migration to the Galapagos Islands has been attributed to the opportunity for profit derived from the booming tourism industry, and resulted in a proliferation of onshore accommodation establishments (in breach of the regulations against such development). Local response also denotes a shift in income derivation, as traditional fishers convert their fishing boats to small tour vessels.

Notably, very little of the revenue is returned to the local community. Largely foreign owned cruise ships transport wealthy foreign tourists to the Galapagos facilitating high-leakage rates. More importantly, incentives for locals to maintain tight controls and regulations are non-existent and they compete to expand their own accommodation and boat tour operations.

The islands ecology is the victim of this poor management. Agriculture is expanding and its effects are proving more disastrous than those of tourism. Depriving locals of their share of tourist revenue leaves them no choice but to expand the agricultural sector. The extinction of 12 native plant species is directly attributable to this expansion *(see Fig. 3.1)*.

Placing locals in control of their tourism industry, or at least returning some of the financial benefits from visitation to local operators may reverse the current trends by providing direct incentives to operate within the regulatory frameworks. This may produce a shift in planning from a short-term reactive response to a long-term pro-active one for the benefit of social and physical environments (Steele, 1995).

SUSTAINABLE TOURISM DEVELOPMENT

As we have seen in Chapter 1, ecotourism is an alternative to mass tourism due to its small-scale infrastructure and the minimization of the environmental impacts that follow from it. This suggests that it can be regulated and controlled at a sustainable level. Sustainable tourism is a tourism that

FIGURE 3.1

*Galapgos Islands.
Photo by Galapgos
Conservancy.*

produces economic advantages, in addition to maintaining environmental diversity and quality thus 'combining conservation with economic development' (Wild, 1994: 12). A primary means of maintaining sustainability is by the limiting of tourist numbers and therefore the possibility for environmental degradation (Inskeep, 1991). In this way ecotourism is a supply-led approach (see Chapter 8) which involves determining visitor numbers based on the environment's capacity (its ability to support) rather than by the demand for it. Therefore, ecotourism seeks to protect those areas still intact that may gain future ecological and economic advantage by remaining so (e.g. Foran, 2007).

However, what often sounds fine in theory is often not always the case in practice. 'Over the last quarter century, both the supply of and demand for ecotourism have grown significantly' (Sharpley, 2006: 7) and most of that growth has been unsustainable (Isaacs, 2000; Kamauro, 1996; Steele, 1995). Sustainable development in relation to ecotourism is difficult to achieve because of the extraordinary expansion of ecotourism and the pressures of demand for access to natural areas. The question here is how should this demand (if it should at all) be controlled?

Unsustainable ecotourism is the result of inappropriate developments taking place in sensitive locations. The problem as Buckley and King (2003) see it is that increasing tourism (including ecotourism) will damage parks in ways that are not predicted or detected until they become irreversible. The environmental effects caused by overcrowding, overdevelopment, unregulated recreation, pollution, wildlife disturbances and vehicle use are more serious for ecotourism than mass tourism (McNeely cited in Hvenegaard, 1994). This is related to the fact that ecotourism is more dependent on intact natural environments and is concentrated in ecologically sensitive areas. Without appropriate regulations, problems of overexploitation, and in particular ecological degradation, may be intensified with the development of ecotourism (Issacs, 2000; Kamauro, 1996; Mieczkowski, 1995). This indicates that in practice the principles of sustainability are difficult to implement on a broad scale without a progressive planning and policy framework.

The negative effects of ecotourism are in large part due to the fact that visitation often precedes effective management and planning (e.g. Sofield, 2003). Thus in reality there is a need for suitable planning strategies to be formulated and implemented to ensure that the future expansion of ecotourism takes place in accordance with the principles of sustainable development. There is a need then for an overall policy framework to facilitate sustainable ecotourism development. Those responsible for ecotourism need to understand its philosophies and their associated requirements and consequences.

PLANNING AND POLICY FRAMEWORKS – WHO IS INVOLVED AND HOW?

Effective planning greatly enhances the sustainable development credentials of ecotourism. Central to the goals of environmental conservation and resource sustainability is the protection and maintenance of environmental quality (Fennell, 2002; Krüger, 2005). Achieving this primary goal requires planning which is grounded in 'environmental protection and enhancement yet fosters the realization of tourism potential' (Dowling, 1991: 128). Planning involves anticipating and regulating change to encourage appropriate development so as to increase the social, economic and environmental benefits of the actual process (Murphy, 1985). Ecotourism can become an important function in protected areas but can cause degradation of natural-landscape values. For this reason, it is necessary to plan and manage carefully tourist movement to achieve the right balance between the use and conservation (Żarska, 2006).

Planning development means not only matching its goals and objectives with the resource capabilities but also with conservation requirements. Sustainability of ecotourism practices is therefore possible if planning balances the demands of development with the supply of the environment in an attempt to manage potential benefits now and in the future (Fennell and Dowling, 2003). However, as yet there are no clearly defined roles as to whose responsibility this is.

Government-led planning and policy initiatives

Sustainable tourism, like its parental concept sustainable development, is inherently political (Bramwell, 2005). It is widely recognized that governments have the greatest potential to shape tourism in dictating how it is promoted, planned, managed and regulated. They are the only body that can provide long-term planning and management as legislative and juridical protection of nature reserves for the benefit of future generations (e.g. Buckley, 2004). Additionally, the importance of government planning and policy is credited to its power to provide an overall harmony, consistency and enforceable standards for the industry as a whole as the independent regulation of small areas is not enough to ensure environmental sustainability (e.g. Mieczkowski, 1995: 467; Sofield, 2003; Tolhurst, 1994).

Government policy, through its ability to enforce necessary environmental regulations, sets broad industry standards and therefore can assist in minimizing negative impacts, and hence has a major role to play in facilitating sustainable ecotourism practices. The significance of government policy and planning in accommodating sustainable ecotourism lies in its ability to effectively administer appropriate guidelines and consistent standards, taking into account possible effects.

Governments at all levels are becoming more involved in ecotourism as it is increasingly valued as an important source of revenue, and where government involvement has been found to be critical to its success For example, the UNESCO-LNTA Nam Ha Ecotourism Project is a community-based ecotourism initiative implemented by the Lao National Tourism Administration (LNTA) in and around the Nam Ha National Protected Area. The Project has been recognized by the United Nation's Development Programme (UNDP) as 'best practice' in delivering poverty alleviation and the conservation of a country's natural heritage (UNESCO, 2001).

CASE STUDY: Ecotourism in Laos – A Government-Led Initiative

The Lao People's Democratic Republic (Laos) has a low-population density, unspoiled diverse ethnic lifestyles and traditions, and perhaps the richest, most extensive network of ecosystems on the Indo-China Peninsula. There are over 800 species of birds and more than 100 large mammals already identified in Laos with new species being discovered every year. Some of the more charismatic species include Tigers, Clouded Leopards, Douc Languar, Gibbons, the Irra-waddy Dolphin, Hornbills, Peafowls, Ibis, Crested Argus and Silver Pheasants. In place to protect and conserve these resources is a network of 20 National Protected Areas, often cited as one of the best designed Protected Area Systems in the world. In addition to the country's vast protected forests and aquatic resources, Laos has two UNESCO World Heritage Sites – the Ancient City of Luang Prabang and the pre-Angkorian Vat Phou Temple Complex. There is also the mysterious Plain of Jars, a forthcoming World Heritage Site that has significant archaeological, historical and natural values. The Lao system of 20 National Protected Areas covers nearly 14% of the country. With large tracts of tropical monsoon forest, diverse wildlife populations, bizarre karst limestone formations and many ethnic minority groups, Laos' protected areas have an abundance of ecotourism attractions (Burke and Vaisutis, 2007).

Eager to position Laos as a premier ecotourism destination, the Lao National Tourism Administration, related government agencies and the private sector are working hard to realize the ambitious vision put forth in the country's National Ecotourism Strategy and Action Plan and are promoting Laos accordingly through a range of mechanisms and partnerships (Lao National Tourism Administration, 2008) *(see Fig. 3.2)*.

Government involvement is especially evident in the Asia-Pacific region. Along with Laos other countries such as the Philippines and Papua New Guinea are in the process of formulating an Ecotourism Act (in the former) and country-wide ecotourism strategy (in the latter) in order to safeguard the fragile eco-systems that draw tourists to these areas (Gabor, 1997; Wearing and Chatterton, 2007). The increased awareness of the potential for negative impacts as a result of ecotourism has led the Yunnan

FIGURE 3.2 *An ecotourism travel agent in the Laos capital Vientiane. Photo by Matthew McDonald.*

provincial government in China to sponsor the Shangri-La Ecotourism Demonstration Project (SLED), a project focused on promoting sustainable development through ecotourism in the area with the involvement of the host community (Morais et al., 2006). Similarly, Tonga in 1997 developed a Sustainable Tourism Strategy with a view to planning and implementing for long-term sustainable development of the tourism industry (Calkin, 1997). However, it has taken additional international funding and consultants to implement the strategy, highlighting the fact that governments alone are not always capable of delivering what they have planned. There is also the issue of local involvement to consider as well. For example, the Solomon Island government instituted a National Sustainable Tourism Policy in 1990; however, it had little effect at the local level because villagers perceived a lack of participation and control (Sofield, 2003: 191–224).

The significance of government planning with regards to sustainability is highlighted by the various National Strategies for Ecologically Sustainable Development implemented throughout the 1990s in many countries around the world.[13] Such strategies recognized that through the use of government planning the tourism industry can be developed and managed in a way that conserves its natural resources and minimizes negative environmental

---

[13] E.g. Sachs (1995: 16).

impacts (e.g. Evans-Smit, 1994). The main tools of government policy aimed at tourism-related environmental problems are

- legislation
- regulation – including revenue collection and redistribution
- control
- the coordination of policies and programs
- infrastructure and incentives
- planning and promotion between national and local level ecotourism ventures

CASE STUDY: Bhutan

The tiny Himalayan kingdom of Bhutan, slightly larger than Switzerland lies between Tibet and the Indian states of Assam and Sikkim. The tourism industry in Bhutan is founded on the principle of sustainability, meaning that tourism must be environmentally and ecologically friendly, socially and culturally acceptable and also economically viable. For these reasons, tourism is carefully monitored and the number of tourists visiting Bhutan is kept to an environmentally manageable level where fewer than 3000 international tourists visit each year. One way to ensure this limit and the generation of revenue has been the levying of a US$200 daily fee for all tourists who enter the country. Those who do visit are usually environmentally conscious and well-informed about Bhutan.

An ecotourism management plan has been developed for a newly established national park along Bhutan's border with Tibet, the Jigme Dorji National Park. Most of the local people are traditional pastoralists who have little experience of tourism and tourists. Their only perceived benefit from tourism is horse contracting. Under the preliminary management plan, community members participated in study tours to neighboring tourist spots in the Himalayas, including the remote Indian state of Ladakh, Nepal and Sikkim in order to explore the pros and cons of tourism and Western 'development' (McLaren, 2003).

The primary means of minimizing impacts is to control tourist numbers and as such much government policy is formulated around this intention. Such controls include quantity controls, for example, zoning or limits to tour group sizes, as well as price controls – such as fees or taxes on local operators.

However, the practice of limiting visitor numbers is often a blunt and simplistic solution. Sustainability is about a process, bringing stakeholders in to address the earliest stage of the problem and managing the visitor.[14]

---

[14] For a comprehensive range of international case studies demonstrating alternatives to regulation, see Hall and McArthur (1998).

Governments also have changing interests and priorities which can lead to policies being inconsistent and unfulfilled. Countries with unstable political systems can often not provide long-term vision and stability in policy and planning for tourism and ecotourism. Even countries where the political and democratic processes are well-established and secure, the frameworks and priorities for ecotourism change frequently.

CASE STUDY: Australian Government Policy

The extent of tourism industry regulation, as an important aspect of government policy, has become a major issue in Australia. Since the late 1980s there has been a move by the Australian Government to deregulate the tourism industry in an attempt to improve service provision. Despite this trend, the significance of conservation issues has meant increased demands for environmental protection regulation and legislation (Hall, 1991). Likewise, it can be argued that ecotourism's survival is reliant on regulation concerned with environmental protection. As such there is a need for increased regulation in regards to minimizing environmental consequences and promoting natural resource conservation. The implication is that while the future of the tourism industry will generally be characterized by decreased regulation, ecotourism's future development may well involve increased regulation, based on its environmental dependence.

The Australian Government established a National Ecotourism Strategy in 1994 with the intention of formulating an overall policy framework for the planning, development and management of ecotourism, to contribute to the achievement of sustainable tourism in natural areas (Evans-Smith, 1994: 4). Such a strategy highlights the importance of the government's role in establishing the necessary guidelines for which ecotourism can be developed in accordance with the principles of sustainability. Through the formulation of a broad framework promoting sustainable ecotourism the Federal Government potentially had a great amount of influence in determining the future direction of this type of tourism and thus its sustainability. However, since the change of government in Australia following a national election in 1996, the National Ecotourism Strategy has not been promoted or recognized as a valid strategy by the newly elected government. In this instance, the government support in implementing this strategy has been withdrawn and leaves the impetus of any further actions with the industry and state governments. Some states in Australia have developed their own ecotourism or nature-based tourism strategies.

Integrated policy and planning

The tourism industry is represented at the ministerial level in the form of specialist portfolios which indicate a government's recognition of tourism's importance. A government's priority for tourism can be derived from the position of the tourism portfolio within larger departments or if it is represented by a department designated solely for it.

Generally, where ecotourism planning occurs, it follows the development of an overall National Development Plan and a Tourism Plan. A Tourism Plan should revolve around the natural and socio-economic environment of a country, taking into consideration domestic and international tourist market groups as well as resident's use of tourist attractions and facilities. Fundamental elements include

- tourist attractions and activities
- accommodation
- transportation and other tourist facilities/services
- other infrastructure
- institutional elements (Inskeep, 1991)

The aim of planning for ecotourism is often to identify major issues that are likely to affect the development and management of ecotourism, as well as to develop policies and programs to assist in making the industry more viable and sustainable. The actual content of an ecotourism plan should include the vision and aims of having such a strategy and a rationale for having it in the first place. The strategy also needs to identify and consult with the many stakeholder groups and representatives of the ecotourism sector before a definition of ecotourism or sustainable tourism is developed. A description of ecotourism impacts in relation to environmental, economic, social and cultural dimensions should raise issues that need to be covered through objectives and actions. Some of those issues can include ecological sustainability, regulation, infrastructure, impact monitoring, industry standards and accreditation, education and marketing. The most important part of any ecotourism plan is the implementation strategy, which needs to attempt to coordinate the actions identified into groupings and responsible stakeholders need to be assigned. A resourcing or funding plan should accompany the implementation plan.

An ecotourism plan should ideally encompass the following steps:

- study preparation
- determination of objectives
- survey
- analysis and synthesis
- policy and plan formulation
- recommendations
- implementation and monitoring

The holistic ambitions of sustainable development and the multidisciplinary nature of tourism entail that only governments and public authorities can coordinate efforts in sustainable tourism policy at both the national and local levels (Bramwell, 2005). Sustainable tourism, viewed as contributing to overall sustainable development, requires coordination between various policy-making levels and agencies to overcome and accommodate sectoral considerations that only government bodies, at all levels of policy-making can provide (Hunter, 1995: 164; McKercher, 1991b: 69). Clearly defined government roles and coordination of government policies are necessary to ensure effective planning for a sustainable tourism product (Hall, 1991). With a consistent and combined effort that seeks community support, governments have the potential to establish effective regulation which incorporates the principles of sustainability: 'its successful implementation requires integrated policy, planning and social learning processes: its political viability depends on the full support of the people it affects through their governments, their social institutions and their private activities' (Gunn, 1994: 244). Integrated regional planning, as outlined by the National Ecotourism Strategy, Australia, has already proven successful in allowing for sustainable ecotourism practices in the Murray-Darling Basin and Cape York Peninsula, for example, where community participation and support has provided a strong foundation for government policy development (Evans-Smith, 1994). Governments also need to examine regional planning across borders.

CASE STUDY: Maasai Mara

The Maasai Mara is one of Kenya's smaller reserves at 560 square miles, yet approximately 290,000 tourists visit it every year, staying in the 25 permanent lodges and camp-sites. At peak times, especially during the migration from June to August, more than 8000 people can be in the park at the same time, leading to lines of 70 or more safari vans queuing at prime viewing points. While the Kenyan Government and local authorities such as the Mara conservancy acknowledge the problems of overcrowding, the park is a major source of hard currency for the country. Entry fees for adult non-Kenyans are US$40 (US$10 for children). However, the various levels of government have decided to act. All new developments in the park have been suspended and a report due in March 2008 is expected to set new targets for the acceptable number of tourists and the corresponding prices that they will have to pay (Pflanz, 2007).

The coordination of government planning with private sector and non-government organizations is also fundamental, as is the establishment of links with tourism operators and local communities to facilitate sustainable practices (Wild, 1994). For sustainability to be achieved at all levels of government, operators and developers, as well as tourists and local communities, must each be involved in collaborative partnerships. Although government has the power to legislate controls through policy and thus contribute to sustainable ecotourism practices, a cooperative approach between all involved parties under government guidance would enhance its ongoing success.

Ideally then a sustainable tourism policy is a policy that stems from government bodies, at various levels, in the form of regulations, official statements or speeches, collaborations made and incentives given. Policy is used here to denote the formulation of goals and objectives and the setting of priorities as expressed in various forms (e.g. choices made, statements, regulations) (Farsari et al., 2007).

CASE STUDY: Government Role in Planning for Sustainable Tourism

Useful guidelines for the role of government in the planning and implementation of sustainable tourism were developed at the GLOBE 90 conference held in Vancouver in March 1990:

- Ensure that all government departments involved in tourism are briefed on the concept of sustainable development. The respective ministers (e.g. environment and natural resources) should collaborate to achieve sustainable tourism development.
- Ensure that national and local tourism development agreements stress a policy of sustainable tourism development.
- Include tourism in land use planning.
- Undertake area and sector-specific research into the environmental, cultural and economic effects of tourism.
- Support the development of economic models for tourism to help define appropriate levels and types of tourism for natural and urban areas.
- Assist and support lower levels of government in developing tourism strategies and conservation strategies and in integrating the two.
- Develop standards and regulations for environmental and cultural impact assessments and monitoring of existing and proposed tourism developments, and

ensure that carrying capacities defined for tourism destinations reflect sustainable levels of development and are monitored and adjusted appropriately.

- Apply sectoral and/or regional environmental accounting systems to the tourism industry.
- Create tourism advisory boards that involve all stakeholders (e.g. the public, indigenous populations, industry, Non-Government Organizations (NGOs), and design and implement public consultation techniques and processes to involve all stakeholders in tourism-related decisions.
- Ensure that tourism interests are represented at major caucus planning meetings that affect the environment and the economy.
- Design and implement educational and awareness programs to sensitize people to sustainable tourism development issues.
- Develop design and construction standards to ensure that tourism development projects do not disrupt local culture and natural environments.
- Enforce regulations relating to illegal trade in historic objects and crafts; unofficial archaeological research and desecration of sacred sites.
- Regulate and control tourism in environmentally and culturally sensitive areas (Ceballos-Lascurain, 1996).

INDUSTRY-LED PLANNING AND POLICY

Planning and policy initiatives in the tourism industry are often seen as preventative methods in striking a balance between self-regulation and external regulation. This issue is of particular importance in managing the relationship between tourism and the environment, due to the fact that a pro-active stance by industry on environmental issues will always be a preferred industry solution rather than reacting to legislative regulations. However, self-regulation of environmental impacts by industry has not always been successful in other sectors, such as mining and agriculture. It remains to be seen whether self-regulation can be effective in the tourism industry (Birtles and Sofield, 1996) as the very nature of the tourism industry as a conglomerate of diverse segments makes it increasingly difficult to regulate such diversity effectively. There are also the problems associated with the influence of global financial institutions. Schilcher (2007) argues that only strategies that are largely in sync with a neo-liberal ideology and the 'World Bank orthodoxy', such as industry self-regulation or government incentives, have much potential to be implemented on a large-scale basis. Furthermore

> *the introduction of certification schemes and private self regulation, reached limits of effectiveness, as implicit prerequisites like common communication codes, coordination of interests between stakeholders, and transparent definition of content of certifications have been missing. (Wink, 2005: 2)*

Industry planning and policy initiatives for sustainable tourism have traditionally focused on improving professionalism, standards, training and quality of customer service, some with a business and marketing emphasis and others with an environmental emphasis. Manidis Roberts (1994) developed an 'Industry Quality Continuum' as a guide to self-regulation. *Table 3.1* shows an adapted version of the continuum including an explanation and examples for each type of measure to improve industry standards. The Continuum can also give an indication of the maturity of the tourism industry in a country or region, assuming that a code of practice is usually the first step in encouraging recognition of the need for environmental standards (Manidis Roberts, 1994).

We will now focus on the three most important measures – codes of practice, compliance and accreditation.

Codes of practice

The development of a code of practice for tourists and tour operators is typically one of the first industry initiatives on the path of sustainable development: 'one of the most promising features of the ecotourism industry is its

Table 3.1 Industry Quality Continuum (Adapted From Manidis Roberts, 1994)

Codes of Practice	Compliance	Accreditation	Quality System	Certification
Explanation				
• Industry general guide to behavior	• Informal	• Formal	• Formal	• Formal
• No requirements for participation by individual or organization	• Complying with codes	• Voluntary	• Voluntary	• Compulsory
• No enforcement	• Voluntary participation	• Administered by industry or other body	• Externally driven	• Externally approved standard
• Little promotion	• Can possibly require the signing of an agreement	• Involves standards of skill, experience or activity	• Conformity with external standard or best practice	• May be regulatory
	• Rarely any enforcement	• May involve audit of individual or organization	• Involves audit and benchmarking	• Involves audit
			• The entire organization participates	• Withdrawal for non-compliance
				• Involves penalties
Examples				
• Ecotourism Association of Australia	• PATA green leaf	• Savannah Guides	• AS3902 (quality in service)	• Builders licence
• Pacific Asia Travel Association (PATA)	• Green Globe	• National Ecotourism Accreditation Program	• ISO 9000	• May include Natural Resource Manager permits
• New Zealand Tourism Industry Association		• Tourism Vanuatu Accreditation	• ISO 14000	
• The Ecotourism Society			• BS7750	
• Tourism Council Australia				

willingness to both educate its operators and provide guidelines for their activities' (Duff, 1993: 18) in the form of codes of practice and guidelines. Today certification and ecolabelling are among the hottest topics in the tourism industry. Around the world there are some 260 voluntary initiatives, including tourism codes of conduct, labels, awards, benchmarking and 'best practices'. Of these 104 are ecolabelling and certification programs offering logos, seals of approval or awards designed to signify socially and/or environmentally superior tourism practices (Honey, 2007). These codes of practice and guidelines seek to establish standards of environmental performance and minimize the environmental impacts of tourism. Numerous codes of practice for ecotourism operators, tourists and developers have emerged in the early 1990s (e.g. Duff, 1993; Dowling, 1991). Examples include the Ecotourism Association of Australia's code of practice for Ecotour Operators (Duff, 1993), New Zealand Tourism Industry Federation Code of Practice (NZTIF, 1991), Pacific Asia Travel Association Code of Practice (PATA, 1992b), the Tasmanian Professional Trout Fishing Guides Association code of ethics (Department of Tourism, Sport and Recreation, 1994) and the Tourism Council Australia Code of Sustainable Practice (Tourism Council Australia, 1998).

CASE STUDY: Kingfisher Bay Resort and Village, Fraser Island, Queensland, Australia

Environmental codes of conduct for developers on Fraser Island were written into all contracts ensuring that environmental protection in the development stages was not neglected (Hackett, 1992). The most important aspect to note in this example is that the guidelines were legally enforceable and as such there were penalties involved for non-compliance.

While environmental legislation in Australia regulates tourism development, it is less effective in operational areas because of the dependency of tourism on environmental resources that are not managed by operators, and the small but incremental nature of operational impacts. The absence of functional environmental standards for tourism means that little guidance exists: a problem compounded by variability in the diversity of operation types and receiving environments, as well as the accessibility of information by a non-technical audience. While legislation and economic considerations may provide impetus to adopt environmental practices, it is proposed that an environmental philosophy is necessary for tourism businesses to seek out and maintain alternative sustainable modes of operation. A review of the environmental audit process used by the Queensland resort – Kingfisher Bay Resort and Village in Fraser Island – suggests that commitment to continual improvement in environmental performance is attributable to individual and corporate ethics. While the case is an ecotourism operation, the literature indicates that these factors have relevance to tourism generally. Although client satisfaction and return on investment objectives are constraints, environmental auditing can provide impetus for practical expression of environmental objectives. Facilitation of ethically motivated voluntary action may be more effective in achieving tourism's environmental objectives than codifying standards in static legislation (Carter et al., 2004) **(see Fig. 3.3)**.

FIGURE 3.3
*Kingfisher Bay Resort.
Photo by Kingfisher
Bay Resort.*

The above example is unfortunately a relatively isolated case. Most guidelines or codes of practice are ineffective as they lack any enforcement policy, statements of objectives, targets or evaluation procedures (Blangy and Nielsen, 1993). Further, such codes of practice and principles have also been criticized as they are usually adopted as narrow checklists, thus creating strict frames of reference that do not encourage actions or thoughts beyond those detailed on the lists (Gertsakis, 1995). As such, although codes of practice and guidelines are an attempt by the industry to minimize its impacts they lack enforcement and as such are limited in effectiveness and value.

Conversely, there are many advocates for the development of codes of conduct for tourists (e.g. Weiler and Johnson, 1991: 125). This would encompass appropriate social, cultural and environmentally responsible behavior. Examples of codes of conduct developed specifically for visitors include the Himalayan Environmental Trust Code of Conduct and the American Society of Travel Agents which was one of the earliest proponents of responsible tourism. While many sensitive regions have regulations governing visitor and operator behavior, such as the regulations governing visits to New Zealand's Sub-Antarctic Islands being some of the most rigorous, none of the codes of practice are in any way binding on the industry or the individual. Distribution and enforcement are major issues that undermine their usefulness (e.g. Hall et al., 1991).

There have also been attempts to introduce affirmation programs, requiring operators to display codes of practice and become signatories. However, their main role has been to create a sense of awareness within the industry and visitors of environmental-responsible practice (Manidis Roberts, 1994).

CASE STUDY: Codes of Conduct – The Arctic

The use of codes of conduct in the Arctic has attracted debate as to the effectiveness of their use particularly in relation to the often inadequate implementation of such codes. A draft visitor code for the Arctic is presented below as an indication of the content which has fueled debate on the effectiveness of such documents:

Conserve Resources

- Please leave wildlife habitats alone; where this is not possible, keep disturbance to a minimum.
- Please do not take plants, animals and other samples from nature – these must be left where found.
- Please limit damage by vehicles such as snow scooters.
- Hunting and fishing are under the strict control of national and regional authorities.
- Accessibility to nature reserves and national parks is restricted through the use of permits.

Stop Pollution

- Please do not leave behind any equipment or litter – this will decay slowly, and may injure wildlife, and could cost you a fine.
- All materials that have been brought in and not consumed during your visit should be taken out.

Respect Indigenous Cultures

- Almost all indigenous cultures in the Arctic have developed in harmony with nature, without overexploiting resources or creating unnecessary waste. Pay respect to these cultures.

Be a Guest

- Please do not expect to come to a wilderness and find all home comforts supplied.
- Be a true guest – one who is welcome in the landscape and amongst the local people.

Enjoy yourself and remember:
Take nothing but photographs,
Kill nothing but time,
Leave nothing but footprints. (Mason, 1997)

Manidis Roberts (1994) in relation to codes of conduct suggests a range of areas of concern, these are

- A need to monitor take up and effectiveness.
- The utilization of codes as a marketing tool.
- The need for coordination.
- Investigating whether self-regulation or external regulation should be utilized.

The critical component to any Code of Conduct is the need to evaluate the effectiveness of the code through an assessment of the effects and recording of the results. The validity of such issues is well-illustrated by the Arctic Case Example, with behavior reliant on the interpretation and honesty of the tourist.

Compliance

Compliance schemes are an attempt to develop environmental constraints for the industry and improve the type and nature of the experiences of visitors. They are similar to the Codes of Practice for, unless binding agreements are made between individual operators and an industry body who is responsible for the enforcement of the principles, the rigor and effectiveness of any such scheme is questionable. However, compliance schemes are distinguished from a Code of Practice in that they may require becoming signatories to a set of principles and intentions.

An example of a compliance scheme in the tourism industry is the Green Globe Programme (GGP) which was developed by the World Travel and Tourism Council (WTTC) in 1994. The Council brings together the chief executives of over 70 of the world's largest travel and tourism companies drawn from the accommodation, catering, recreation, transportation and travel-related services sector. The GGP was designed to help tourism businesses take targeted environmental action to enhance both business and environmental performance (Hawkins, 1995). It is a worldwide environmental management and awareness program for the travel and tourism industry, open to any companies of any size, type and location (WTTC, 1994). Research which focuses on environmental impacts where operational changes to minimize or negate adverse effects on the environment have a cost to the individual operator, will not necessarily induce the operator to introduce the required changes (Birtles and Sofield, 1996). The GGP, however, is based on the assumption that tourism operators will be motivated to introduce operational changes for cost savings, increased turnover and profit, moral pressure or a competitive advantage.

The promised services to members of the program include a telephone hotline information service, training, education and information guides, a global network of environmental advisers, annual survey, member's directory and extended support services. To become a member of the program, an organization is required to complete an annual survey on the state of environmental practice and targets for the coming year, as well as make a formal commitment to improvement in environmental practice and accept the Green Globe goals.

While there are many positive elements that the GGP achieves in the greening of the tourism industry, there are also some questionable aspects. While the WTTC has the potential to have a global influence due to its high profile amongst the international industry, government and policy makers, it is difficult to provide one set of guidelines and training materials for the diverse range of tourism destinations and operations in the world. Its objectives are also constrained by the lack of rigorous controls to ensure that standards are met. Often, however, some sort of environmental conservation program is better than no program at all. The WTTC advocates the self-regulation approach of the industry with the rationale that if the industry acts now it may through self-regulation be able to prevent constrictive governmental regulation (e.g. Birtles and Sofield, 1996).

A study conducted by Sirakaya and Uysal (1997) investigated the compliance behavior of 127 tour operators with ecotourism guidelines in the USA, Canada and Ecuador. The study tested major factors that promote the adherence to codes of conduct and compliance schemes. Those factors included rewards, sanctions and enforcement, education and communication of policies as potential predictors of compliance within the setting of the ecotourism industry. The study results showed that within a voluntary system of compliance, sanctions and deterrent measures did not play an important role in achieving the conformance behavior to the guidelines. Instead the positive reinforces, such as education of tour operators with respect to the benefits of compliance, were identified to be far more effective in achieving adherence to the guidelines. Scarpaci et al. (2004) investigated voluntary compliance by operators concluding that in many cases such compliance cannot be assumed, and that operators appear to comply better with conditions that are easily quantified. Accreditation programs involve a far greater degree of rewards and education than codes of practice or compliance schemes and therefore have the potential to be a more effective instrument in managing sustainable tourism.

Accreditation

Choice, risk, involvement and interaction with the natural environment are vital parts of the ecotourism experience. The ecotour operator (provider) needs to instil trust in the ecotourist (client) in order to attract and encourage them and this can be achieved through professionalism and accreditation (Font and Wood, 2007). However, while these provide the ecotourist with security, they can, in turn, reduce the excitement and interaction found in the natural environments visited.

Accreditation has been proposed as one solution to the provision of security and a quality of experience. It offers the opportunity to improve industry standards generally and the opportunity to provide a degree of quality assurance in a highly competitive market. It may also improve the protection of the natural environment on which ecotourism depends and ensure appropriate practices and more informed decision-making by ecotourists.

Accreditation involves the formal acknowledgment of adherence to agreed standards (Allcock et al., 1994). Benefits often associated with accreditation include quality assurance to both operators and tourists and the creation of a competitive edge in marketing. In accreditation systems, the primary responsibility for the integration and adoption of changes is with the tourism operator, through the identification and evaluation of a number of the environmental best practice initiatives within the ecotourism industry. However, a number of issues limit the effectiveness of 'environmental best practice' initiatives of the ecotourism industry, one of which was highlighted by PATA (1992a) in that the industry does not control or own any major part of its assets. As such this leads to the industry developing a 'selling mentality to the resource as distinct from a sense of ownership and stewardship' (PATA, 1992a: 9). Although this is the case, the diversity of not only the bodies involved in ecotourism but also destinations make it extremely difficult to create and implement a national accreditation scheme, as indicated by both Allcock et al. (1994) and the Department of Tourism, Sport and Recreation (1994). The high level of fragmentation of the tourism industry further reinforces such anticipated difficulties (Forestry Tasmania, 1994; Gilbert, 1984).

Nevertheless, the world's first National Ecotourism Accreditation scheme was developed and launched by the Ecotourism Association of Australia and the Australian Tourism Operators Network in 1996. The program is based on ecologically sustainable development principles and gives operators the opportunity to be innovative and continually improve their practices. The application process involves the completion of self-assessment in relation to minimum standards, compiled in a comprehensive application document and the nomination of three referees. An appropriately qualified and appointed Ecotourism Accreditation Assessor evaluates the self-assessment and forwards the application to the Ecotourism Accreditation Committee for approval or rejection. Apart from the referee checks there are other forms of verification used to determine if the application is bona fide, such as feedback from clients and random audits on a certain percentage of accredited operators. Should it be revealed that an accredited business is not fulfilling their nominated criteria, their accreditation status may be suspended or revoked. The aim over time is to increase the minimum standards on a regular basis and to ensure that best practice can be realized on an ongoing basis (Ecotourism Association of Australia, 1996). While initiatives such as the National Ecotourism Accreditation Programme are more accountable and enforceable than any code of practice or compliance scheme, there are still concerns over the credibility of its self-assessment component. However, this concern will most likely decrease with the increasing amount of accredited ecotourism operators who have the capacity to act as 'watchdogs' amongst themselves, and the continual review and raising of the minimum standards:

> *if we have switched the emphasis from defining ecotourism to improving its performance, then we have come a long way in a short time. The challenge now is to go beyond rewarding bona fide ecotourism operators to establish measures that help other operators change their practices and become bona fide themselves. (McArthur, 1997b: 25)*

CASE STUDY: Great Barrier Reef Marine Park, Queensland, Australia

The issuing of license and permits is one method that is used to control both the numbers and types of users of a particular area. An example of their use is in the Great Barrier Reef Marine Park where commercial tourist operators require a permit to operate. Before any activity is undertaken in the Marine Park they must check the *Great Barrier Reef Marine Park Zoning Plan 2003* to see if the activity is allowed, and whether the activity requires a Marine Park's permit. All permit applications are assessed for possible impacts upon the conservation of the park's natural resources in order to reduce or prevent potential adverse impacts. In this way access is restricted to a select number who have met certain conditions or criteria which are seen as being compatible with the area's values and desired uses. The main strength of the use of licenses and permits is that they are legally enforceable. An associated problem or issue with regard to industry-led best practice is that it is dependent upon the resource manager and not the user (such as the ecotour operator) to establish and instigate the conditions or criteria for the granting of the licenses and permits. As such, all the operator has to do is to fulfill the required conditions of the use situation (Great Barrier Reef Marine Park, 2008a).

COOPERATIVE GOVERNMENT AND INDUSTRY INITIATIVES: COMMUNITY INVOLVEMENT AND COOPERATIVE APPROACHES

Depending on the political and economic system of a country, the ideal solution to the debate over 'self-regulation' versus 'regulation' is a cooperative approach to tourism planning and policy. A critical ingredient in the success of self-regulation is community involvement, which is a major issue in the sustainable tourism principles literature (Inskeep, 1991; Eber, 1992). Sustainable tourism relies heavily then on the stakeholder involvement and efforts must be made to improve the links between nature conservation, local community development and the tourism industry (Ceballos-Lascurain, 1996; Weaver, 2001). Stakeholder involvement needs to consider two main points: (1) who should be considered stakeholders in the tourism planning and development stage, and (2) how should planners and developers involve stakeholders in the development of tourism (Byrd, 2007). The managers of protected areas and other primary stakeholders often do not have sufficient knowledge, skills, capabilities and tools to ensure that protected areas can more effectively respond to the challenges posed by global change. Enhanced capacity is essential and is needed at a range of levels, including for protected areas agencies, park managers and nearby communities. Skills and competencies need to be more specialized than in the past, requiring a range of innovative and adaptive approaches to protected area management (Bushell and Eagles, 2003).

As well as capacity building for stakeholders there needs to be development of models to monitor and manage tourism activity that has been established with their endorsement and support (Prosser, 1986). Stakeholders from the local tourism sector and community are critical to implementing these models. The stakeholders can provide valuable input into desired conditions and acceptable standards, and are usually essential in providing the economic and political support necessary to maintain monitoring programs and implement management decisions.

However, there has been a consistent failure to establish sufficient stakeholder support for sustainable management models – such as the Visitor Impact Management Model (VIMM) and the Limits of Acceptable Change (LAC) which we discuss further in the following chapter – largely due to the fact that management organizations responsible for these models simply are not attuned to attracting wider stakeholder involvement. There are three primary impediments to achieving this outcome:

- the use of the terms 'impact' and 'limits', which the tourism industry has interpreted as being discouraging to growth and thus business

- the conventional narrow focus on the condition of the physical environment and to some extent, the nature of the visitor experience

- the lack of cooperative involvement of the tourism sector in identifying indicators and standards that are acceptable to the industry

Without the involvement of all stakeholders the monitoring of results becomes conflictual and prone to conjecture, particularly if they reveal surprising or controversial implications (McArthur 1997a).

USING POLICY TO ACHIEVE BEST PRACTICE

Tourism has the potential to be an 'environmentally friendly' industry. Yet, there are well-documented examples of tourist destinations becoming polluted, degraded and congested by mass market travel (PATA, 1992a: 7). One way of attempting to deal with such problems of increasing environmental degradation of the natural environment is through the incorporation of 'environmental best practice'. This concept not only plays a role in the ecotourism industry but also in the 'mainstream' tourism industry. We will now turn our attention to 'environmental best practice' in ecotourism as a practical and effective approach to generate solutions to environmental management and its potential to give direction to the rest of the tourism industry with regard to the environmental issues the industry is facing as a whole. In order to address these issues, a number of specific areas will have to be discussed. We will begin by discussing best practice and its relation to ecotourism and environmental management. This will lead to the identification of a number of forms of environmental best practice, with emphasis on their relative strengths and weaknesses.

Best practice involves striving for excellence, keeping in touch with innovations, avoiding waste and focusing on outcomes which are in the community interest (Edwards and Prineas, 1995). It involves managing change and continual improvement and in this way it encompasses all levels of an organization. Examples of best practice include aiming to increase customer service, improvements in productivity or in the management of people. Best practice is neither limited to particular types of organizations or bodies, nor is it to particular aspects or issues within those organizations or bodies. Rather it is an extremely diverse practice, which can be implemented in an array of different situations to serve different purposes. However, its central concern is related to change within an organization.

Bushell and Eagles (2003) suggest that the best practice initiatives promote and support national and international collaborative capacity-development activities with tourism stakeholders at all levels. This approach the authors argue would go some way to ensuring that best practice is widely disseminated, provides assistance for stakeholders to develop appropriate responses to change and thereby enable and empower themselves to play their full role in protected area management. Following from this, it seems fairly straightforward that best practice can be associated with tourism or ecotourism, especially in regard to the increasing levels of environmental concern and awareness worldwide. An example of this is the World Commission on Protected Areas Best Practice, Protected Area Guidelines

(WCPA, 2007). The form of best practice in this case can be referred to as environmental best practice, which is defined by the Ecologically Sustainable Development Steering Committee (ESDSC, 1992) as business/industry culture and practices which align operational competitiveness to improved environmental performance. In this way it links environmental management and operational management in a positive way, leaving the primary responsibility for both with the organization itself. Numerous forms of environmental best practice are currently employed by ecotourism operators, ranging from the issuing of licenses and permits for access to the development of codes of practice for tourists, operators and developers. A number of these forms will be discussed below, with emphasis placed on their relative strengths and weaknesses. Tourism is no different from any other industry in its imperative for profitability. This profitability imperative is somewhat limited in ecotourism ventures as they must realize and incorporate limits to growth and volume. (The following chapter will elaborate on operational techniques to achieve these objectives.) There is an inverse relationship between how environmentally friendly a local nature tourism operation is and how economically powerful it can ever hope to be (Cohen and Richardson, 1995). In this sense the environmental best practice initiatives of ecotourism are often not adopted within the greater tourism industry as they can be seen to place limits on profitability. This issue is further compounded by the general tourism's overt pursuit of ever increasing volumes and the measurement of performance being exclusively linked to this increase (PATA, 1992b).

CASE STUDY: The Canadian Tourism Industry

In recent years, the Canadian tourism industry has moved from a system of 'ecolabelling' to one of 'benchmarking', culminating in the Catalogue of Exemplary Practices in Adventure Travel and Ecotourism in order to facilitate and disseminate best practice (Wight, 2001).

It would be a grave mistake, however, for the tourism industry to disregard the environmental best practice initiatives of ecotourism. As we have seen, the most effective forms of regulation are those instigated by the industry itself and ecotourism is a leader in recognizing its environmental responsibilities by attempting to address these responsibilities through the establishment of codes of practice, guidelines and suggested accreditation schemes. Even though such initiatives are not yet supported by penalties for non-compliance, they provide a starting point or springboard with which to further foster and encourage environmentally sound practices in the tourism industry into the future. However, the major drawback with ecotourism-led environmental best practice is that actions are only adopted if they are seen as desirable within the organization. If they are not legally enforceable their use and effect is limited to those organizations already oriented toward environmental philosophies or which have the aspiration to incorporate such values.

In understanding the mechanisms for policy and planning we may be able to achieve certain flexibility in approaching ecotourism development by adopting a broad range of approaches which may assist in:

- achieving lower infrastructure cost

- reducing the number of inbound visitors – which could conserve natural and cultural sites

- an increase in the quality of visitor experience through understanding group and community interactions

- a means to increase long-term benefits for local communities

The extent to which ecotourism adheres to the principles of sustainability appears to be greater with cooperative approaches between government and stakeholder planning and policy. The principal role of such planning and policy, which mainly occurs through legislation and regulation, is therefore to ensure that ecotourism does not negatively impact on the environment, but rather creates environmental, economic and socio-cultural benefits.

CASE STUDY: Rwanda Diversification of Ecotourism Product

In lesser developed nations, a shift to reliance on ecotourism as a primary source of income, in preference to traditional agricultural pursuits, is observable. In such cases, management of this shift may be strengthened by diversification of the ecotourism products promoted.

In Rwanda, data available suggest that 93% of the country's tourism income is derived from gorilla visitation (Mazimhaka, 2007). The revenues in 1989, estimated at $1 million through direct expenditure and $9 million via indirect expenditure, are derived through international visitation, as high-tourism costs in the country deter domestic visitors to gorilla populations (numbers of visitors and income generated from tourism in Rwanda fell dramatically after this period due to the 1990–1994 war and genocide) (Mazimhaka, 2007).

Most visitors to Rwanda are attracted to the Parc National des Volcans which houses the gorilla population, however, the country has been attempting to promote its other protected areas. The Parc National d'Akagera, created in 1954 and covering an area of 2500 square miles, and the Nyungwe Forest Reserve in Southern Rwanda, one of the largest untouched montane forests with 250 species of birds, are two such areas. With Rwanda still reeling from the recent civil war, genocide and mass population exodus, advertising of new ecotourism destinations has been given lesser priority. The effects of economic and political upheaval in less-developed nations illustrate the influence external factors may have on already limited government expenditure on tourism, and that such volatility threatens successful ecotourism ventures which operate in areas of significant natural beauty. Where governments cannot afford to promote the region/attraction operators are left to bridge a large gap with finite resources (Shackley, 1995).

There is a pressing need to follow the principles of ecotourism in Rwanda's tourism industry in order to best conserve the indigenous primates. Without taking into account the best interests of their conservation needs, it is unlikely that a sustainable future for the primate tourism industry can be attained. Using tourism as a strategy for conservation must also take into account local community needs, as people who benefit from nature are more likely to protect nature.

Land use zoning is associated with the use of carrying capacity. Generally carrying capacity attempts to establish the level of use possible within the given environment without environmental deterioration. Hall (1994) takes the issue of carrying capacities a step further, highlighting that they must include social and cultural aspects as well as the above-mentioned environmental issues. An example of the effective use of an environmental carrying capacity is at the Point Nepean National Park in Victoria, Australia where once the assigned quota of daily visitors is reached the gates to the park are simply closed (Wescott, 1993). Once again though, the identification and implementation of the carrying capacity is the duty of the resource manager and not the user. Furthering this, there are inherent difficulties involved in quantifying the associated environmental, social and cultural impacts (Dowling, 1991; Garrod and Wilson, 2003; Norris, 1994).

Zoning

Land use zoning divides sections of land into areas based on their sensitivity and conservation values (Buckley and Pannell, 1990). They also aim to establish systematic recreational use management. By doing so areas are designated for different purposes in an attempt not only to protect the valued areas but also to balance this with use. It has the ability to facilitate sustainable tourism through the regulation of development and the implementation of design standards for tourist facilities to ensure that they do not impact to the detriment of the environment in which they are developed (McIntyre et al., 1993). The main advantage of zoning is that it is one way in which conflicting activities can be separated, enabling the identification of the suitability of particular sites/areas for particular uses, and the protection and conservation of selected sites or areas (Simmons and Harris, 1995: 14). Zoning is an effective means to limit the extent of tourism activities within the sustainable boundaries of the region. In order for zoning to work effectively it is essential to clarify each zone's recreational characteristic and management goal in the area, and develop recreation facilities and manage the area in keeping with these goals (Yamaki et al., 2003).

CASE STUDY: Great Barrier Reef Marine Park Zoning Plan 2003

The Great Barrier Marine Park Zoning Plan 2003 superseded all previous zoning plans, coming into effect on 1 July 2004. The new zoning plan was brought into effect for the entire marine park, and has been widely acclaimed as a new global benchmark for the conservation of marine ecosystems. The Great Barrier Reef Marine Park is now the largest protected sea area in the world after the Australian Government increased the areas protected from extractive activities (such as fishing and sand mining) from 4.6% to 33.3%.

The current method of zoning is called the 'Representative Areas Programme', which chooses typical areas of the Great Barrier Reef Marine Park. The area has now been divided into 70 bioregions, of which 30 are reef bioregions and 40 are non-reef bioregions, each with their own rules and regulations.

In 2006, a review was undertaken of the 'Great Barrier Reef Marine Park Act 1975'. Some recommendations of the review are that there should be no further zoning plan changes until 2013, and that every 5 years, a peer-reviewed Outlook Report should be published, examining the health of the Great Barrier Reef, the management of the reef and environmental pressures (Great Barrier Reef Marine Park, 2008b).

FURTHER READING

Bramwell, B. (2005). Interventions and policy instruments for sustainable tourism. In *Global Tourism*, third ed. (W.F. Theobald, ed.). Elsevier, New York, pp. 406–25.

Fennell, D.A., and Dowling, R.K. (eds) (2003). *Ecotourism Policy and Planning*. CAB International, Oxford, UK.

Bramwell's chapter and Fennell and Dowling's edited text explore the range of challenges that ecotourism managers face in delivering sustainable tourism experiences. They outline policies and procedures based on various case studies from around the world and how these affect the business of ecotourism.

Wight, P.A. (2003). Supporting the principles of sustainable development in tourism and ecotourism: government's potential role. In *Global Ecotourism Policies and Case Studies: Perspectives and Constraints* (M. Lück, & T. Kirstges, eds). Channel View Publications, Clevedon, UK, pp. 50–72.

Using the provincial government of Alberta, Canada, as a case study, Wight tracks its involvement in ecotourism from the early to the late 1990s. She contrasts the government's initial 'strong sustainability' mode with its later 'weak sustainability' mode and its lack of support for the principles of sustainable development.

CHAPTER 4

Ecotourism and Protected Areas: Visitor Management for Sustainability

Conservation issues are now at the forefront of public awareness. Climate change, the decline of rainforests, loss of endangered species and increasing land degradation have galvanized public support for conservation. It is no accident that the interest and growth of ecotourism and nature-oriented tourism have coincided with this worldwide concern (e.g. Wearing et al., 2002).

Ecotourism and nature-oriented tourism often take place in protected and remote regions, areas of exceptional beauty, ecological interest and cultural importance. Today, these areas are established to conserve biodiversity and to halt the large-scale loss of natural ecosystems. In 1962, there were 1000 protected areas covering 3% of the earth's surface, now there are 102,100 covering 18.8 million square kilometers or 11.5% of the Earth's land surface (Bushell and Eagles, 2003). This represents a phenomenal growth in both the public desire and political will to see natural areas protected in perpetuity.

While the number of protected areas around the world has grown they are also coming under increasing pressure on a range of fronts including

- the demands for 'multiple use' parks allowing extractive industries

- the demands of lobby groups seeking access for a range of recreational activities – four wheel driving, horse riding, hunting, fishing, mountain biking, bushwalking and skiing

- and the aspirations of indigenous groups for title and management of parks

These demands raise distinct challenges for protected areas. Indeed, in the face of these increasing challenges can (indeed, should) these areas remain as protected refuges?

The traditional conception of protected areas is the uninhabited, minimal interference park, as we have seen in Chapter 2, this is an overtly 'preservationist' position. However, in much of the world population pressures are

CONTENTS

Tourism and Protected Areas

Protected Areas and Capitalist Realism

Tourism as a Key

Sustainable Management Techniques

A Short History of Protected Areas and Sustainable Management Strategies

Managing Visitor Use

Further Reading

dictating that excluding human presence from protected areas is no longer feasible.

The preservationist position is also under attack from the opposite end of the spectrum, by those who believe nature has one primary value or function – for human use. 'Use' adherents range from industry representatives seeking access to park resources, such as the logging, grazing and mining industries to the many diverse special interest groups who are generally hostile to nature-centered management, such as hunters and off-road vehicle enthusiasts.

Historically protected area policy has moved significantly in the direction of human use. In the Caracas Action Plan, the major strategy document to come out of the IVth World Congress on National Parks and Protected Areas in Venezuela in 1992, the shift away from an overt preservationist position toward a human-needs orientation is unambiguous: 'Protected areas must be managed so that local communities, the nations involved and the world community all benefit' (IUCN, 1992: 14). These sentiments were echoed more recently in the Durban Action Plan which stated that protected areas cannot be managed without regards to the communities and the economic activities within and around them (IUCN, 2004).

We can see here, in both the use and preservationist positions, the centrality of the anthropocentric premise. Nature conservation's most acceptable and prevalent form[15] is a utilitarian one in that such areas are deemed necessary to preserve or protect for their potential human benefits, be it for 'aesthetic', 'gymnasium', 'cathedral' or 'laboratory' potential (see Chapter 2). Thus the use and preservationist positions are constrained by two orientations: at one extreme lies the emphasis on human needs being met in parks, while the other leads to overt opposition to the preservation and protection of natural areas as valueless 'locking up' of land. This conflict intensifies with the pressures of an exponentially increasing global population and the concomitant consumption of resources this entails.

As we have seen in Chapter 2, ecocentrically oriented philosophies have raised significant challenges to the anthropocentric focus on nature's value lying in its relation to human needs. However, an extreme ecocentrist approach would actually challenge the fundamental rationale of protected areas themselves as a 'Noah's Ark solution', for protected areas are in effect isolated islands of biodiversity. An ecocentric perspective would argue that we would not need protected areas if we did not have such an exploitative relationship with nature (see Chapter 2) and this is the heart of the protected area debate, particularly in relation to ecotourism.

---

[15] This is often the only grounds accepted for its argument.

TOURISM AND PROTECTED AREAS

Nowhere are the conflicting views over intrinsic and utilitarian value more evident than the current debate over the function and purpose of protected areas. It is a conflict over two primary orientations, 'preservation' versus 'use', and tourism in protected areas embodies precisely this dilemma. For tourism is in essence a recreational activity in which the value for nature aligns with both the 'cathedral' and 'gymnasium' dimensions that we have discussed in Chapter 2. Protected areas seemingly are incompatible with such activities for their primary function lies in the preservation of natural ecosystems (Zarska, 2006). Such an opposition is illustrated and reinforced through accepted institutional arrangements in which tourism and conservation goals are pursued by independent organizations. The current focus of the debate on tourism in parks is the extension of a long controversy, a controversy that has existed since the conception of protected areas and equivalent reserves. The originating conception of national parks placed recreation rather than conservation at the center of park functions (Nash, 2001). Yellowstone National Park in the United States of America, for example, was originally conceptualized as 'pleasuring grounds for the benefit and enjoyment of the people...for gaining great profit from tourists and pleasure seekers' and as 'a national domain for rest and recreation' (Strom, 1980: 3). Similarly, The Royal National Park, established in Australia in 1879, was originally established as an area for leisure. Historically then parks were established for utilitarian reasons but since the early conception of parks there has been a significant reorientation away from a predominant recreational/tourism focus toward conservation objectives. Recreation and tourism were only a minor threat to parks because of the distance and difficulty in access and the low levels of visitation. However, this has changed significantly in the last 40 years as protected areas are becoming much more popular through increases in mobility, leisure and environmental awareness (Sheppard, 1987; Eagles and McCool, 2004).

To accept increased levels of visitation as the price of support significantly compromises the natural qualities upon which parks are founded. Everyday we witness increasing pressure on natural resources and a need for escalating protection of resources, particularly those found in protected areas and equivalent reserves. The major problem is in deciding what directions and actions should be taken to ensure the future of such areas.

Although protected areas are not conceived identically across the world, the International Union of the Conservation of Nature provides a general definition:

An area of land and/or sea especially dedicated to the protection and maintenance of biological diversity, and of natural and associated cultural resources, and managed through legal or other effective means.

Within the definition, six different categories have been identified (see below), which provide an underlining approach to management *(see Table 4.1)*.

These definitions clearly identify nature conservation values as a major purpose. This includes the protection of genetic and biological diversities, and the provision of settings for baseline measurements of biological conditions for the comparison of effects associated with development. However, it also recognizes the legitimate right of public entry 'under special conditions' – recreational purposes, for example.

Table 4.1	
Category Ia	Strict Nature Reserve: protected area managed mainly for science
Category Ib	Wilderness Area : protected area managed mainly for wilderness protection
Category II	National Park: protected area managed mainly for ecosystem protection and recreation
Category III	Natural Monument: protected area managed mainly for conservation of specific natural features
Category IV	Habitat/Species Management Area: protected area managed mainly for conservation through management intervention
Category V	Protected Landscape/Seascape: protected area managed mainly for landscape/seascape conservation and recreation
Category VI	Managed Resource Protected Area: protected area managed mainly for the sustainable use of natural ecosystems

PROTECTED AREAS AND CAPITALIST REALISM

Across the industrialized west the role of government is shrinking with many former government controlled sectors – insurance, health, education, energy, water, transport, and banking – being increasingly removed from public ownership and control in a shift toward a corporate/profit rather than public interest model. The impacts of this change have seen no sphere of government exempt from the market-based rationale. In this way protected area agencies have also found themselves under intense pressure to be more 'commercial', 'customer focused' and to produce more of their revenue from the services provided by parks.

CASE STUDY: Funding US National Parks

With the drive to meet budget targets and increased discussions on corporate sponsorship the National Parks Service has been forced to pursue alternative funding options whilst still maintaining their stewardship role. In 1997, in budget submissions to the Department of Interior, the Park Service requested (US$) 1.5 billion. Congress allotted (US$) 1.42 billion. For the 1998 fiscal year, the agency is seeking (US$) 1.6 billion, including (US$) 100 million for an ambitious upgrading of the Everglades National Park. Although funding has steadily increased from (US$) 900 million in 1984 to the 1997 figure of (US$) 1.4 billion, if this figure is measured in constant 1983 dollars, the appropriations have decreased by 14%.

Increased land management responsibilities have increased the strain on resource managers – consider these statistics alongside the decline in real funding:

- Visits have steadily risen from 210 million in 1984 to over 272 million in 2006.
- The number of national parks has increased from 335 in 1984 to 391 today.
- In the past 10 years, staff numbers have been reduced by 10%.

In addition, there are estimated costs of (US$) 7–10 billion required to rectify a backlog of repairs and improvements. A debate rages over appropriations, budgeting and priorities, but the essence of the argument is that parks need more money. One critical concern is that the Park Service maintains its stewardship role in the face of the funding crisis. Congress approved a 3-year pilot program to introduce entrance fees at 100 parks. Nearly all of the money collected goes back into parks, providing in 1998 an estimated (US$) 48 million for repairs and maintenance.

Congress is considering

- Concession reforms legislation. This could generate $50 million annually from private businesses operating within the park.
- A revenue bond program, allowing private, non-profit groups to finance capital parks projects by issuing bonds.
- A bill to let taxpayers check off part of their return to go toward funding parks.

However, the primary fear for the parks service is that the reduction in appropriations due to such an offset would in effect defeat the purpose of such fund raising (Mitman Clarke, 1997) *(see Fig. 4.1)*.

FIGURE 4.1 *Half Dome (2693 m) in the Yosemite National Park, California. Photo by United States National Park Service.*

Contemporary questions about whether to utilize or conserve are really questions about who controls natural resources (Stretton, 1976; Worboys et al., 2005). They are therefore like any other question of distributive justice and are inherently political. In our current economically rationalist world-view protected areas are considered as no different from competing land use claims and most argue for their survival on these terms.

The imperative for conservation advocates becomes *how* to conserve rather than whether or not to conserve. However urgent it may be to wake people up to physical and ecological changes, environmental reformers also need political philosophies (Stretton, 1976) and for quite practical purposes (Weaver, 2001a). In this way ecotourism, as a sustainable development strategy, is increasingly being turned to as part of a political philosophy for protected area managers and conservation agencies as a means of providing practical outcomes in the struggle to provide a basis for continued protection for these areas. These outcomes include

- a source of finance for parks and conservation and therefore providing a justification (economic) for park protection

- an alternative form of economic development

- the broadening of conservation issues within the general public

- the facilitation of a private conservation ethic

To operationalize conservation goals in a context which involves decisions on the allocation of scarce resources dictates that arguments for protected areas will almost inevitably involve economic rationalist and utilitarian premises. Being realistic (some would say pessimistic) it also seems unlikely that the potential value of protected areas to future generations will be a sufficiently strong argument to cause current generations to set aside scarce resources for future generations.

However, to argue that protected areas are a resource that can be enjoyed for recreation and tourism poses a serious dilemma. This dilemma is one of current protections based on utilitarian objectives and of future conservation based on intrinsic value. Are these approaches compatible or, more importantly, can either contribute toward conservation?

> With such a variety of pressures on natural resources, the need for more and more intensive protection of those resources which are currently found in protected areas and equivalent reserves is all too evident. The manpower and financial resources which are needed for the protection of the 2% of the Earth's terrestrial surface that are currently in protected areas are far from adequate. Can we rest with any confidence that the 98% of the globe which is not covered by the UN list of protected areas and Equivalent Reserves is adequately managed? [P]rotected areas are but one mechanism for attaining conservation objectives. They are an important mechanism but in themselves they are inadequate. (Eidsvik, 1980: 187)

A number of authors (e.g. Nash, 1989; Runte, 1997) suggest that the use versus preservation question is an 'appropriate use' dilemma. This dilemma of 'appropriate use' is a conflict of values which will always arise in any anthropocentric approach to conservation and management of ecosystems:

> Wilderness, however defined, belongs to all Americans, yet to enjoy the wilderness is to destroy it – particularly if the enjoyment is seen in terms of mass recreation. (Coppock & Rogers, 1975: 510)

Although protected areas are considered as primarily conservation based (e.g. Bruggemann, 1997; Runte 1997; Strom, 1980) there will always be conflicts between use and conservation.

> Protected areas have been, are, and will continue to be used by people, irrespective of what park management agencies say and do. (Sheppard, 1987: 23)

Section 72(4)(e) of the New South Wales (Australia) National Parks and Wildlife Act (1974) requires of protected areas

The encouragement and regulation of the appropriate use, understanding and enjoyment of each national park, historic site and state recreation area by the public.

TOURISM AS A KEY

Society expects optimal use of natural resources as an integral part of the process of continual economic development. In this circumstance the economic justification of ecotourism in protected areas offers a means of providing outcomes that can demonstrate to society the benefits of protected areas. Increasingly, tourism is often used to provide an economic rationale to preserve natural areas rather than developing them for alternative uses such as agriculture or forestry. In current analyses of natural or protected areas it is this element that has become central, pushing debate onto the question of maintaining an area in its natural state as opposed to exploiting the resources it contains.

This economic valuation is increasingly being used to justify the existence of protected areas through the demonstratable 'value' of both the wildlife and ecosystem features. Tourism is becoming increasingly central to these strategies given that tourists are willing to pay to experience these natural areas.

Many studies are now being used to show that protected areas make an economic contribution of some significance (e.g. Bushell, 2003; Butler et al., 1994; Buultjens and Luckie, 2004; Herath and Kennedy, 2004; Pearce, 2006; Prideaux and Falco-Mammone, 2007). These studies have variously used econometric modeling, input–output analysis and multiplier analysis to estimate the impact of natural resource-based recreation and tourism on local and regional economies.

CASE STUDY: Amboseli National Park

Mount Kilimanjaro is the majestic backdrop for this park which features five different wildlife habitats: the seasonal lake bed of Lake Amboseli, sulfur springs surrounded by swamps and marshes, open plains, woodlands and lava rock thornbush country. These habitats support elephant herds, black rhino, lion and cheetah as well as Masai giraffe, eland, Coke's hartebeest, waterbuck, impala and gazelle.

Amboseli National Park is estimated to be worth 18 times the annual income of a fully developed commercial beef industry covering the same area. Estimates indicate that Amboseli National Park brings in US$3.3 million a year from park fees and related tourist activities. The value of a single lion as a tourist attraction is estimated at US$27,000 a year, while an elephant herd may be worth as much as US$610,000 per year – thus they are 'worth' more alive than dead (MacKinnon et al., 1986). The total net return for a park such as Amboseli in utilizing tourism, is estimated to be 50 times more per hectare a year than the most optimistic agricultural returns.[16]

In fact there are many potential economic benefits related to the park. For example Okello (2005) estimates that extending wildlife tourism and conservation beyond the park boundaries of Amboseli, through an adjoining community conservation area could potentially generate US$147,867 annually for surrounding villages.

Tourism in protected areas can lead to increased economic benefits through both the direct expenditures of tourists and the associated employment opportunities it generates, both within and adjacent to the park. This can be capitalized upon in promotional strategies – a poster in Tanzania reads: 'Our protected areas bring good money into Tanzania – Protect them' (Nash, 1989: 344). The Terai Arc Landscape, a UNESCO World Heritage Site in Nepal, carries a slogan that shares the same sentiments: 'People for natural resources and natural resources for the people' (Gajurel, 2004). This economic rationale in support of parks (e.g. Machlis and Tichnell, 1985; MacKinnon et al., 1986) is especially important where competing resource uses, such as agriculture or forestry, are involved.

The economic benefits of tourism have the potential to provide additional support for park protection and for giving parks a role in supporting rural development. However, there are questions about the distribution of the economic benefits of tourism. Large-scale developments involving millions of dollars may be appearing to contribute to local or regional economies but, in fact, such benefits may only be illusory. Rates of leakage of tourist expenditures can be very high and are generally found to range from 30% to 45% in first round leakages thus leaving limited income for local communities (e.g. Lea, 1988, 1993; Mowforth and Munt, 2008).

The question of who gets the benefits and who pays the costs is complex. Although visitors expect some tourism money to directly benefit the local population surrounding the area, in some cases little of that money is actually distributed to the local communities. Moreover, much of the economic impact literature focuses only on benefits. Limited attention has

---

[16] Similar studies abound in the literature: one study in Costa Rica showed that the value of a tropical rain forest reserve in its natural state was at least equal to or twice as high than the economic 'price' of the land itself; a macaw in Peru is estimated as generating between $750 and $4700 annually in tourist revenues (Munn, 1991: 471).

been given to the economic costs imposed by the infrastructure developed to attract, accommodate and facilitate tourism or to the costs of maintaining and/or restoring park resources that are adversely affected by tourists. This raises the concern of whether the perceived economic returns of tourism in or associated with protected areas will lead to inappropriate developments and/or use levels that threaten the conservation objectives upon which the park is founded.

Arguments for tourism's ability to generate employment is also problematic as often employment goes to persons residing outside of the area. Wages also are typically low and tourism is highly seasonal in many areas. Economic benefits are also subject to external changes, such as shifts in exchange rates that can rapidly change the 'attractiveness' of a location as the cost of holidaying is one of the most important factors in determining the desirability of a region.

This illustrates several key limitations in the economic justification of protected areas. Current economic analyses are capable of extending only to those more tangible economic measurements, such as willingness to pay, travel costs and expenditure rates. These methods have been effective to an extent in evaluating some human behavior associated with national parks and protected areas, but they have not been widely accepted as adequate methods for estimating accurately the value of national parks and protected areas.

Economics is by definition a zero sum equation and must therefore take account of all costs that are associated with a particular project in order for the economic equation to balance fully. In terms of natural areas, a large proportion of the costs in changing the use of an area are social costs which, in many cases, are intangible and difficult, if not impossible to measure.

Economic concepts do not readily adapt to measurement of the intangible values of protected areas. The valuation of natural areas has its basis in the framework for land use planning in developed countries which centers on the idea of 'highest and best use'. For an economic cost, the highest and best use of land invariably refers to the most economically viable purpose. Inherent in this judgment are the limitations of economic indicators to value all relevant factors with a consistent degree of accuracy. Clearly it is easier to quantify the value of raw materials, land (as private real estate) or development opportunities in accurate monetary terms, than it is to identify the more intangible social impacts of utilizing a resource.

When an economic valuation of a natural area is proposed, it is usually done so in order to compare alternative uses of the resource. This comparison is almost always for the purposes of decision-making, and this decision-making process is inherently political. While the concept of economic cost seeks to provide a figure that provides a platform upon which a political argument is built, almost inevitably this argument moves to analysis of non-economic matters or the concept of 'social cost,' or, in economic terms, externalities.

In basic economic terms a quality environment is a 'good' producing 'satisfaction' and therefore must be accounted for in some way. Environmental impact assessment has been developed as a mechanism to begin accounting for these less tangible values. However, the consideration of social costs presents significant problems for economic analyses. Economic analysis has, in the last decade, expanded its theoretical parameters to include non-financial benefits. However, there is an inherent bias for measurable economic returns.

It is found that although global property rights in biodiversity and ecotourism can provide some positive support for biodiversity conservation, they cannot be relied on to conserve biodiversity to the extent desired globally. This is because they only allow appropriation of economic use values, and then probably do this only partially (Tisdell, 2004: 269). The solution to the problem should not be based on the development of better economic and social indexes.

Indexes cannot alter the fact that what one citizen sees as goods another sees as costs or waste. What one wants to consume another wants to leave in the ground. Indexes of net welfare have to be constructed by controversial judgments of good and bad. They are still worth having (though every person may want their own). Better accounting can serve all sorts of good purposes, and reconcile some mistaken conflicts of opinion, but it cannot reconcile real conflicts of interest outside (Stretton, 1976: 314). Ecocentrically informed management recognizes that modern science and technology cannot prevent environmental degradation if the current economic growth and resource use trends continue, and that a change in philosophy, politics and economics is needed to ensure that a sustainable human population can exist in balance with its environment. This is a preservationist position which reemphasizes the need for prior macro-environmental constraints, such as government legislation. Such an approach is based on the idea of 'ecological economics' (or full-cost accounting) which comprehensively takes resource depletion and environmental damage into consideration and thereby addresses issues of natural debt (ShuYang et al., 2004).

Conservation then involves the management or control of human use of resources (biotic and abiotic) and activities on the planet, in an attempt to restore, enhance, protect and sustain the quality and quantity of a desired mix of species, ecosystem conditions and processes for present and future generations (Dunster and Dunster, 1996: 69).

Resource conservation is thus a form of 'restrained development' in that, at a minimum, development must be sustainable in not endangering the natural systems that support life on earth – the atmosphere, the waters, the soils and all living beings. An ecocentric systems approach to protected areas management allows a shift from the utilitarian/instrumental justification toward the intrinsic values of the protected areas. However, without this change in values the long-term future of protected areas could be placed in jeopardy.

SUSTAINABLE MANAGEMENT TECHNIQUES

While more conventional forms of tourism modify the surrounding environment to suit the specific needs of their clients, ecotourists do not expect or even desire substantial modifications of the natural environment. Rather than measuring the quality of the tour by conventional standards such as predictability and uniformity of experience, 'ecotourism's success is based on the unexpected' (Williams, 1990: 84). Ecotourism provides the tourist with opportunities to discover and actively participate and interact with the surrounding environment, encouraging the tourist to assume a pro-active role in creating their own tourism experience.

Despite increasing interest from larger tour operators, ecotourism remains largely an activity of small operators (O'Neill, 1991). Thus it occurs at a different scale to traditional mass tourism as small operators are restricted in the numbers of clients that they are able to handle at any one time. (e.g. Choegyal, 1991: 94; Williams, 1990: 85). Due to the small scale of operations, political support, market stability, business costs and employment are not as reliable as conventional tourism (e.g. Orams, 2003). However, limited group size provides a higher quality experience for the tourist. There is concern, however, that ecotourism will act much in the same manner as mass tourism only destroying the resource at a slower rate (Bauer, 2001; Butler, 1992). In the short-term ecotourism is viewed as less conducive to causing change in destination areas than mass tourism, in part because of its dimensions and in part because of the need for fewer and smaller facilities (Butler, 1990). However, it is thought that, over time, the cumulative effects of this activity may penetrate deeper into the environment and the surrounding communities, paving the way for mass tourism development (Duffy, 2002). For example, many forms of alternative tourism, such as ecotourism, are located in highly sensitive and vulnerable environments, some of which cannot withstand even moderate levels of use, and which often have little or no infrastructure to deal with development (Butler, 1999).

This is a fundamental issue for ecotourism and protected areas. Ecotourists prefer to experience natural areas in an unspoilt state; therefore there is a significant cross-over of interest for conservation objectives. However, although ecotourism to natural areas may have positive outcomes, it is important for management to be aware of possible adverse effects so that they might be addressed through careful planning and effective management strategies (Buckley, 2003; McNeely and Thorsell, 1989). The overriding aim for managers is to carefully plan for and monitor tourist movement in order to achieve a balance between the use and conservation (Zarska, 2006). Protected area agencies may be attracted to the economic benefits of tourism which may significantly compromise conservation objectives. Managers must be clear of the park's objectives along with the significant differences between forms of tourism and their impacts. Common issues associated with tourism in natural areas that need to be considered by managers include visitor crowding, conflict between different user types, littering, user fees and information distribution (Eagles and McCool, 2004; Lucas, 1984).

Thus, an important consideration for management involved in ecotourism activities in natural areas is ecological planning to prevent intensive usage from causing future damage (Cengiz, 2007). It is essential here to note that even when ecotourism is deployed in order to supply protected areas with economic benefits, the park itself must be strictly managed, monitored and controlled through protective measures to prevent degradation of the site by tourists. Most protected areas with the highest biodiversity are fragile and even the smallest human impacts have significant environmental effects. Protected areas are themselves areas that are in much demand for nature-based tourism because of the very features that they are designed to protect – their biodiversity, remoteness and pristine ecosystems. However, many of these areas lack infrastructure and park managers therefore have few resources to cope with increasing tourist levels.

The defense of protected areas for their intrinsic value alone has proven to be difficult. In capitalist free market societies, expensive and often expansive claims on scarce land resources must be based on broad grounds and integrated within a robust management framework; ecotourism has presented an opportunity to achieve this.

As we have seen in previous chapters, one critical element of ecotourism is sustainability. Ecotourism's goal then is sustainability which attempts to provide a resource base for the future, and seeks to ensure the productivity of the resource base, maintain biodiversity and avoid irreversible environmental changes while ensuring equity both within and between generations.

Ecotourism seeks to capitalize on the increase in tourism to protected areas renowned for their outstanding beauty and extraordinary ecological interest and return the benefits of this to the host community. Ecotourism is premised on the idea that it can only be sustainable if the natural and cultural assets it is reliant upon survive and prosper. This involves reducing social and biophysical impacts caused by visitors, reducing the leakage of potential benefits away from developing countries, increasing environmental awareness and action among tourists and opportunities for the people who would otherwise depend on the extraction of local resources.

Management guidelines for natural attractions are frequently expected by nature-oriented tourists. Management control serves to protect and conserve the area, ensuring that the expectations of visitors are met thus ensuring that patronage continues along with the natural resource bases. Factors which should be under management control, which may affect natural attractions as well as tourist expectations include tourist infrastructure and development, visitor levels, guides, vandalism, souvenir collection, access to areas, driving off-road at night, feeding animals and others.

Ecotourism groups ideally should be small in scale in order to provide a higher quality experience to the customer as this aids in the ability to keep environmental stress and impact levels to a minimum, as well as allowing the tourists intrinsic goals to be realized. Ecotourism is able to foster an appreciation of natural areas and traditional cultures by enabling the tourist to experience an area first hand. It is this first-hand experience with the natural environment, combined with the quest for education and other intrinsic enjoyment that constitutes a true ecotourism experience (Butler, 1992).

Carrying Capacity, Recreation Opportunity Spectrum (ROS), Limits of Acceptable Change (LAC), Visitor Impact Management (VIM) and Visitor Activity Management Process (VAMP) are sustainability decision-making frameworks used in protected area management. When implemented they help to protect a country's natural and cultural heritage, enhance public appreciation of the resource, and manage the conflict between resource and user (Graham et al., 1987: 292; Jenkins and Pigram, 2006; Pigram and Jenkins, 2005). To gain an appreciation of these strategies and their relationship to managing ecotourism operations, protected areas will be used to elaborate the specific issues relating to sustainability practices, their historical development within the context of an increasing environmental awareness and the ability to consider broad social factors will be examined.

A SHORT HISTORY OF PROTECTED AREAS AND SUSTAINABLE MANAGEMENT STRATEGIES

The balancing of the tension between the resource and the user during the late nineteenth century and into the late 1960s was largely achieved by focusing research, planning and management efforts on the resource base in determining infrastructure and facilities in the park. Social and economic factors were not an integral component of park planning and management and little was known about the dimensions and nature of human use. In this respect, management did not have an understanding of the interdependent relationship between social and biophysical systems. There was no overall approach to the selection and management of visitor opportunities, and the effectiveness of services could not be measured with incorrect decisions often being made about the size and location of facilities with little public involvement in the development of park plans and often confusing information was given to the visitors (Graham, 1990: 276).

As we have seen so far in this book increasing recreational and tourism use of protected areas is generally accompanied by negative environmental and social impacts. These impacts have to be managed to conserve ecological and recreational values. Numerous planning and management frameworks have been developed to assist managers in preventing, combating or minimizing the effects of recreational use on natural environments.

The concepts of Carrying Capacity, the ROS, LAC, VIM, VAMP and the Tourism Optimization Management Model (TOMM) are examples of visitor planning and management frameworks. Each is intended to complement existing management and decision-making processes (Pigram and Jenkins, 2005).

Carrying Capacity is fundamental to environmental protection and sustainable development. It refers to the maximum use of any site without causing negative effects on the resources, reducing visitor satisfaction, or exerting adverse impact upon the society, economy and culture of the area. Carrying capacity limits can sometimes be difficult to quantify, but they are essential to environmental planning for tourism and recreation.

Carrying capacity

The carrying capacity concept originated in the 1970s. Its central idea 'is that environmental factors set limits on the population that an area can sustain. When these limits are exceeded, the quality of the environment suffers and ultimately, its ability to support that population' (Stankey, 1991: 12). It was believed that objective, biological studies could determine the capacity of an area's natural resources, establishing how much use the environment could cope with and regulating access to the resource. According to Stankey (1991: 11) this 'scientific' basis explains the wide appeal of carrying capacity as a recreation and tourism management concept.

There are three main elements of tourism carrying capacity:

- Biophysical (ecological) – which relates to the natural environment.

- Socio-cultural – which relates primarily to the impact on the host population and its culture.

- Facility – which relates to the visitor experience.

Carrying capacity varies according to the season and, over time, factors such as tourists' behavioral patterns, facility design and management, the dynamic character of the environment, and the changing attitudes of the host community will all vary in differing ways, thus affecting its determination.

However, carrying capacity has not been as useful as anticipated. Perhaps it was expected to reveal precisely 'how many is too many?' Instead, depending on assumptions and values, the result has been 'widely varying capacity estimates' of types and levels of use (Stankey, 1991: 12). There are a wide range of differing values and perceptions of what an 'unacceptable impact' is. There are no absolute measurements of the resource's condition that can be defined as constituting 'crowding' or 'resource damage' (Stankey, 1991: 13).

As social issues, management as well as natural resources, affect the calculation of carrying capacity, it is not possible to come up with a number beyond which unacceptable impacts occur: 'To prevent most impact it would be necessary to limit use to very low levels' (Stankey, 1991: 13). People continue to use an area for recreational activities even when it is obviously having an impact on the resource. This stems from the absence of an adequate framework that links the relationship between visitor expectations, use and impact and management decisions (Stankey and McCool, 1985).

Carrying capacity analysis then has been virtually ignored because of the complexity of the parameters, and although tourism operators can be conscious that too many visitors will degrade the environment and diminish the experience of their clients in both recreation and tourism, there are very few examples of it being used by agencies to successfully limit tourism (McCool and Lime, 2001).

Solutions to the problems of overuse and crowding differ depending on the policies of agencies managing wilderness (Watson, 1989: 394). A study conducted in 1987, for example, found that only 6 out of 38 wilderness managers had estimated recreational carrying capacity, even though most were concerned about overuse of parks (Watson, 1989). McCool and Lime (2001) argue that the conditions needed to establish carrying capacity are rarely achieved in the real world and that it is only applicable to limited situations where numerical capacities may be appropriate such as parking lots. In its stead they suggest that the planning frameworks such as Visitor Experience, Resource Protection and LAC are better suited to address the issues of visitor impacts.

Canada, for example, recognized the concept's deficiencies, such as ignoring the social aspects, and went on to develop more broad-based concepts. ROS is based on assumptions and tenets borrowed from other lines of research (Driver et al., 1987: 210). Nevertheless, Viñals et al. (2003) provide an innovative approach to carrying capacity by steering it away from empirical approaches toward developing a sequenced approach that could be extrapolated to other sites. This approach offers a particular research methodology as opposed to a generalized formula. The methodology involves a sequence of phases for analyzing a wetland's recreational carrying capacity (e.g. physical carrying capacity, actual carrying capacity and permissible carrying capacity). It also considers all components and factors that should be included in the analysis (wetland environment, profile of users, resources involved, type of recreational activity), and includes systems of indicators and quick assessments

The recreation opportunity spectrum (ROS)

ROS is a framework for prescribing carrying capacities and managing recreational impacts. The process is largely a judgmental one, but establishes explicit standards regarding appropriate conditions for each opportunity class. Determining carrying capacities for recreational areas establishes conditions of use which are considered appropriate for each opportunity type, and provides a means of assessing the relative numbers of persons as a result of changing opportunity types (e.g. Stankey, 1991).

The ROS approach shifted attention from the type and amount of use an area receives to the biophysical, social and managerial attributes of the park setting (Prosser, 1986: 7). ROS was further developed to provide a logical series of interrelated steps for natural area planning. This new framework is known as the LAC system (Prosser, 1986: 6).

The ROS focuses on the setting in which recreation occurs. A recreation opportunity setting is the combination of physical, biological, social and managerial conditions that give value to a place (Clark and Stankey, 1979). ROS has been described as a framework for presenting carrying capacities and managing recreational impacts. The ROS provides a systematic framework for looking at the actual distribution of opportunities and a procedure for assessing possible management actions.[17]

---

[17] For an applied example of the ROS, see McDonald and Wearing's (2003: 163-8) case study of Avoca Beach, Australia.

Clark and Stankey (1979) initially proposed a series of four levels of development, or management classes under the ROS system:

- semi-modern
- modern
- semi-primitive
- primitive

Factors used to describe management classes were

- access
- other non-recreational resource uses
- on-site management
- social interaction
- acceptability of visitor impacts
- acceptable level of regimentation

More recently the ROS has been used to establish the classification criterion and framework for a local ecotourism venture in Taiwan. A number of opportunity classifications were identified including 'specialized and middle adventure', 'specialized', 'middle and popular ecotourism experience' and 'cultural scanning' (Huang and Lo, 2005).

Limitations of the ROS are related to its basis in recreational carrying capacity, which is seen as the product of technical assessments, as opposed to value judgments that weigh resource and social impacts, along with human needs and values (McCool, 1990).

Limits of acceptable change (LAC)

LAC methodology is an extension of the ROS concept and recognizes both the social and environmental dimensions of recreational impacts. It involves both resource managers and stakeholders in:

- identifying acceptable and achievable social and resource standards
- documenting gaps between desirable and existing circumstances
- identifying management actions to close these gaps
- monitoring and evaluating management effectiveness. (Payne and Graham, 1993)

The LAC planning system consists of nine steps.

1. Identifying concerns and issues.

2. Defining and describing opportunity classes.

3. Selecting indicators of resource and social conditions.

4. Carrying out an inventory of resource and social conditions.

5. Specifying standards for the resource and social indicators.

6. Identifying alternative opportunity class allocations.

7. Identifying management actions for each alternative.

8. Evaluating and selecting an alternative.

9. Implementing actions and monitoring conditions (Stankey et al., 1985).

Like the ROS, the LAC framework offers more opportunity for public participation which results in a consensus planning approach to natural area management (e.g. Ahn et al., 2002). However, few LAC systems generated in Australia for instance have been implemented with any great success and this is thought to be due to a lack of political and economic support from stakeholders (McArthur, 1997c; Lindberg et al., 1998). LAC systems also require considerable resources to establish inventories of resource and social conditions, which make it particularly difficult to implement in developing countries (Rouphael and Hanafy, 2007).

The LAC system is a technical planning system. It provides a 'systematic decision-making framework which helps determine what resource and social conditions are acceptable and prescribes appropriate management actions' (Stankey, 1991: 14). The LAC framework mitigates the conflict between recreation, tourism and conservation. It defines the impacts associated with different levels of environmental protection. It also helps to set the basis for allowing environmental change consistent with, and appropriate and acceptable to, different types of recreational opportunities (Stankey, 1991: 13). By establishing specific indicators and standards related to conservation values, coupled with monitoring, it is possible to define what impact levels can be permitted before management intervention becomes necessary (Stankey, 1991: 12).

Significantly, the LAC system does more than developing and extending the ROS framework. It also represents an important reformulation of key elements of the carrying capacity concept (Prosser, 1986: 8). By directing attention away from the question 'how much recreation use is too much?'

toward desired conditions, the LAC approach skirts around the use/impact conundrum. Because the resource and social conditions of an area are most important, the LAC emphasis is on the management of the impacts of use (Lucas and Stankey, 1988).

Visitor impact management (VIM)

VIM process involves a combination of legislation/policy review, scientific problem identification (both social and natural) and analysis and professional judgment (Payne and Graham, 1993). The principles of VIM are as follows.

- Identifying unacceptable changes occurring as a result of visitor use and developing management strategies to keep visitor impacts within acceptable levels.

- Integrating VIM into existing agency planning, design and management processes.

- Basing VIM on the best scientific understanding and situational information available.

- Determining management objectives that identify the resource condition to be achieved and the type of recreation experience to be provided.

- Identifying visitor impact problems by comparing standards for acceptable conditions with key indicators of impact at designated times and locations.

- Basing management decisions, to reduce impacts or maintain acceptable conditions, on knowledge of the probable sources of, and interrelationships between unacceptable impacts.

- Addressing visitor impacts using a wide range of alternative management techniques.

- Formulating visitor management objectives, which incorporate a range of acceptable impact levels, to accommodate the diversity of environments and experience opportunities present within any natural setting (Graefe et al., 1990).

Both LAC and VIM frameworks rely on indicators and standards as a means of defining impacts that are deemed unacceptable and place carrying capacities into a broader managerial context. However, VIM makes reference to planning and policy and includes identifying the probable causes of impacts, whereas LAC places more emphasis on defining the opportunity classes (Payne and Graham, 1993; Graefe et al., 1990).

Visitor activity management process (VAMP)

Whereas ROS and LAC rely on management of the resource, the emphasis with VAMP shifts back to the user of the resource. VAMP was built upon the previously developed VIM. It has received relatively little attention in recreation management journals, whereas VAMP has been written about extensively in the USA and Canada, where it was originally developed (Graham et al., 1988).

VAMP relates to interpretation and visitor services. This framework involves the development of activity profiles which connect activities with:

- the social and demographic characteristics of the participants

- the activity setting requirements

- trends affecting the activity

The VAMP framework is designed to operate in parallel with the natural resource management processes. It is a pro-active, flexible, decision-building framework which can contribute to a more integrated approach to management of protected areas. It has the potential to develop better information about customary users, stakeholders, visitors and non-visitors (Graham, 1990: 280). Information on both natural and social sciences is used to 'build' decisions about access and use of protected areas. It also incorporates a format for evaluating the effectiveness in meeting public needs (Graham, 1990: 281).

VAMP is not a process to justify random development at a site; rather it is an aid to understand visitor behavior and, where necessary, to modify it. The questions that guide the process include needs and expectations, what interpretive services and educational opportunities should be offered at a site, level of service for current and projected use and visitor satisfaction (Graham, 1990: 283).

VAMP provides a framework to ensure that visitor understanding, appreciation and enjoyment of the resources are just as carefully and systematically considered as protection of natural resources. 'Its strength is recognizing the demand and supply side of natural area management' (Newsome et al., 2002: 176). VAMP does not stand alone, but operates within a strong planning and management context as it represents how social science data are integrated within a park's management planning process.

The application of the basic VAMP concept to management of visitor programs follows the traditional approach to planning used by most resource management agencies. However, a major emphasis throughout each stage is on understanding park visitors (Taylor, 1990). The task is to determine the current situation when comparing the park's expectations to the visitor's, and then to assess the actual activity on offer in terms of services, their use and visitor satisfaction (Taylor, 1990). VAMP's pro-active approach to profiling visitor activity groups, suggesting target messages, and evaluation before the development of interpretive programs, may lead to more effective interpretation and environmental education programs (Graham, 1990: 291).

Tourism optimization management model (TOMM)

The Tourism Optimization Management Model was developed by Manidis Roberts Consultants (1997). It builds on the LAC system to incorporate a stronger political dimension and seeks to monitor and manage tourism in a way that seeks optimum sustainable performance, rather than maximum levels or carrying capacities. TOMM involves the following.

- Identifying strategic imperatives (such as policies and emerging issues).

- Identifying community values, product characteristics, growth patterns, market trends and opportunities, positioning and branding and alternative scenarios for tourism in a region.

- Identifying optimum conditions, indicators, acceptable ranges, monitoring techniques, benchmarks, annual performance and predicted performance.

- Identifying poor performance, exploring cause/effect relationships, identifying results requiring a tourism response or other sector response, and developing management options to address poor performance (McArthur, 1997a).

In Australia the TOMM model has been used to address the tourism impacts on the community, economy and environment of Kangaroo Island; a popular tourist destination that lies off the coast of South Australia (Miller and Twining-Ward, 2005).

MANAGING VISITOR USE

The frameworks we have discussed above are effective means to assess and project the sustainable and desired limits of human impact on natural

CASE STUDY: TOMM, Kangaroo Island, South Australia

The implementation of a tourism planning and monitoring model on Kangaroo Island in South Australia has attracted worldwide attention due to its strong focus on involving all relevant stakeholders from local and state government to tourism operators, the island's community and natural area managers (Manidis Roberts, 1997). Its success was largely due to the Tourism Optimization Management Model (TOMM) which builds on the LAC system developed by Stankey and McCool (1985). (See Chapter 4 for a full discussion of the LAC system and other sustainable management models.) TOMM was designed to serve a multitude of stakeholders with a multitude of interests, and can operate at a regional level over a multitude of public and private land tenures. Specifically, TOMM has been designed to monitor and quantify the key economic, marketing, environmental,

socio-cultural and experiential benefits and impacts of tourism activity; and assist in the assessment of emerging issues and alternative future management options for the sustainable development and management of tourism activity (Manidis Roberts, 1997).

TOMM is being used to help change the culture of the tourism industry and its stakeholders by generating tangible evidence that the viability of the industry is dependent upon the quality of the visitor experiences it generates, and the condition of the natural, cultural and social resources it relies on. In a recent survey carried out in 2007 it was shown that the overall visitor's satisfaction rated 95% and that visitors are willing to contribute to an environmental program via a levy (Tourism Optimisation Management Model, 2008) *(see Fig. 4.2)*.

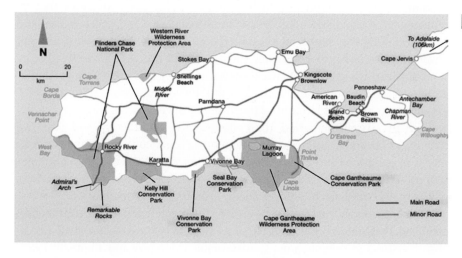

FIGURE 4.2

Kangaroo Island. Photo by South Australian Visitor and Travel Centre.

ecosystems. Once identified these limits must be strictly monitored in order to ensure that the baseline sustainability limits are maintained. Protected area authorities must then implement strategies to ensure that these limits are maintained.

Use limitation

*However much proponents of development may ignore the fact,
implicit in the concept of sustainable development is the idea of
limits. (Butler, 1999: 7)*

One fairly common and direct, regulatory type of visitor management is
that of the 'use limitation'. For instance, in the Grand Canyon National Park,
private and commercial rafting parties have been limited to approximately
2000 per year (Todd, 1989). Also, Skomer Island, Wales, is a bird sanctuary
with access controlled by a daily ferry, limiting the quota of visitors to 100 per
day (Valentine, 1991). While the small size of ecotour operators serves to limit
tourist numbers somewhat, there may also be a need for managers to
implement built in limits to control the size and number of tour operations
acting within natural areas (Bunting, 1991). Westwood and Boyd (2005) argue
that one way of limiting impacts in areas of high conservation is to offer scenic
flights which have become popular in the South Island of New Zealand.
Private operators may also be restricted by permit or other such regulations to
guard against excessive or destructive impacts (Ceballos-Lascurain, 1990). As
well as controlling the negative impacts on the natural environment, this
would also serve to increase the quality of the visitor's experience, as most
ecotourists perceive crowding to be a problem. Research indicates that by
reducing crowding, particularly in camping areas (e.g. Cole, 2001; Farrell and
Marion, 2000), the quality of visitor experience tends to increase, although
fewer people are able to experience the benefits of this.

Therefore, the intensity of use (how many people are engaged in particular
activities) is an important consideration for managers of natural areas.
Regulations can be used to control the numbers of visitors entering a particular
area in any given time period, their access points and the types of activities
they may undertake. As well as implementing these controls, managers may
find it necessary to employ some form of deterrent to the breaching of regulations. These deterrents are usually in the form of fines and other penalties
which may be difficult to enforce due to limitations to surveillance.

In order to limit the number of visitors to an area, management must first
establish a visitor carrying capacity – an estimate of the capacity of an area to
absorb visitors so that such use is sustainable (McNeely and Thorsell, 1989;
Saveriades, 2000). Environmental, social and managerial resources must be
evaluated as all of these factors represent constraints on the carrying capacity
of a given area. One problem associated with the establishment of carrying
capacities is that it is a subjective issue, each interest tolerating various levels

of environmental degradation. Thus management must determine the level of visitor use that an area can accommodate, 'maintaining high levels of visitor satisfaction and few negative impacts on the environment' (McNeely and Thorsell, 1989: 33). Butler adds:

> *While thinking on carrying capacity has been modified greatly since the 1960s, when researchers were seeking the 'magic number' of visitors who could be accommodated at a specific site, the issue of volume still remains. Although it is generally accepted that numbers alone are not an entirely satisfactory measure of the effects of tourism, there is little doubt that, in almost all tourism contexts, there is a maximum number of tourists who can be successfully accommodated (however 'successful' is defined). Once this number is exceeded, a range of negative and sometimes irreversible effects take place. These impacts may take some time to manifest themselves in certain areas (e.g. changes in environmental quality), whereas in others their effects may be felt almost immediately (e.g. resident attitudes). (1999: 7)*

One method used to achieve a more sustainable level of use is 'redistribution'. Such techniques are most commonly used by managers to reduce the concentration of use in general, by shifting some visitors from heavily to lightly used areas (Lucas, 1984), or from peak to off peak periods (Manning and Powers, 1984). It is believed that tourists tend to confine themselves to small segments of wilderness in accordance with the ease of access and viewing attractions (Todd, 1989). Although this may not be desired by the ecotourist, they are often restricted in their experiences by the operators or guides of such tours who, whilst seeking to provide their client with the best view of wildlife, produce a highly commercial activity. An example of this includes operators in the Serengeti National Park in Tanzania, where tour bus drivers 'concentrate on the "Big 5" – lions, leopards, elephants, buffalos and rhinos' (Todd, 1989: 78). Use redistribution has been implemented in East Africa's Amboseli Game Park where, in the late 1970s, it was estimated that 80% of visitors used only 10% of the total area of the park. This technique was used to disperse visitor movement throughout the park, allowing carrying capacity to rise from 80,000 to 250,000 visitors annually, for the same level of impact (Todd, 1989: 78). This may not be conducive to the ecotourism experience as impact levels spread, making it more difficult to experience a truly unspoilt wilderness tract.

Managers may wish to shift use in site-specific ways, to reduce use in particularly fragile or overused areas and shift some of it to specific places better able to sustain it. This can be achieved through zoning measures and the restriction of access points to control the movements of ecotourists and other visitors within wilderness areas.

Zoning

Zoning may also be used to control different uses in different parts of the region. It is a multidimensional technique that is driven by ecological data in order to balance the demands between protection and use in determining the most appropriate levels of use for specific areas within the park. Zoning is often used to support wider management frameworks such as the ROS (e.g. Ruschano and Yaotanee, 2007). One of the most important outcomes is to ensure that 'activities in one zone do not impinge on the planned functions of another' (Buckley and Pannell, 1990: 29). Where tourism is concerned, zoning should include areas that are not open for visitation in order to minimize the impact of infrastructure on wildlife. For example,

> tourism and recreation in the upstream part of a catchment may adversely effect water quality in the downstream region; so if the latter has been zoned purely for conservation, it may suffer water quality deterioration even though there are no recreational activities in the conservation zone itself. (Buckley and Pannell, 1990: 29)

As ecotourism involves low impact travel requiring few facilities and minimal disturbance to the environment and other wilderness users, it is not so prevalent to zone ecotouristic activity from other users as it is to zone more commercial activities from them. For example, it is necessary for managers to limit or prohibit areas in which mechanized recreation, horse riding and other such activities are not permissible in order to minimize the negative impact on the wilderness area, as well as to protect other visitor experiences. Visitor facilities act as a powerful management tool. They allow managing authorities to attract tourists to areas of significance/interest, control activities within these areas and divert visitors from more sensitive areas. Thus more traditional forms of tourism may be restricted from areas important to ecotourism by simply a lack of facilities that adequately satisfy their needs. This indirect management technique of restraint in providing facilities in natural areas seems to be consistent with what is known about wilderness visitor preferences. Wilderness visitors desire a landscape that is natural, wild, uncrowded and free (Cole, 2000). In management terms this means the absence of built facilities, and in areas where crowding is a problem, a system for limitation (Hendee and Dawson, 2002).

Trial system design

Trail system design is also an indirect management action that may not only be effective in the redistribution of use, but also for improving the quality of visitor experiences by, setting the level of challenge, the scenic quality and opportunities to observe and learn about natural communities and processes (Lucas, 1984). In protected areas, trails are the linkage between visitors and the natural ecosystem, so most of the adverse impacts caused by visitors can be concentrated on trails (WenJun et al., 2005).

The design of trail systems may be an important factor in improving the quality of the ecotourists experience as they rely on trails to provide an experience in themselves, rather than just a route to attractions. For example, the artificial maintenance of trails, such as the establishment of wooden trails, flagstone trails and bridges can create a point of interest, particularly if signage and construction reflect cultural aesthetics (WenJun et al., 2005). Much of the negative impact that occurs in natural areas can be specifically related to visitor behavior and actions, rather than to sheer numbers of users. It is the minority 'few unskilled, uninformed, careless groups rather than the many typical parties' that cause most of the damage (Lucas, 1984: 133). Perceptions of natural areas may be altered through various means of providing visitors with information. This indirect management technique can act to increase the visitor's enjoyment of the area and also to stimulate 'modes of behaviour which enhance the environmental quality of the site' (McNeely and Thorsell, 1989: 37). It is recognized by Buckley and Pannell (1990) that education as a management option may be the most effective of all management techniques, particularly in natural areas where it may well be the only option. Lucas (1984: 133) notes that wilderness visitors 'tend to be highly educated, most with university educations and often with graduate study, as well as strongly committed to wilderness'. Ecotourists possess these same characteristics and it is thought that these allow education programs to be successful in informing tourists of how to minimize the negative impacts of their visit on the surrounding environment. It is important, however, that the information provided to visitors be interpretative in nature, explaining possible interactions between visitors and the environment as well as methods to reduce any impacts that might occur from these interactions, and if possible that such messages be delivered by trained ecotourism guides (Buckley and Littlefair, 2007; Weiler and Ham, 2001). This information may be provided in such forms as brochures, maps and pamphlets and are preferred by visitors to be distributed prior to entering the resource area. The majority of information aimed at changing visitor behavior deal with the reduction of environmental impacts through minimal impact camping and hiking information. These education programs commonly address issues such as littering, campfire use and vegetation impacts (Lucas, 1984; Marion and Reid, 2007).

Education

No natural resource can be effectively managed without the support and backing of its users. It follows that no system of natural area reserves can adequately fulfill its roles without the guidance of appropriate management objectives. Failure to fulfill such roles and provide appropriate information is likely to alienate some recreational users and decrease the level of public support for the reserve system as a whole. This would be a very serious situation, for without public support it is unlikely that we would have such a diverse and extensive range of environments protected. The fate of reserve systems are determined largely by social and political pressures (Hall and McArthur, 1996). As Buckley notes

> Conservation interests hope to use tourism as a tool in conservation, whereas tourism interests want to use conservation as a tool in tourism development. Both promote partnerships, but with different political aims. (2004: 75)

Even the best-planned management procedures will fail without public support. A strong base of public support for the aims and objectives of protected areas is one of the first prerequisites for their management. From this comes the political will, financial support and staffing necessary to achieve the aims and objectives of management. For this reason it is essential that the natural areas management provide information that seek to change behavior, not just awareness (Forestell, 1990). As we shall see in the following chapter, interpretation and education are the key components of ecotourism and protected areas providing one of the essential ingredients for successful park management. Interpretation provides the opportunity for natural processes to be observed, for the interrelationship of natural ecological systems to be appreciated and for the consequences of human change and ultimate degradation to be understood (Kenchington, 1990). Outdoor recreation has been the major function of all parks and reserve areas, even though conservation may be the more vital and immediately necessary role of these areas (Cameron-Smith, 1977). Recreation in this context is generally limited to those activities that are consistent with preserving the natural state of these areas, although this definition in itself can cause problems. Activities such as bush walking, picnicking, camping and nature photography, for example, are generally considered acceptable within national park and reserve areas; however, even such restricted recreational use can cause problems, including physical damage to ecological and cultural resources. User/user or user/manager conflicts in the perception of what constitutes acceptable recreational behavior at any given site can and do still arise (e.g. Beckmann, 1991; Dear and Myers, 2005).

Priorities in outdoor recreation management should therefore include a balancing of supply and demand, a matching of resource adequacy with human recreational needs and desires (Kenchington, 1990). Management strategies which reconcile recreation with other priorities such as conservation have become essential with increasing visitor demand. Visitor, rather than resource management, is now regarded as the most important component of recreation management (Wearing and Gardiner, 1994).

Ecotour operators in wilderness and other protected areas must also assume responsibility for minimizing the impacts of their operations in the destination region. Examples of education techniques that may be applied by tour operators include 'slide shows, lectures and discussions to further familiarize guests with the wildlife, history and culture of the remote area in which they find themselves' (Choegyal, 1991: 95). It has been identified that a vital component in the successful management of enhanced visitor experiences and appropriate environmental behavior is the training of the tour guides themselves (Buckley and Littlefair, 2007; McGrath, 2007). It has been argued that in developing countries such training should form one component of a wider capacity building program, where the involvement of stakeholders has been found to play an important role in securing positive outcomes for local communities (McGrath, 2007; Strasdas et al., 2007).

A more direct benefit of education and interpretation is as a visitor management tool to manage visitors and reduce visitor impacts. One of the chief criticisms of ecotourism is that it threatens to destroy the environment which it is trying to protect. Interpretation is an effective way management can encourage appropriate behavior thus alleviating any potentially damaging behavior of ecotourists. For example, the ecotourist trekking through the Himalayas in Nepal in search of an understanding of subalpine environments may leave trails strewn with toilet paper, empty cans and bottles, which contribute to erosion and leave ashes from fires used for cooking. However, through education by interpretive means, they may be made aware of on-site problems and learn skills to minimize their own impacts.

While other strategies for reducing environmental impacts from visitor pressure have been developed and implemented in protected areas and national parks, interpretation is a key approach due to its long-term effects (Buckley and Littlefair, 2007; Cameron-Smith, 1977). Interpretation can help visitors to understand and appreciate the differences in permitted activities, management practices and conservation values among national parks, state forests, reserves and privately owned bushland, as such interpretation is an important part of any strategic management plan.

Although interpretation is believed by many to be the most powerful tool for visitor management it has rarely been incorporated fully into major planning mechanisms (Roggenbuck, 1987). Nonetheless, the relationship between interpretation and management is now recognized as a fundamental and that such programs should stem directly from management policies (Newsome et al., 2002). For example, interpretation significantly influences the carrying capacity of an area. By limiting the number of unwanted encounters or experiences in a recreational environment and restricting unsuitable behavior in the area and reducing conflicts between users, the current acceptable carrying capacity limits can be increased.

User fees and charges

User fees and charges have been gaining increased consideration as natural areas have become more popular for recreational use. There are a range of each and they are the methods of capturing revenue from visitation that is essential to channel back into conservation objectives:

- *User fees*: charges on 'users' of an area or facility such as park entrance, trekking fees, etc.

- *Concession*: a fee for the permission to operate within a location for groups or individuals that provide certain services to visitors such as food, accommodation and retail stores.

- *Sales and royalties*: fees levied on a percentage of earnings that have been derived from activities or products at a site such as photographs or postcards.

- *Taxation*: an additional cost imposed upon goods and services that are used by ecotourists, such as airport taxes.

- *Donations*: tourists are often encouraged to contribute to maintaining a facility (e.g. Hedsrom, 1992; Marriott, 1993).

Fees can provide an important source of revenue for managers, particularly in developing countries where protected areas are traditionally underfunded (Swanson, 1992). The rationale supporting user fees is that most foreign visitors travel to remote protected areas to experience their very isolation and unspoilt natural features. Research suggests that ecotourists are willing to pay a fee for the conservation of wildlife when observing wildlife that is part of a tour (Tisdell and Wilson, 2005).

> *User fees on both the ecotour operators and the ecotourists cover management costs. The visibility of these fees to the operators and the tourists makes an important connection between use and the need for management costs. (Jenkins and Wearing, 2003: 215)*

This chapter has presented the issues relating to ecotourism and protected area management. It has reflected upon the compromise between current views on management of our natural resources, and allows for evolution toward future management based on ecocentric management using ecotourism as a catalyst. Given the dominance of economic rationalism and increasing competition for scarce resources, protected areas are going to come under more and more use pressure. Park supporters need to join the political debate and look at ecotourism as a means of achieving the economic justification that will ensure the short-term survival of protected areas while developing a political constituency enabling a longer-term perspective. Conservation and preservation of natural resources and cultural heritage are global as well as local concerns. For tourism to be sustainable, the type and extent of tourism activity must be balanced against the capacity of the natural and man-made resources available.

FURTHER READING

Worboys, G., Lockwood, M., & De Lacy, T. (2005) *Protected Area Management: Principles and Practice*, second ed. Oxford University Press, Oxford, UK.

Newsome, D., Moore, S.A., & Dowling, R.K. (2002) *Natural Area Tourism: Ecology, Impacts and Management*. Channel View Publications, Clevedon, UK.

Both of these texts provide an introduction to the management of tourism and recreation in natural and protected areas. They describe the potential for environmental impacts, and strategies for how managers can plan, develop and deliver appropriate solutions to ensure nature conservation.

McDonald, M., & Wearing, S. (2003). Reconciling community's expectations of ecotourism: initiating a planning and education strategy for the Avoca Beach Rock Platform. In *Marine Ecotourism: Issues and Experiences* (B. Garrod, & J.C. Wilson, eds). Channel View Publications, Clevedon, UK, pp. 155–70.

McDonald and Wearing's chapter provides an Australian case study on how the ROS system can be implemented and the way in which it can take pressure off popular areas experiencing environmental and social impacts.

CHAPTER 5

The Role of Interpretation in Achieving a Sustainable Future

Environmental interpretation involves translating the technical language of a natural science or related field into terms and ideas that people who aren't scientists can readily understand. And it involves doing it in a way that's entertaining and interesting to these people. (Ham, 1992: 3)

It has been suggested that there is limited value in science (which provides the data upon which conservation is based) and management (which provides the tools) without communication to share their respective insights and directions (McCurdy, 1985). Past experience has shown us that many of the answers to today's environmental problems are far from clear, based as they are on scientific prediction only after the accumulation of evidence and therefore after significant impacts have already occurred. This is compounded by scientists being notoriously poor at imparting information that is readily understandable to the lay person and as such the message is often lost to the community at large. As science informs ecology it is essential for it not only to communicate the facts and current theories, but also to promote under-standing of resource management as a dynamic process with a continuing need for monitoring, assessment and research.

As we have seen in Chapter 1, it is this recognition of interpretation and education's centrality to ecotourism that helps to differentiate ecotourism from other forms of nature-based tourism. A focus on the dimensions of visitor experience reveals that the visitor is concerned not with simply looking at a setting or object, but with feeling and realizing some of its *value*. In this way, interpretation is oriented toward a visitor's cognitive and emotional state in order to raise awareness, enhance understanding and hopefully, clarify or enlarge each participant's perspective and attitude. In this way, interpretation is essential to conservation goals.

CONTENTS

Defining Interpretation

Changing Understanding, Attitudes and Behavior

Interpretation Techniques

Principles for Successful Interpretation

The Benefits of Interpretation

Further Reading

Regulations and restrictions do not necessarily change people's activities or attitude toward our environment (Cameron-Smith, 1977). Few people are satisfied in the knowledge that small pockets of natural wilderness exist if they cannot gain access to the areas. We can focus on regulation, but as we have seen in previous chapters, that there could never be enough resources – rangers, firearms or patrol vehicles – to protect parks from visitors who do not care about it (McCurdy, 1985; Cameron-Smith, 1977). Visitors to sensitive protected area sites who lack awareness of the value of the place can become bored, and then directly or indirectly cause impacts which could have been avoided if they had been offered a more enriching experience pitched at their interests. For example, one study investigated the non-compliance behavior by tourists to a voluntary Code Of Conduct concerning the viewing of marine turtles attempting to nest in the Ningaloo Marine Park in Western Australia. The research found that 77% of tourist groups breached the Code Of Conduct, with 51% of these breaches resulting in a disturbance to marine turtles attempting to nest (Waayers et al., 2006).

Interpretation is effective because rather than regulating and enforcing behaviors and practices, it works with, rather than against the visitor.

DEFINING INTERPRETATION

Before exploring some of the interpretive techniques utilized by ecotourism, we need to clearly define what interpretation is and understand how attitudinal and behavioral outcomes are generated by interpretation. Many definitions of interpretation limit it to a kind of 'dressing-up' exercise for facts and figures, usually the translation of the technical language associated with natural science into terms and concepts that people can easily understand and enjoy (Ham, 1992). While this may be a part of what interpretation is, it is not limited to this aspect alone. Indeed, Freeman Tilden (1977), in providing one of interpretations most recognized definitions states that it is 'an educational activity which aims to reveal meaning and relationships through the use of original objectives, by first-hand experience, and by illustrative media, rather than simply to communicate factual information' (Tilden, 1977: 8).

Tilden stressed that interpretation was not simply 'jazzed up information', it had a larger purpose – that of revelation. Although an environmental interpreter may use factual information to illustrate points and clarify meanings, it is concepts and ideals that they are first trying to communicate, not simply facts. This is what distinguishes interpretation from conventional education and instruction and it is in these terms that effective interpretation can be used as a basis for developing a conservation ethic within the community.

The Queensland National Parks and Wildlife Service (Carter, 1984) defined interpretation as: 'a special process of stimulating and encouraging an appreciation of the natural and cultural heritage of a region, as well as a means of communicating nature conservation ideals and practices'. This definition suggests that the service uses interpretation to get visitors to appreciate the heritage it is responsible for managing. This single perspective or value base is commonly known as a 'unicentric' approach (Machlis and Field, 1992). From the visitor's perspective, interpretation is a means of value-adding to their experience because most sights become a little bit more interesting when you know a little more about them. Ecotourism operators have recognized this value-adding and incorporated it into their product. For the operator interpretation and education are important because they provide an opportunity to offer something extra that may lead to market advantage.

However, interpretation and education need not necessarily focus on natural and cultural heritage and the raising of appreciation. Ecotourists are, after all, on a holiday, and are therefore resistant to the imposition of 'too much information' and particularly of having it 'shoved down their throats', meaning that they are sensitive to the continual presentation of one perspective and position. As a result, interpreters and educators have widened their definition and use of interpretation to present a range of values, perspectives and positions. This approach, known as a 'multicentric' approach, places the responsibility back with the visitor to arrive at their own understanding based on their collective experiences.

The definition of interpretation provided by the Interpretation Australia Association is worth noting because it was generated after extensive consultation with its 400 members who work in various professions associated with interpretation. Interpretation 'is a means of communicating ideas and feelings which help people understand more about themselves and their environment' (Interpretation Australia Association, 2008). This definition builds on the multicentric view and Tilden's stress on revelation, then adds the concept of empowerment, so that the end benefit rests with the audience of the interpretation – the visitor, or the ecotourist.

It is worth contrasting interpretation from education, particularly since in the field of ecotourism the two are so often used interchangeably. Education is a more formalized version of interpretation. Whereas interpretation tries to capture the attention of visitors, education typically has a 'captive audience' and can therefore develop facilities and programs specifically designated for education. Environmental education mirrors the basic philosophy and characteristics of interpretation in that it also takes place in the natural environment and its subject matter concerns the environment.

CASE STUDY: New Zealand

Customized educational resources for tour operators and their customers have been designed for a series of themed heritage trails in New Zealand with the aim to enhance the tourist experience. The production of something tangible or physical, through the provision of interpretive materials and certificates as a result of participation on the trails, has been clearly identified as value-adding and building on the natural competitive advantage of New Zealand's ecotourism industry (Hall et al., 1991).

CHANGING UNDERSTANDING, ATTITUDES AND BEHAVIOR

In order to understand how interpretation works, it is important to understand how interpretation relates to attitudinal and behavioral change in contributing to environmental awareness. This in turn requires an understanding of what attitudes are and what kinds of cognitive processes are involved in their change. If we argue for greater use of interpretation as a means of generating attitudes and behavioral choice that will assist in conserving our environment we must have some idea of how the process of gaining an environmental consciousness occurs.

In order for natural areas to stimulate environmental awareness, people presently uncommitted to conservation must be encouraged to visit both national parks and reserves. In order to achieve a change in attitude, they must be provided with much more than simple information and propaganda when they visit (e.g. Mayes et al., 2004; Tubb, 2003). Research by Beaumont (1997) suggests that interpretation can induce a change in understanding and a positive shift in attitude among individuals who already have some form of conservation ethic. Otherwise there is little evidence to support that on-site interpretation altered visitor attitudes toward sustainable tourism (Hill et al., 2007; Hughes and Saunders, 2005). A recent analysis by Munro et al. (2008) of interpretation evaluation literature indicates that few studies extend to the measurement of behavioral change. Therefore, due to the large number of possible variables and small number of studies undertaken on this topic, it is difficult to make any substantive conclusions on the role of interpretation in promoting more sustainable visitor behavior. Thus, interpretation may neither necessarily lead to a conservation ethic and flow-on behavior, nor even retention of a positive environmental attitude.

However, this may be due to the standard of interpretation being delivered not reaching a level that induces visitors to shift their position. Fundamentally, they require an experience that will change their basic thinking of the environment and its preservation (Forestell, 1990).

Clearly, the ability of interpretation to enact attitudinal change is in large part dependent upon the availability and effectiveness of resources to provide material that can be understood by the general public and is able to maintain their interest both on-site and post-experience. Given the relative lack of research on interpretation finding its way back to interpreters, this situation seems to be intractable for the short-to-medium term. The effects of limited research and subsequent poor planning in the past were largely responsible for a culture of interpreters that was overtly focused on technique delivery, at the expense of a sound rationale (McArthur, 1996). It, therefore, seems pertinent to briefly examine some of these techniques that interpreters typically concentrate on providing.

INTERPRETATION TECHNIQUES

There are more ways to interpret than one could hope to cover because each technique is like a piece of artwork, crafted from the creativity of the interpreter. In this sense, some of the most creative interpretation is barely recognized as such.

For example, within the lobby of an ecolodge or museum the materials used in construction, the pattern of pavers on the floor and the choice of music, all suggest ideas and feelings of which the visitor may or may not consciously be aware. Another example is the presence of staff within a site and the way in which they present themselves to visitors (WTO, 1990; McIntyre et al., 1993). As staff move about their normal duties they can casually engage visitors in conversation, provide relevant information and obtain some feedback. In order for the contact to be effective, however, the staff must be knowledgeable, which may require training in visitor communication and hospitality.

The most widely recognized interpretive techniques therefore tend to be the more tangible ones, such as visitor centers, publications, educational activities, displays, exhibits, signs and guided tours. Guided tours are particularly popular for visitors as they have been found to enhance the tourism experience (Periera, 2005).

Visitor centers

Visitor centers are special buildings or rooms in which exhibits and displays can be presented in relative comfort and controlled surroundings. Exhibits may include photographs arranged in wall or panel displays, map models, mounted specimens or diagrams. Visitor centers are very useful for showing 'the big picture' such as processes, histories and other features that cannot be easily depicted on-site. Visitor centers often house permanent and continuous audiovisual presentations in an auditorium. The visitor experience within a visitor center typically finishes with a gift shop selling extension material such as detailed guidebooks and maps. Where necessary, visitor centers can be enlarged or combined with education centers. The most effective visitor centers are designed from the inside out, meaning that their interpretive theme and purpose drives the design and construction of the building, rather than vice versa.

Education centers

Education centers are designated buildings, or separate spaces within a visitor center, designed to deliver educational activities and house facilities and supporting material. Education centers usually feature low-key classrooms to hold activities and discussion sessions, though the surrounding environment outside the environment center is critical to delivering many of the activities. The most effective education centers are those containing one or more full-time education officers who have developed their programs to dovetail with school curricula.

Displays and exhibits

Displays and exhibits are typically developed as permanent features within a museum or visitor/education center, or as a mobile 'mini-center' or mobile display. They typically feature objects and specimens, dioramas, scale models, live exhibits, panels of text, diagrams and photographs. Displays and exhibits are useful because they are relatively cost effective, and are portable enough to be located indoors or outdoors. The most effective exhibits are designed with a specific audience in mind, and the most effective mobile displays are those that are staffed to add a more personal touch to the interpretation.

CASE STUDY: Cape Otway Centre for Conservation Ecology

The Cape Otway Centre for Conservation Ecology is upheld internationally as an outstanding example of ecotourism. Based in Victoria, Australia the centre runs a number of environmental education programs based on experiential learning. Volunteers to the center have the opportunity to get involved in a number of ongoing projects. These include planning and developing sustainable living strategies, conservation of the surrounding area and rehabilitating wildlife affected by bushfires, road accidents and illness. Guests have the opportunity to undertake a number of 'ecology experiences' which include guided tours of the surrounding area with an emphasis on the interpretation of native flora and fauna (Cape Otway Centre, 2008).

Publications, websites and dvds

Publications, websites and DVDs are a cost effective way of reaching a large numbers of people. Publications can come in the form of brochures, leaflets, fact-sheets, maps, books, posters, postcards, calendars and stickers. Publications tend to be based around information rather than interpretation. For example, the standard brochure promoting a region or site tends to be more information oriented. Nonetheless, there have been some highly interpretive posters that use layered presentations of images and ideas to progressively reveal underlying concepts. Websites and DVDs on the other hand have the ability to combine information and interpretation by including interactive activities, moving images and text. Some of the disadvantages of publications, websites and DVDs are that they have limited capacity to respond to different visitor needs, they can be difficult to distribute and manage and they can quickly go out of date requiring regular updating and upgrading.

CASE STUDY: Dancing and The Fire Devil, Uncovering the Hidden History of the Victorian Alps, Australia

Dancing and The Fire Devil is the title of an award winning interpretative DVD developed by Parks Victoria, the state government agency responsible for managing protected areas in the Australian state of Victoria. The DVD has strong and emotive visuals illustrating the attachment Aboriginal people have for country. It shows the spiritual impact of the new understandings revealed through the post 2003 Alpine fire archaeological survey program, which revealed the Aboriginal occupation of the Alpine region. It also shows the encouragement that the new findings gave Aboriginal people to connect to the cultural values of the region. This project illustrates how new technological mediums can provide park visitors, government, management, students and indigenous communities with an interactive, informative and enjoyable interpretation experience (Parks Victoria, 2008).

Self-guided trails

Self-guided trails involve a series of prescribed stops along a route that visitors travel. The route may be a road, a walking track, a river or a railway line. Each stop provides a feature that is interpreted via a brochure, a sign or an audio facility such as radio or cassette. Each stop is usually marked by a numbered post, label or sign. A self-guided trail allows the visitor freedom to move at their own pace, stopping for as long as they want. Self-guided tours have similar problems to publications but are similarly cost effective per visitor contact. A study in Sweden of self-guided tours for campers found that it was much easier to attract the independent travelers to the self-guided tours for exactly those reasons (Hultman, 1992).

Guided tours

Face-to-face interpretation is considered to be one of the most powerful and worthwhile interpretive techniques available because it can be continually tuned to the type of visitor(s) participating. In terms of commercially run ecotourism, guided tours are perhaps the most widely used technique. The method is especially useful with school children and formal tour groups or as a means of controlling where visitors go and what they do. A trained guide accompanying a group discusses features along a predetermined route, adding additional detail or perspectives according to the interests and responses of the group (Noam, 1999). One of the strengths of guided tours is that the guide can adapt what is said to the particular interest of each group. Guides working for ecotourism operators must be knowledgeable about many aspects of the attractions and be fluent in the major languages of visitors. One of the limitations of guided tours is their high cost per visitor, and their continual reliance on the personality and commitment of the guide to deliver a high-quality experience. In addition, large proportions of visitors may find guides an interference that impinges upon their desired sense of freedom.

CASE STUDY: The National Geographic Traveller

The National Geographic Traveller is an American-based magazine publication, whose mission is to 'increase and diffuse' geographic knowledge. The editor, Richard Busch, stated in his address to the 1994 World Congress on Adventure Travel and Ecotourism that publications such as the *National Geographic Traveller* had two responsibilities – one to their readers and the other to the environment. The readers need to be provided information on worthwhile places to visit, and simultaneously informed on the importance of protecting the environment.

The publication 'communicates with a conscience' by following several important steps. Firstly, the editor insists that writers discuss relevant ecological issues in the stories themselves. This is often supplemented by side stories and sidebars on the subject. Secondly, an 'Econotes' component of the trip-planning section details the environmentally friendly do's and don'ts, and often covers policy governing the subject area. Thirdly, the editor's notes have often addressed ecotourism specific issues, particularly when they relate to articles.

Busch used an example article on the Amazon to illustrate the type of article produced. The piece centered around an Amazon ecotour that took the photographer from Belem, near the mouth of the river, westward to Iquitos, Peru, 2300 miles upriver. The article illustrated the forest flooding during the rainy season and the role of fish in seed dispersal as they swam among trees. The article also depicted tree-top lodges at the The Explornapo Camp, a low-impact ecolodge facility near Iquitos, and most importantly, the native guide who interprets the rainforest. Thus, there was a balance between environmental and cultural presentations.

Busch's presentation ended in a reiteration that the needs of the environment and reader are not mutually exclusive, and that if other publications took care to inform readers on the fragility of ecosystems, and ways to minimize impacts, such advertising could benefit both the environment and the consuming public (Busch, 1994).

PRINCIPLES FOR SUCCESSFUL INTERPRETATION

Successful interpretation typically reflects a number of key principles:

- people learn better when they are actively involved in the learning process

- people learn better when they are using as many senses as appropriate. It is generally recognized that people retain approximately 10% of what they hear, 30% of what they read, 50% of what they see and 90% of what they do

- insights that people discover for themselves are the most memorable as they stimulate a sense of excitement and growth

- learning requires activity on the part of the learner

- being aware of the usefulness of the knowledge being acquired makes the learning process more effective

- people learn best from first-hand experience (Lewis, 1980)

With these factors in mind it should be possible to develop an effective communication network that promotes ecotourism and subsequently a conservation ethic. Interpretation should leave the ecotourist with a sense of enjoyment and satisfaction, and a perception that environmental conservation and the principles of sustainability are worthwhile thus satisfying conservation objectives (Forestell, 1990).

Protected areas provide one of the essential ingredients for successful interpretation. They provide the opportunity for natural processes to be observed, for the interrelationship of natural ecological systems to be appreciated and for the consequences of human change and ultimate degradation to be understood (Kenchington, 1990). If these opportunities are realized, then people can look forward to a more informed society, capable of weighing up the implications of local, national and international decisions which may affect the environment, fostering a willingness to actively participate in the decision-making process (Ham, 1992).

THE BENEFITS OF INTERPRETATION

Along with interpretations role in value-adding to the visitor experience through enhancing and facilitating the setting being explored, there are four key areas of potential benefits:

- promotional benefits

- recreational benefits

- educational benefits

- management/conservation benefits

- economic benefits (Beckmann, 1991)

In practical terms these benefits may overlap significantly but for clarity we will discuss them individually (e.g. Almond, 1994).

Promotional benefits

Because interpretation generally requires contact between the public and the agency staff it often crosses into the public relations role of effective management. The interpretation services of the Canadian National Parks, for example, have been described as a 'propaganda service' due to promotion,

not only of the need to manage the natural resources, but also of an understanding of the management agency itself (Sharpe, 1982).

The potential promotional benefits of interpretation are summarized in
Table 5.1.

Effective interpretive services can be of use in promoting the 'image' or
'visual identity' of the agency. This is particularly beneficial for protected area
and conservation agencies as a favorable image and prominent visual identity
is fundamental for conveying the objectives of an organization. Many people
make a rapid appraisal of an organization based on the 'image' presented and
since most conservation authorities communicate their message and ideas
with the use of visual media, the relevance of an interesting and easily
recognizable design or logo is central.

An easily recognizable graphic design will improve communication of the
conservation message by allowing the public to identify the management
agency and the management practices associated with that agency. It will also
promote a favorable corporate image for the organization and thus promote
support within the local community. Although a prominent visual identity as
such is hardly a prime objective of a conservation agency, it necessarily plays
a leading role in creating an independent, competent and forcefully
competitive impact.

The political leverage which can be exerted by interpretation is a promotional benefit that should also be identified and utilized. Interpretation is
often used to achieve political objectives and to control volatile conflicts
between advocacy groups. For example, the US National Park Service was
able to promote valuable community support for its management policies by
presenting interpretive seminars on local natural history and by placing
qualified interpreters into uniform to capitalize on the well-accepted ranger
image of the management authority (Beckmann, 1991).

Table 5.1   The Promotional Benefits of Interpretation

Promotional Benefits	Explanation of Benefits
Diversity of subjects that can be promoted	Interpretation can promote values, sites, land tenures, management objectives and practices and the corporate mission of the managing authority
A subtle and sophisticated form of promotion	Interpretation can weave promotion into a story without making it sound too promotional and self-centered
Added dimensions for follow on promotion	Interpretation can provide ongoing advisory services to reinforce and expand initial ideas

Recreational benefits

One expectation common to most people in an outdoor leisure setting is a relaxed atmosphere and activities which enhance the feeling of relaxation (Wearing and Gardiner, 1994). Many park visitors seek some level of recreational involvement with the landscape, flora, fauna and/or cultural sites, although social interaction with other visiting groups may be either actively sought or actively rejected. To be effective, therefore, any educational activity offered within such a setting must retain this informal, relaxed atmosphere (Ham, 1992) and cater for the level of friendly interaction required by the visitor. Compulsory activities will be rejected, while the diversity of visitors can be satisfied by an equally diverse range of educational experiences (Sharpe, 1982). Interpretation, by focusing on the visitor's desire to be involved in their surroundings, provides educational opportunities while at the same time enhancing recreational experiences (Lewis, 1980). By helping visitors to match their recreational needs and expectations with the available resources, and by influencing visitor behavior, interpretation may aid recreation management directly. Satisfied visitors may be encouraged to make return visits, with a more realistic idea of what to expect from the site and of the most appropriate behavior for the area. This provides benefits for managers through a reduction in depreciative behavior and increased community support for the protection of the site. Pre-visit interpretation may be as important as on-site interpretation in maximizing visitor satisfaction, and establishing visitor expectations prior to visiting the area (Sharpe, 1982).

Outdoor recreation has been the major function of all parks and reserve areas, even though conservation may be the more vital and immediately necessary role of these areas (Cameron-Smith, 1977). Recreation in this context is generally limited to those activities that are 'consistent with preserving the natural state' of these areas, although this definition in itself can cause problems. Activities such as trekking, picnicking, camping and nature photography, for example, are generally considered acceptable within national park and reserve areas; however, even such restricted recreational use can cause problems, including physical damage to ecological and cultural resources. User/user or user/manager conflicts in the perception of what constitutes acceptable recreational behavior at any given site can and do still arise (Beckmann, 1991).

Priorities in outdoor recreation management should therefore include a balancing of supply and demand, a matching of resource adequacy with human recreational needs and desires (Kenchington, 1990). Management strategies which reconcile recreation with other priorities such as conservation have become essential with increasing visitor demand. Visitor, rather

Table 5.2	The Recreational Benefits of Interpretation
Recreational Benefits	**Explanation of Benefits**
Value added to the visitor experience	Interpretation is an added activity to those typically expected. For example, interpretation signs enhance a walking track just as interpretive guides are preferred over one that merely points out significant attractions as they come into view
Making the experience more enjoyable	Interpretation that is stimulating and connects with emotions tends to make the experience more enjoyable
Enhance a sense of meaning to recreational activity	Interpretation provides a greater sense of meaning to activities such as sightseeing

than resource management, is now regarded as the most important component of recreation management (Wearing and Gardiner, 1994). *Table 5.2* illustrates some of the recreational benefits of interpretation.

Educational benefits

Tilden's (1957) original definition of interpretation refers to an educational activity. However, educating simply to improve the satisfaction gained from recreational experiences has ceased to be the only or even the dominant role of interpretation in protected areas and equivalent reserves. Although these areas are recognized as important resources for environmental change, management agencies now recognize that it is not enough simply to interpret the site itself (Cameron-Smith, 1977). Interpretation should also be used to educate. The emphasis on managing visitor experiences should allow a more holistic perspective to be employed, 'in which the visitor can be put within a context that includes both the destination community and the environment visited. Such an approach, it is argued, should not only lead to better informed and behaved visitors, but a reduction in negative visitor impacts' (Mason, 2005: 181). As the US National Park Service emphasizes in all its interpretive programs, interpretation should communicate an environmental consciousness both within and beyond the park (McCurdy, 1985). As a result, environmental interpretation is rapidly becoming an adjunct to formal environmental education programs. *Table 5.3* presents some of the educational benefits of interpretation.

Many environmental educators and interpreters alike identify that the knowledge base of the individual is the key to attitudes, and that with changing attitudes comes an instinctive change in behavior (Lewis, 1980). However, it must be stated that knowledge is not alone sufficient to change

Table 5.3	The Educational Benefits of Interpretation
Educational Benefits	**Explanation of Benefits**
Opportunity for learning	Interpretation generates learning experiences for visitors who increase their knowledge and understanding of the environment
Opportunity for self-discovery	Interpretation generates experiences for visitors to gain a clearer understanding of their role within their environment, and this aids in self-discovery and self-actualization

attitudes. With knowledge must come the understanding (Cockrell et al., 1984). It is not enough for an individual to know that a plant is the main food source of a given species of bird. What must be taught is that without this plant being present in the area the bird life of the area will change. This gives the individual a reason to ensure that their activities do not affect the potential survival of the plant or bird species found in the area. This change in attitude also has some value for interpretive planners in the evaluation process. If attitude changes can be identified then interpretive programs can be evaluated accordingly. Popular outdoor recreation sites obviously attract large numbers of visitors and on-site interpretation can expand latent interests in nature and scenery of an area into a more active concern for conservation (Carter, 1979).

The fundamental differences between interpretation and environmental education lie not in the basic philosophy but in the procedures and methodologies used to present the message.

Interpretation as a conservation management tool

A more direct benefit of interpretation is as a visitor management tool to manage visitors and reduce visitor impacts. One of the chief criticisms of ecotourism is that it threatens to destroy the environment which it is trying to protect. Interpretation is an effective way of management that can encourage appropriate behavior, thus alleviating any potentially damaging behavior of ecotourists. For example, the feeding, swimming with and touching of wildlife have the potential to create a number of unforeseen impacts, however, the proper management of these interactions can provide an excellent vehicle for highlighting issues around the protection of wildlife and their habitats (Rodger et al., 2007).

Natural area management agencies use on-site interpretation, in part, to communicate messages based on themes of conservation. This then provides the context onto which management overlays their emphasis on protection of often fragile and unique ecosystems (Hughes and Saunders, 2005).

Table 5.4 presents some of the conservation and protected area management benefits of interpretation.

While other strategies for reducing environmental impacts from visitor pressure have been developed and implemented in protected areas and national parks, interpretation is a key approach due to its long-term effects (Cameron-Smith, 1977). For example, interpretation can help visitors to understand and appreciate the differences in permitted activities, management practices and conservation values among national parks, state forests, reserves and privately owned bushland. As such, interpretation is an important part of any strategic management plan.

Although interpretation is believed by many to be the most powerful tool for visitor management, it has rarely been incorporated fully into major planning mechanisms (Roggenbuck, 1987). Nonetheless, the relationship between interpretation and management is now recognized as a fundamental one and the two are often linked directly in management policies (Wearing and Gardiner, 1994).

Economic benefits

Tourism that utilizes interpretation as a key part of its product generates economic benefits. Whether the tourism is ecotourism, cultural tourism or

Table 5.4	Conservation and Protected Area Management Benefits of Interpretation
Conservation Benefits	**Explanation of Benefits**
Stimulation of an environmental consciousness and broad-based conservation ethic	Interpretation stimulates thoughts of personal responsibility for using resources and contributes to improvements in quality of life
Raise awareness of regulations and codes designed to minimize impacts	Interpretation programs such as minimal impact campaigns can subtly present requirements for changed visitor behavior in a way that is non-confrontational
Stimulation of behavioral change to minimize personal impacts upon the environment	Interpretation presents ideas for people to adopt
Support for protected areas	Interpretation presents the value of protected areas from a range of perspectives
Support for protected area management organizations	Interpretation presents the challenges for management in a candid way that exposes the constraints facing protected area management agencies

some other form, the delivery of interpretation can give the product additional value that attracts higher yield markets (Garrod and Wilson, 2003: 257).

Similarly, by encouraging conservation and modifying visitor behaviors that effect damage to natural resources, effective interpretation programs can reduce the costs of managing recreational resources (Sharpe, 1982).

While *Table 5.1* illustrates that effective interpretation has important economic benefits, these benefits are not always easy, or indeed possible, to prove to management agencies (Hill, 1993). Economists have spent vast amounts of time in recent years attempting to place a dollar value on natural resources. Techniques such as measuring the actual costs incurred in attaining a recreational experience or in identifying people's willingness to pay for an interpretive experience have all been attempted, but it seems to underestimate the value of our natural resources. However, measuring benefits in monetary terms is particularly important when cost-benefit analyses are required as management is interested in the cost effectiveness of different interpretive methods in order to rationalize its continued use given budgetary constraints.

Table 5.5	The Economic Benefits of Interpretation
Economic Benefits	**Explanation of Benefits**
Business activity	Tourism operations utilizing interpretation contribute significantly to wealth. For example, the turnover for Australia's ecotourism industry in 1995 was estimated to be $250 million (Econsult, 1995)
Direct employment	There are many people employed as interpreters. For example, the Interpretation Australia Association has a membership of 450, most of whom are interpreters for heritage managers (Interpretation Australia Association, 2008). In 1995 some 6500 people or 4500 full-time equivalent staff were employed in the Australian ecotourism industry (Econsult, 1995). The payroll from ecotourism employment in 1995 was estimated at $115 million (Econsult, 1995)
Indirect employment	The business activity generated by organizations employing interpreters itself generates additional indirect jobs and wealth. For example, interpreters need training providers, graphic artists, sign and display manufacturers and visitor center builders
Investment	Investment in tourism businesses to deliver interpretation via facilities (e.g. visitor centers, signs, displays, etc.) and services, e.g. guides and counter staff. Total expenditure in North Queensland by visitors to the Wet Tropics World Heritage Area (WHA) equated to $425 million in 2007, a significant portion of which was generated by interpretation goods and services (Prideaux and Falco-Mammone, 2007)

Problems limiting interpretation

Interpretation has suffered from the perception that it is simply 'the icing on the cake' instead of being an integral part of the ecotourism product base. Indeed, Australia's National Ecotourism Accreditation Program in its first year of operation found the quality and commitment to interpretation to be one of the weaker elements of the operators seeking accreditation (McArthur, 1997a).

No natural resource can be effectively managed without the support and backing of it users. It follows that no system of natural area reserves can adequately fulfill its roles without the guidance of appropriate management objectives. Failure to fulfill such roles and provide appropriate information is likely to alienate some recreational users and decrease the level of public support for the reserve system as a whole. This would be a very serious situation, for without public support it is unlikely that we would have such a diverse and extensive range of environments protected. The fate of reserve systems are determined largely by social and political pressures (Hall and McArthur, 1996). Even the best-planned management procedures will fail without public support. A strong base of public support for the aims and objectives of protected areas is one of the first prerequisites for their management. From this comes the political will, financial support and staffing necessary to achieve the aims and objectives of management. For this reason it is essential that the natural areas management provides information that seek to change behavior and not just raise awareness (Forestell, 1990).

Although the premise underlying interpretation and interpretive services is that it is worthwhile and valuable, it would be naive to consider it as a field without flaws. The implementation of effective interpretation is not without its problems and it is for this reason that any interpretation should include monitoring and periodic evaluation (Munro et al., 2008).

CASE STUDY: Savannah Guides, Australia, Interpretation with a Difference

The Gulf Savannah of Northern Australia, along the Gulf of Carpentaria, is a remote 200,000 square kilometer wilderness, which up until the early 1980s was virtually unassessed. The new breed of 'recreational explorers' which emerged about this time began to accelerate negative environmental impacts in the region. The local response was the development of a Wilderness Management Plan by Gulf Local Authorities Development Association (GLADA). GLADA is a grouping of four remote local authorities specifically responding to the emergence of tourism.

One major recommendation was the establishment of a ranger/guide organization that was professional, and moved beyond interpreting the environment to being empowered to protect it. A community/ranger guide system was subsequently established across Northern Australia, and these were the founders of Savannah Guides.

The mission of Savannah Guides is

'*To be economically sound, community-based, identifiable professional body maintaining high standards of*

Interpretation

Public education

Tourism and resource management

Leadership, and

Staffing

And through ecologically sustainable tourism principles to enhance and maintain the regional lifestyle and encourage the protection and conservation of the environment and cultural resources of the Gulf Savannah region'.

From its inception, founding members agreed to fund the setting up of the Savannah Guide system. This included an agreement to collectively fund a biannual 5-day training school at a Guide Station, where professionals such as behavioral scientists, geologists and Aboriginal elders, etc. would lecture. Additionally, a grant of US$10,000 was secured from the PATA Foundation to produce educational material for use in interpretation, and the development of Guide Station signage.

All Savannah Guides are long-term residents, whose role covers both education and training of visitors and the community to protect natural and cultural assets. Each Guide Station is administered by one Savannah Guide. Any other employees are classified following their completion of on-site training and Joongai (local indigenous community)

assessment as site interpreters. In the event that a guide leaves the service, it is from this pool of employees that a new guide would be selected.

The Savannah Guides use education as their tool for managing impacts and visitation. The guides are able to access stations and national parks often closed to individual visitors. Each national park or grazing lease has an associated management regime, which the local guide is very familiar with, thereby eliminating conflicts that may arise with a tour party and generating additional income for landholders, charged at a per head basis.

The keywords which have been used to describe the interpretation skills of Savannah Guides are 'accurate' and 'authentic'. Each guide is encouraged to have a reference library, which is utilized in the event that they and the client do not know the answer to a query. Communication skills are considered a critical aspect to continued training within the ranks of Savannah Guides. Each guide utilizes these verbal communication skills in conjunction with a more traditional marketing effort to distribute information on other stations across the Savannah.

The Savannah Guide concept has facilitated the development of positive benefits from tourism, introduced ecotourism to numerous cattle properties and provided an opportunity for small businesses in creating environmentally sensitive tourism products. Currently, this system is one of the few private organizations that manage a national park. It demonstrates the potential success of a pro-active and managed wilderness scheme.

John Courtenay, Savannah Guides, Australia. British Airways Tourism for Tomorrow Awards 1996 Pacific Region.

Interpretive services have a role in developing visitor expectations for their recreational experience of an area and thus inappropriate interpretation may result in disappointment being experienced. Even something as simple as the photograph chosen for use in a promotional poster can convey an inappropriate message to visitors. Inaccurate promotion has proven to lead to unsatisfied visitors and inappropriate behavior (Jenkins and McArthur, 1996).

Inappropriate interpretive facilities and services can in fact diminish the natural resources of an area. No one who visits a wilderness area or marine reserve known for its natural beauty wishes to be confronted with a series of unattractive and overpowering concrete signs conveying information about the area. Similarly, a visitor center that dominates the landscape and reduces the aesthetic appeal of an area is not an effective management tool. For this reason, many sound interpretation plans actually prescribe 'Interpretation Free Zones'

CASE STUDY: Dolphin Discovery Tours, Port Phillip Bay, Victoria, Australia

Dolphin Discovery Tours operates a luxury charter yacht which ferries tourists to Port Phillip Bay, Victoria, to learn about and interact with dolphins. The tour was designed to educate and develop awareness about the environment in Port Phillip Bay and the need to protect the area and its wildlife populations. At present, 12% of revenue is redirected to support of the Dolphin Research Institute, and the yacht itself is made available to media and sponsorship special events.

The educative component of the tour is what sets it apart from other such ventures. The delivery of information to passengers if achieved through comprehensive commentary and access to guides, all of whom are actively involved in the Dolphin Research Institute or its research and education programs. In addition, a booklet, *The Dolphins of Port Phillip Bay*, is made available for purchase at a significantly reduced price.

The tour itself commences with a familiarization and safety demonstration, during which participants are invited to ask questions during the course of the tour. On route to dolphin prone waters, the vessel sails to Chinaman's Hat, the site of a colony of Australian Fur Seals. The passengers are provided with information on the biology and behaviors of the animals, and informed about the detrimental effects of sealing during the last century. Other unique islands and channels en route provide the commentator with a multitude of topics to which all passengers are encouraged to listen. Unique ecosystems and wildlife species such as Gannet Rookeries and Defence Forts bearing testimony to the development of early Australia provide a historical and biological context to the area.

Dolphin Discovery Tours operates with a definite community focus, with the aim to give participants a direct experience which is properly and thoughtfully interpreted. Interpretation itself is channeled primarily through crew members, professionals and volunteer guides. A comprehensive training program educates guides to the standard required by the management, and the inclusion of volunteer guides provides all passengers with the opportunity to seek information in a relaxed and informal way – without the necessity of approaching the principal commentator.

Minimization of environmental impacts, interpretive quality and the management of visitor expectations are critical to the owner operators of this product. The emphasis of the commentary is on the diversity and value of Port Phillip Bay's ecosystems, the need to protect it, threats currently posed and most critically, what individuals can do to help preserve the area.

The dolphins themselves are not interfered with in any way. Dolphin Discovery Tours is the only tourism experience in the Bay that operates within the whale watching guidelines of not approaching the mammals within 100 meters. The quality of interpretive strategy is summarized by Bill Fox, Tourism Manager for Parks Victoria – 'The high quality interpretation of the natural environment of Port Phillip Bay offered to tourists by this operator plays a significant role in enhancing awareness and understanding of the need to protect and sustain our natural assets…. Dolphin Discovery Tours offers an excellent example of a partnership between conservation and tourism interests, and the value of an ecologically sustainable tourism industry'.

Philip Tubb, Victoria British Airways Tourism for Tomorrow Awards 1997 Pacific Region.

for, in some cases, the most effective interpretation is no obvious interpretation at all, just the right setting for individual inspiration and imagination.

Interpretation is not just the communication of information, regardless of how jazzed up and enjoyable it becomes. Interpretation seeks to reveal the meaning and stimulate a cognitive and emotional response. This response should impel people into reconsidering their value base and behavior. The way in which interpretation is delivered can be as varied as the individual imagination, and, generally speaking, the more imaginative the approach, the more successful the interpretation. Interpretation is a core part of any ecotourism experience. As such, interpretation adds real value for the operator, distinguishing the product from nature-based tourism. Interpretation is also critical to the protected area manager, as it offers a chance to present values and conservation ethics, and at a more practical level, provides the opportunity to minimize visitor impact. Within both these sectors, interpretation is yet to realize anything like its full potential. When it does, it will become quite an awe inspiring player in the world of ecotourism, conservation and personal commitment to a sustainable future.

FURTHER READING

Ham, S.H. (1992) *Environmental Interpretation: A Practical Guide for People with Big Ideas and Small Budgets*. North American Press, Golden, CO.

Although this text is now over 15 years old it provides one of the best practical guides for managers wanting to institute an interpretation program. The book covers a range of topics including how to prepare and present a talk, tips on using visual aids, how to develop and undertake a guided tour or walk, case studies on school and community programs and how to plan and prepare inexpensive exhibits.

CHAPTER 6

Linking Conservation and Communities: Community Benefits and Social Costs

A significant contribution to ecotourism's global following has been its potential to deliver benefits to communities remote from centers of commerce, benefits that do not involve widespread social or environmental destruction.[18] Too often in the past the only opportunities for many communities remote from urban centers, particularly in the developing world, were provided by the extractive industries – mining, logging, fishing or slash and burn livestock production – all of which have detrimental impacts on local communities and often leave an unacceptable legacy of long-term environmental damage.

Ecotourism is often advocated as a way of solving some of the problems that have arisen in developing nations through inappropriate economic growth (Weaver, 1998). Tourism is a diverse and decentralized industry, which affects other sectors of local economies. It is a 24-hour a day, 7-day a week industry, labor-intensive, creating employment opportunities across all sectors and skill levels. However, conventional tourism brings with it many of the problems we have found in the exploitation of developing nations in the past.[19] It is often driven, owned and controlled by the developed nations with a high return to these nations – conventional package tours in many cases, for example, utilize local people through the use of their resources and labor at a minimum (or often zero) cost to the operator. Employment is often seasonal and lowly paid in contrast to the profits accruing to investors and operators. Such practices are defended on the pretext that if these operators did not initiate tourism then there would be no money injected into the community at all. However, tourism can no longer be justified on its supposedly low impact-high return.

CONTENTS

Ecotourism and Local Communities: Conflict, Compromise or Cooperation?

Ecotourism and Local Communities

The Issues and Problems

Local Planning and Development

Further Reading

---

[18] For an example of this see Taylor et al.'s (2003) case study on the economic impact of ecotourism on the remote Galapagos Islands.

[19] E.g. Archer et al. (2005), Butler (1991), Holden (2007), Lea (1993) and Robinson and Boniface (1998).

It is this dominant economic focus that serves to obscure significant dimensions of tourism impact. Tourism produces a diverse range of both social and environmental impacts that are often complex and mutually related. Some indigenous communities often put it in simple terms: 'Tourism is like fire. It can cook your food or burn down your house'. The tourism industry makes extensive use of natural assets such as forests, reefs, beaches and parks, but what does it contribute to the management of these assets? The provision of tourism infrastructure, and the costs of managing the impact of tourism on host communities, is often borne by the environment, the local community and the government. A significant body of research has challenged the claims of industry and government agencies that the aggregate benefits of tourism far outweigh the costs: benefits are rarely uniform, accruing to those actively involved in the tourist industry, while costs are often borne by those who derive no compensatory benefits from tourism (Holden, 2007).

Local communities are significantly vulnerable to the deleterious impacts of tourism development – particularly indigenous cultures – as they directly experience the socio-cultural impacts of tourism (e.g. Mbaiwa, 2004). The subsequent impact of tourism's dynamic growth on communities has in some cases precipitated strong protests by community groups, which, being sensitive to the impacts of tourism, have actively opposed large-scale tourism developments for their locality (e.g. Brammer et al., 2004). Other community groups have been more accepting of a gradual growth in tourism to their region over many years, only to become aware of the negative impacts at a later date when these impacts cannot easily be ignored.

Disruption to established activity patterns, anti-social behavior, crime and overcrowding caused by tourism development can also have a negative impact on local lifestyles and the quality of life of both indigenous and non-indigenous communities.

In many cases indigenous cultures are used extensively to promote destinations to overseas markets yet opportunities for visitors to interact with and experience their cultures and lifestyles are limited while the opportunities that are provided for tourists often trivialize or exploit those involved and the communities they represent. Many indigenous people rightly feel that the tourism industry has a poor track record, in disregarding their legitimate interests and rights, and profiting from their cultural knowledge and heritage.

The tourism potential of local areas is also compromised by the environmental impact of other industries. According to the Economist Intelligence Unit, the entire tourism industry is under attack from other business interests which are virtually stealing its assets (Jenner and Smith, 1991). In the late 1980s, the development boom initiated the emergence of many so-called tourism developments which were nothing more than land speculation, or a means of making otherwise conventional residential developments acceptable to planning authorities. It led to bankruptcies, inflated profits, overloaded infrastructure, residential sprawl and unwanted social and environmental impacts which lead to many local communities suspicions about the benefits of the tourism industry. The ecological, cultural and social impacts of tourism often lead to diminished community and political support for the industry, particularly at local levels.

The interdependence of tourism and the social and physical environment is fundamental to the future of each and seeking a way to accommodate the needs of all parties, without control being external to those who experience its effects most directly, is essential. Features of the natural and cultural environments and supportive host communities are the foundations of a successful industry. Neglect of conservation and quality of life issues threatens the very basis of local populations and a viable and sustainable tourism industry.

As we have discussed in Chapter 1, ecotourism involves travel to relatively undisturbed or protected natural areas, fostering understanding, appreciation and conservation of the flora, fauna, geology and ecosystems of an area as well as local community culture and its relationship to the land. The flora, fauna, geology and ecosystems of an area highlight the nature-based aspect. There is thus a significant overlap between conservation and sustainability between the natural and social environment. As we have seen in Chapter 2, sustainability is at the forefront of government tourism policy; however, it is rare for discussion to take place about the sustainability or otherwise of communities adjacent to, or surrounding, protected areas where many ecotourism ventures take place.

Ecotourism has the potential to create support for conservation objectives in both the host community and in the visitor alike, through establishing and sustaining links between the tourism industry, local communities and protected areas. As social and environmental benefits are essentially interdependent, social benefits accruing to host communities as a result of ecotourism may have the result of increasing overall standards of living due to the localized economic stimulus provided for in increased visitation to the site. Similarly, environmental benefits accrue as host communities are persuaded to protect natural environments in order to sustain economically viable tourism (Ceballos-Lascurain, 1990). Many tourists, and especially ecotourists, are sensitive to decreases in water quality and air quality, loss of vegetation, loss of wildlife, soil erosion and a change in the character and visual appeal of an area due to development. Degradation of the natural environment will severely reduce visitor demand in the long term because the natural attributes on which ecotourists depend will be perceived as less attractive, less legitimate and less able to provide satisfying ecology-based experiences.

CASE STUDY: Global Code of Ethics in Tourism

One of the most significant achievements to stem from the International Year of Ecotourism (2002) was the inclusion of tourism in the World Summit for Sustainable Development implementation agenda. This inclusion was an important step toward recognizing tourism as a tool for international development. Tepelus (2008) argues that this leads to a shift in the conceptualization of tourism from a conservation tool to an instrument for poverty alleviation and development. As a result the World Tourism Organization (WTO) changed their definition on sustainable development of tourism and promoted the Global Code of Ethics for Tourism, which is a set of 10 articles promoted as 'rules of the game' for tourism development. The code of ethics is a 'comprehensive set of principles whose purpose is to guide stakeholders in tourism development'. Article 5 notes that local populations that live in and around tourism sites should be associated with tourism activities and share equitably in the economic, social and cultural benefits they generate. Tourism policies should also be applied in such a way as to help raise the standard of living of local communities as well (WTO, 2008).

ECOTOURISM AND LOCAL COMMUNITIES: CONFLICT, COMPROMISE OR COOPERATION?

Local communities comprise groups with different and potentially conflicting interests *(see Fig. 6.1)*. That is, not all groups want the same things.

The tourist industry seeks a healthy business environment with:

■ financial security

■ a trained and responsible workforce

FIGURE 6.1 Stakeholders and their needs.

- attractions of sufficient quality to ensure a steady flow of visitors – who stay longer and visit more often

- a significant return on investment

Those interested in the natural environment and cultural heritage issues seek

- protection of the environment through prevention, improvement, correction of damage and restoration

- to motivate people to be more aware – and therefore 'care for' rather than 'use up' resources

Community members seek a healthy place in which to live:

- food, adequate and clean water, health care, rewarding work for equitable pay, education and recreation

- respect for cultural traditions

- opportunities to make decisions about the future

Some concerns that each may hold in common include

- issues of access, such as when, where and how tourists visit and move from place to place

- host and guest issues, such as cultural impact or common use of infrastructure

- land use issues, such as hunting/wildlife habitat, agriculture/ recreation, preservation/development, etc.

ECOTOURISM AND LOCAL COMMUNITIES

There are a number of reasons why local communities may consider ecotourism:

- a desire to be part of strong growth in tourism generally and see the potential of catering for special-interest tourism (niche markets)

- an awareness of the high value of natural attractions in the locale

- empathy for conservation ideals and the need for sustainable tourism

- a desire to responsibly rejuvenate the local tourist industry

CASE STUDY: Using Ecotourism to Rebuild After the 2004 Indian Ocean Earthquake and Tsunami

It has been over 5 years since the 2004 Indian Ocean earthquake and tsunami devastated Koh Mook, in the Katang district of Thailand. Once a fishing village with 90% of the population working as fisherman, the locals have now become more open to tourism, which is generating higher incomes than they previously gained from fishing. For tourists, mainly westerners, this is a newly discovered destination. Its popularity is stemming from its remoteness and pristine environment. Activities in and around the village include caving, diving and kayaking. Accommodation is home-stay with local families. Thanks to the money from the Tsunami Relief Fund the villagers have repaired their boats and constructed a new boat yard in a more protected cove in order to provide shelter from strong winds, storms and other natural disasters. Many of the villagers have adapted and now use their fishing boats to transport tourists. It takes about 40 minutes from Trang on the mainland to Koh Mook by boat. In response to the interest in the area by tourists the village has set up their own community rules to better protect the sea and natural resources by refraining from using destructive fishing techniques in the hope that there will be more fish and marine animals for the next generation and for tourists to come and enjoy (Intathep, 2008).

As we have seen in Chapter 1, one of the main principles or elements of ecotourism is its ability to maximize the benefits of tourism, not only as far as income to a region but also the preservation of social infrastructure and biosphere conservation. Specifically, these benefits include

- increased demand for accommodation houses and food and beverage outlets, and therefore improved viability for new and established hotels, motels, guest houses, farm stays, etc.

- additional revenue to local retail businesses and other services (e.g. medical, banking, car hire, cottage industries, souvenir shops, tourist attractions)

- increased market for local products (e.g. locally grown produce, artefacts, value-added goods), thereby sustaining traditional customs and practices

- employment of local labor and expertise (e.g. ecotour guides, retail sales assistants, restaurant table waiting staff)

- source of funding for the protection and enhancement/maintenance of natural attractions and symbols of cultural heritage

- funding and/or volunteers for field work associated with wildlife research and archaeological studies

- heightened community awareness of the value of local/indigenous culture and the natural environment.

As these benefits suggest, ecotourism is about attracting visitors for the 'right' reasons, and not simply promoting tourism for the sake of the 'tourist dollar' at the expense of a community's natural and cultural attributes. However, local communities are not immune from ecotourism impacts.

THE ISSUES AND PROBLEMS

The conflictual issues expressed by representatives of host communities to tourism development generally fall into a number of interrelated categories.

- The lack of opportunities for involvement in decision-making relating to ecotourism.

- Inadequate responses from governments when administrative or legislative mechanisms have been established to involve them in such decision-making.

- The lack of financial, social and vocational benefits flowing to these communities from projects that commercially exploit what they regard as their resources.

- The need to establish better tools for evaluating socio-cultural impacts and ensuring this is completed over the more emphasized environmental impacts on the natural environments which are usually of more interest to the outside investors and conservation groups.

- Impacts on community cohesion and structure.

- The rapidity of tourism development that in many cases significantly accelerates social change.

These concerns embrace a wide range of issues relating to the management of natural resources adjacent to these communities. The central issue is the inadequate levels of participation perceived by these communities in the management of what they regard as their traditional domains (Mowforth and Munt, 2008; Sofield, 2003). Control is exerted over local communities both economically and culturally. Tourism involves an interactive process between host (both human and environment) and guest and therefore 'the culture of the host society is as much at risk from various forms of tourism as physical environments' (Sofield, 1991: 56). In many cases tourists view indigenous cultures and local communities as 'products' of the tourism experience that exist to be 'consumed' along with all the other elements of their trip. As tourists are often paying to watch and photograph indigenous people the tourist feels that it is their 'right' to treat them accordingly – as providing a service, and as a product that they are purchasing as a component of their travel cost. Significantly, however, many local cultures may actively 'construct' what appears (to the tourist's camera) to be an 'authentic' cultural display but which in reality is a staged event specifically for tourist's consumption. This phenomenon is also known as 'staged authenticity' (e.g. Chhabra et al., 2003; MacCannell, 1976) and in many cases this serves a strategic purpose in satisfying the tourists' curiosity while allowing the maintenance of actual cultural rituals to escape the hungry tourist's lens. This is the positive side (from the indigenous culture's perspective) of the commodification of tourism as in many cases it is the interest in local cultures that helps to sustain and even revive traditional cultural practices. A good example of this is the 'Ngadha' on the Indonesian Island of Flores, where small-scale tourism based on local ownership and control of the resource base has been effective in reviving aspects of their culture.

> *The villagers of Ngadha like tourists for a number of reasons: they provide entertainment, bring economic benefits and service provision, provide friends from far away places, and are a source of information. Importantly, they make the locals proud of their cultural heritage…The cultural commodification of their difference has led to a recognizable 'ethnic group' identity. This process of commodification of the villager's identity is bringing them pride and a self-conscious awareness of their traditional culture, which has become a resource that they manipulate to economic and political ends. (Cole, 2007: 955)*

However, the commodification of culture can also have exact significant impacts on local communities. 'Staged authenticity' is actively encouraged by operators whose chief concern is often with providing a 'cultural experience' for tourists that can be experienced in comfort, safety and which are aesthetically pleasing. These cultural performances often become detached from their actual cultural meaning and begin to be performed purely for the viewing public. Too often cultural attractions become overtly commercialized in nature, satisfying the visitors' needs but losing all meaning and significance for the indigenous population. Similarly, indigenous communities often have little or no say over whether they want tourism and they derive few real benefits from their 'performance'. Sustaining the well-being and the cultural traditions of the local community where ecotourism takes place becomes fundamental to the definitions of ecotourism. While one could argue that community participation is fundamental to the definitions of ecotourism, Garrod (2003) argues that the full and effective participation of local communities in the planning and management of ecotourism is rarely a feature of ecotourism ventures.

CASE STUDY: The Commodification of Culture, The Arctic

Over the past 20 years, much of the presentation of indigenous Sami culture has been by those who have lost their traditional Sami heritage or by non-Samis. This has led to the overt commercialization of Sami culture with an often manufactured culture being promoted with the economic benefits being diverted away from the traditional Sami groups to those involved in the provision of unauthentic services: 'The danger is that the people of the north will become human animals in a cultural zoo, mere objects of curiosity for adventurous southerners wealthy enough to enjoy the temptations of glossy travel magazines, luxury cruises through the icebergs, reindeer round-ups or photographic safaris amongst the walrus and polar bears' (Hall, 1987: 217).

To become something to see (a tourist attraction) indigenous peoples have to keep alive an image where features assumed to be modern have no place. This is not an image that only relates to a global discourse. By analyzing the sites tourists encounter, it is shown how these exposures are embedded in different local and national discourses that still have consequences in the contemporary everyday life (Olsen, 2006).

As we have seen in Chapter 3 ecotourism is in large part a sustainable development strategy whereby natural resource amenities, the local community and the visitor benefit from tourism activity (e.g. Pearce et al., 1996). As the following definition of ecotourism highlights

> *Ecotourism is a multifaceted concept that involves travel to fragile, pristine and usually protected areas. It strives to be low impact and (usually) small scale; helps educate the traveller; provides funds for conservation; directly benefits the economic development and political empowerment of local communities; and fosters respect for different cultures and human rights. (Honey, 1999: 25)*

Similarly, many organizations are now beginning to recognize the integral part that local indigenous people play in tourism by including cultural understanding and appreciation in their definitions of ecotourism. As Palmer (2006) notes ecotourism is a concept linking natural resources and cultural environments with a key focus on 'local'. In this way ecologically sustainable tourism is increasingly becoming aligned to conservation, environmental and cultural understanding and appreciation (e.g. Ecotourism Association of Australia, 1996).

Thus, ecotourism aims to promote and foster a respect and an increase in awareness of other cultures, in fostering mutually beneficial relationships between hosts and tourists.

CASE STUDY: The Anangu and Tiwi Island Response

For the indigenous Australians of the Northern Territory, tourism was perceived as being able to 'offer some employment in remote parts of the Territory where alternative economic opportunities were few' (Burchett, 1992: 6). Guided walks, demonstrations of tracking skills and food processing techniques and other aspects of Aboriginal life are carried out at Uluru. Performances of traditional dance are undertaken by three different groups who maintain control of their dance routines. This business venture is based on a joint management philosophy of Uluru Kata-Tjuta National Park, which means that the board of managers comprised members of the Anangu, the traditional owners of the country (Howitt, 2001: 43–45).

Similarly, specialized small group tours are undertaken by the Tiwi community of Melville Island who saw 'the development of an isolated, comfortable safari camp as being an ideal way for them to combine their needs for employment, cash flow and cultural underpinning' (Burchett, 1992: 7). Produce from traditional hunting and fishing activities undertaken by tourists is returned to the local community with only sufficient amounts for tasting for the tourists left at the safari camp. Tourists experience the traditional and authentic activity and can taste the 'catch', but these vital resources, necessary food stocks for the Aborigines, are not depleted just for the sake of the tourist (Burchett, 1992).

While it is important for the traditional values of local and indigenous communities be maintained, indigenous people must not be asked to maintain their traditional practices simply for the sake of tourist entertainment. However, it must also be recognized that cultures undergo a constant process of change and it is this process of *genuine* culture change and exchange that is a fundamental component of ecotourism. 'Genuine' in this sense may be read as synonymous with *sovereignty*. Local communities must be in an empowered position rather than a subordinate position from which they have autonomy over their culture, its artefacts and rituals, its very direction, while engaging in and with cultures that interact with them but that do not exploit them (Fuller et al., 2007; Scheyvens, 1999; Sofield, 2003).

In this way, both the visitors and the hosts benefit from the tourism experience while at the same time avoiding negative cultural impacts on the indigenous population. Participation of local communities in the activity of tourism, therefore, is an essential element to sustain the well-being of local people.

Through the interactive process between the visitor and the host population both can benefit experientially from ecotourism. By developing an appreciation of local communities and their customs and traditions 'a process of mutual respect and understanding between societies can be greatly enhanced' (Burchett 1992: 10) and the achievement of successful interaction between hosts and guests will only benefit and sustain the well-being of local communities. An ecotourism venture may also in some instances bring villagers together to work collaboratively on planning and delivering products and services to visitors (Morais et al., 2006).

Local communities can benefit from ecotourism economically if they play a greater participatory role in the tourism process. The greater the control over tourism in their region, the more culturally sustainable they will become.

CASE STUDY: Pro-poor Tourism and the World Tourism Organization

For some time now tourism researchers and practitioners have acknowledged the potential for tourism to reduce poverty. Nevertheless, it has only been in the last 10 years that a specific response to this goal has taken shape in the form of pro-poor tourism (PPT). The principle of PPT is 'tourism that generates net profits for the poor...(it) is not a specific product or sector of tourism, but an approach to the industry...PPT strategies aim to unlock opportunities for the poor – whether for economic gain, other livelihood benefits or participation in decision-making' (Ashley et al., 2000: 2). In many ways PPT overlaps with ecotourism and sustainable tourism more generally in its approach to provide sustainable development for local communities so that they might achieve a higher standard of living. The difference between PPT and ecotourism is that PPT focuses on countries in the less-developed South. 'Poverty is the core focus, rather than one element of (mainly environmental) sustainability' (Ashley et al., 2001: viii).

WTO has become committed to exploring ways in which tourism can contribute to the well-being of poor communities and their environment. 'The World Tourism Organization is convinced that the power of tourism – one of the most dynamic economic activities of our time – can be more effectively harnessed to address problems of poverty more directly' (WTO, 2002: 1). Using tourism as a tool to reduce poverty makes sense given that international tourism makes important contributions to the economies of developing countries, particularly to foreign exchange earnings, employment, and Gross Domestic Product (GDP) (Roe and Urquhart, 2001: 3). The focus of PPT is generally economic benefits. Therefore, strategies attempt to achieve outcomes with this goal and include expanding business and employment opportunities for the poor, enhancing collective benefits, capacity building, training and empowerment (Roe and Urquhart, 2001: 5–6).

Employment

One of the most obvious and immediate benefits of tourism associated with local communities is the increase in employment opportunities and income generation for the host region. Tokalau (2005: 173) notes that ecotourism has the potential to improve 'the economic opportunities of local beneficiaries through income and employment generation, increased local entrepreneurship and improved proficiency in time management resulting in rises of labour productivity'. The benefits of employment as a result of tourism impacts on three main economic areas include

- direct employment (associated service industries such as hotels, restaurants, concessions)

- indirect employment (generated as a result of increasing industry inputs such as employment at a retail souvenir outlet, interpretation centers, protected area land manager) (Beeton, 1999: 7–8)

- induced employment (generated as a result of increased spending capacity of local residents due to increased receipts from tourism, consumption of goods for example) (Healy, 1989: 21)

Unfortunately, however, employment opportunities for local communities are often restricted. Tourism is extolled as a major employer in local communities due to the assumption that high levels of capital investment equate with a corresponding increase in employment. Conversely, tourism is often advocated as a major employment generator due to its labor-intensive nature. However, these assumptions are often misleading as tourism often does not essentially generate significant amounts of employment and is less labor-intensive than sometimes espoused by operators seeking community support.

The primary employment opportunities through ecotourism are in the areas of hotels, craft makers, shop owners, tour operators, government agency staff, park wardens/rangers, guides and the like. Moreover, the majority of tourism, and certainly ecotourism businesses are small in scale and familyowned (Getz et al., 2004). Nevertheless, ecotourism may not be the panacea for solving endemic unemployment, particularly in remote and rural areas.

In many circumstances little (if any) employment benefits have accrued to local communities because infrastructure, such as accommodation establishments have already been developed (and staffed) in the area. Furthermore, locals living in remote and rural areas often lack formal qualifications, finding it difficult, if not impossible, to compete with outsiders when employment opportunities arise. Consequently, the general lack of skills and resources has meant that many ecotourism ventures are owned and operated by expatriates (Weiler and Hall, 1992). Often it is unfeasible to expect the local population to automatically assume employment positions within ecotourism. 'The hard truth is that a local farmer, fisherman or plantation worker cannot always be changed overnight into a tourist guide or hotel manager' (Clark and Banford, 1991: 9). Remote and rural destinations are also constrained by tyranny of distance. The location of training and education opportunities are usually offered only in large capital cities that maybe many hundreds and thousands of kilometers away (Mader, 2002).

CASE STUDY: Papua New Guinea

Papua New Guinea is the most rapidly westernizing nation on earth, and as a consequence there are growing social problems, unemployment and a rapidly diminishing traditional culture (Bates, 1991: 4). The Ambua Lodge in the Highlands of Papua New Guinea is an example of an ecotourism establishment providing employment opportunities to local people which, in part, assists in halting the urban drift toward the crime ridden major cities, and thus providing the incentive not only to preserve the natural environment, but also the unique features of the local culture. The construction and operation of Ambua Lodge provides a diverse range of long- and short-term employment to locals, in the positions of construction workers, art and crafts makers, performers, waiters, cooks, guides, gardeners, room cleaners, laundry operators, maintenance personnel, vegetable growers and the like (Bates, 1991: 4).

Map 3 Papua New Guinea Map.

It is often common that the planning, staff and management of parks are done by developed country personnel or expatriates in developing countries and this can have negative effects on the effected local communities, often leading to 'homogenization' of cultures, and in many cases the trivialization of local and traditional methods of managing the natural resources, as well as hostility and bitterness.

Training and education should not solely be concerned to utilitarian skills that may enhance employment opportunities. Partnerships between the tourism industry, government agencies and the local population are needed in which local populations are able to articulate their initial concerns, wants and needs in relation to any development, and which allows them to evaluate in their own terms whether they wish to benefit from tourism (even before they gain employment).

However, participation by local communities in tourism must not be limited simply to employment opportunities. Local communities must be involved in the complete tourism development process, from the planning stage to the implementation and management of tourism projects, through avenues of consultation and partnership. In conjunction, tourism ventures need to be driven by the local communities themselves in all aspects, particularly through locally owned operations or vested interests in local operations which would see greater economic benefits accruing to local communities (Sofield, 2003). Joy and Motzney (1992: 457) suggest that locals should buy and manage small accommodation establishments. However, despite the lack of capital intensity of ecotourism, it may not be a viable economic possibility for many local populations to enter the market.

Extensive training and education is needed before local communities can gain meaningful benefits from ecotourism, particularly language, environmental and natural history skills (Jithendran and Baum, 2000). While the skills for running private business enterprises may not be available within the local community, gaining local expertise and knowledge can be a powerful tool for tourist guides and park wardens in protected areas:

> *proper management of protected areas requires employment of park rangers and guards, as well as workers to maintain park buildings, roads and trails. Ecotourism in protected areas creates demand for guide services…providing employment for…local people familiar with the flora and fauna of the area. (Bunting, 1991: 3)*

According to Ceballos-Lascurian (1992: 5) local people not only possess the 'practical and ancestral knowledge of the natural features' of the area, but they also have the incentive to become dedicated to ecotourism in positions such as park rangers since 'their subsistence would depend in a major degree on the sustained preservation of the natural qualities of their environment'.

Similarly, instead of promoting a colonialist model of development which would seek to bring locals 'up to speed' through training in 'necessary' skills, a recognition of the particular range of skills *already* possessed by local communities matched with their own expectations and outcomes for tourism projects proposed for their locale would be more beneficial in any real sense. Local communities must be involved in the complete tourism development process, from planning, through to the implementation of tourism projects, through avenues of consultation. Consultation can aid in incorporating stakeholder preferences into the design and evolution of conservation policy instruments, as well as reconcile economic development and its potential impact on a local community's social and cultural environment (Bienabe, 2006; World Wide Fund for Nature, 1992).

CASE STUDY: Sakau Rainforest Lodge, Borneo, an Ecotourism Model

Sakau Rainforest Lodge was developed with the intention of blending in with the socio-cultural and physical environment of the region, and to create an alternative source of employment for the local population, particularly those being retrenched from the logging industry. The lodge is located 130 kilometers from Sandakan, with a further 15-minute boat trip up the Kinabatangan River from Sakau itself. A 7-acre land site was purchased in the remote location on the Kinabatangan River bank, but in order to minimize disturbance of natural vegetation, the built up area is limited to 10,000 square feet.

The management recruits local people as boatmen, gardeners, general workers and kitchen hands. All boats used to ferry passengers are built by local fishermen, with other jetty and furniture requirements sub-contracted to the local trade's people in the event that the lodge operates at maximum capacity, local boats are hired for use in ferrying and guiding guests.

Staff slide shows are the primary tool used to upgrade current local interpretive skills, understand the conservation policies of the company and government and of course, the needs of the tourists.

The lodge is sited 100 feet from the river and separated by a buffer zone of trees to prevent soil erosion and minimize the effects of noise on proximal areas. Sakau Rainforest Lodge is built on stilts 5 feet above the ground with a 10-foot ceiling to optimize air circulation and cooling. To maximize the benefits of the location, solar lighting and a supplementary generator are used wherever possible. Rainwater and river water are collected for showering, toilet and household usage, with no waste discharged into the river.

In order to minimize the effects of lodge-controlled tours along the river, all boats are painted green and powered by the smallest possible engine size of 15 HP. When the tour group stops to observe wildlife, power is derived from a solar charged battery, connected to an electric engine.

The management of Sakau Rainforest Lodge set aside 1000 room nights in 1996 for volunteers to clear weeds in the nearby Kelenanap ox-bow lake. Wildlife, birdlife and local fishing have been affected as a result of weed infestation. Working in cooperation with the University of Malaysia and overseas students, the problems of weed infestation and waterway eutrophication are being addressed.

Finally, Sakau Rainforest Lodge has begun to raise funds from overseas tour operators – the money being channeled to a local Non-Government Organization (NGO) – Sabah Environmental Protection Association, and used for research purposes. In the near future, an area of the lower Kinabatangan River will be gazetted as a wildlife sanctuary. Management is using this sustainable lodge as a catalyst and incentive in preserving the natural and cultural environments, encouraging a move from illegal logging and bribery of local enforcement officers to sustainable ecotourism, where locals receive long-term benefits.

Albert Teo – Managing Director, Sakau Rainforest Lodge, Malaysia: British Airways Tourism for Tomorrow Awards 1996 Pacific Region.

Even small-scale development may have significant negative impacts. As a result of tourism to various areas, local people have lost access to land and resources they had previously enjoyed. According to Walpole et al. (2001) ecotourism often leads to a change in resource ownership and management particularly when the land is set aside for protected area status, which is beneficial to the tourism industry but detrimental to the local people.

Similarly, 'flourishing employment, living standards and consumption levels for some, added to the unequal distribution of benefits to a portion of the population, can contribute to social tensions and hostility' (World Wide Fund for Nature, 1992: 19). This has significant import for protected area agencies for local resentment toward designated conservation areas often arises when the park is viewed as principally of benefit to tourists with no reciprocal benefit for the local population. This is often due to the fact that local people no longer have the right to use land they consider was theirs, but at the same time see it frequently visited by foreign tourists.

In extreme cases this resentment can lead to the destruction of natural areas as 'malicious destruction may occur if landowners believe that their lands are being singled out for protection...and they are not receiving the benefits' (Kusler, n.d.: 2). Therefore, care should be taken with assumptions that tourism based on indigenous cultures will necessarily produce significant developmental benefits for indigenous peoples. This can only come about if indigenous people have the necessary resources, or they have recognized rights to their heritage (van Veuren, 2003).

LOCAL PLANNING AND DEVELOPMENT

The important strategies for indigenous success in operating ecotourism enterprises... include the importance of consultation and planning processes, the availability of suitable education and training to indigenous business owner–operators and the availability of joint-venture partnerships with actors in the mainstream economy. (Fuller et al., 2007: 141)

Such a process would involve goal setting at the national, regional and local levels. Clark and Banford (1991: 7) suggest the development of a tourism master plan to document the desirability and limits of acceptable tourism for the area. Ideally, communities could develop their own master plan, but presently it is dependent on the priorities of those in positions of power to determine.

Several examples exist where local people have taken moves to ensure that they both personally, and as a community, benefit directly from ecotourism. In many small communities such as that living on Easter Island accommodation becomes a key factor; on Easter Island over 300 beds within local houses are open to tourists, providing the major source of accommodation on the island (Stanton, 2003). The additional income gained has been spent beautifying homes and providing for local infrastructure. In Papua New Guinea's highlands, villagers have a source of income from the accommodation huts they have built on their land (Bates, 1991: 4) which, with the co-operation of the local tour operators, provide accommodation to groups of tourists.

Similarly, the Pax World Friendship Tours and Co-op America's Travel Link programs are all designed specifically so that the local community can benefit from ecotourism to that area. The programs involve local people opening their homes to tourists, who in turn use this time in the local community to work on 'community development projects' (Johnson, 1993: 3)

CASE STUDY: South Pentecost, Vanuatu

The Pentecost Land Dive is a traditional ceremony of the villages in this area that occurs annually in April/May. In response to increasing negative cultural impacts as a result of tourism, the local chiefs of the villages established 'The South Pentecost Tourism Council' to manage the event, its 'primary responsibility [being] to safeguard the cultural integrity of the event' (Sofield, 1991: 59). This involves maintaining customs with tourist visits, preventing filming of the event and limiting numbers of tourists attending the performance. These actions were declared in response to growing concerns about the increasing distortion of the ceremony due to growing commercialization and the lack of transparency in the distribution of fees paid by foreign film companies to communities to film this event. The moratorium on filming provides the tourist with an 'authentic' cultural experience while maintaining the cultural significance of the ritual to the villagers themselves and allows them some degree of control over the activity of tourism (Vanuatu Cultural Centre, 2008).

However, it is often the power struggle at national, state or local level which is the determining factor of where tourism occurs, what is seen and done, and who, among the local community, receives the economic benefits (e.g. Sofield, 2003: 191–224). In practice, the planning system itself is often set up in a way that gives indigenous people little or no opportunities for input. According to Johnson (1993: 4) 'development projects are often designed and implemented in a political context in which indigenous people have minimal voice in policy and management'. In contrast, Nepal has developed a system (through a resource management plan) specifically benefiting local people by giving them increased power and a greater role in decision-making.

Increasing access to information for indigenous people provides them with greater scope for involvement in planning and decision-making. Education plays a powerful role in increasing local involvement.

CASE STUDY: Costa Rica

Costa Rica's joint UNESCO-MAB and Costa Rica National Park project, intentionally prefers residents to foreign involvement. The restoration of denigrated forests (known as the Guanacaste project) emphasizes Costa Rican residents, employing and training locals in the areas of park maintenance, management and habitat restoration. This program has the long-term benefit of the gradual transfer of control over the research, management and public education sectors from the currently dominant North Americans to Costa Rican industry (Johnson, 1993: 3).

Programs such as these will eventually lead to greater local control over protected areas and the tourism industry. Therefore, when local people are involved in studying, discussing and devising strategies to control, or capture control over the development decision-making process they are taking a critical step toward increasing their role in ecotourism (Johnson, 1993: 4).

Consideration for local cultures can be incorporated into the planning and marketing of ecotourism destinations and products in many ways. Blangy and Epler-Wood (1992: 4) recommend those government agencies, tourism boards, the tourism industry and local inhabitants that could all play a role in the education of tourists about cultural issues by the implementation of social guidelines. They suggest that government should be responsible for developing guidelines but recommend significant input from the local community. The local community can be incorporated into the development of these guidelines by using government funding (if available) to get assistance with the preparation and editing of brochures for distribution. Alternatively, the local community could collaborate with international and local non-governmental organizations and become involved with environmental education projects.

Social guidelines[20] could incorporate desirable and acceptable behavior in the following areas:

1. Local customs and traditions

2. Permission for photographs

3. Dress

4. Language

5. Invasion of privacy

6. Response to begging

7. Use and abuse of technological gadgetry

---

[20] See Lorimer (2006) for other practical social, economic and environmental guidelines for ecotourists.

8. Bartering and bargaining

9. Indigenous rights

10. Local officials

11. Off-limits areas (Blangy & Epler-Wood, 1992: 4)

Another source of potential assistance is tourist boards. Blangy and Epler-Wood (1992: 4) suggest that boards should allocate funds for all stages of the education process, through the generation, printing and distribution of local guidelines. Distribution of brochures and printed matter at tourist centers and at on-site is an effective means of reaching the tourist. Tour guides could play an important role by briefing tourists on what is acceptable and unacceptable in the region being visited.

However, despite the often good intentions of tourists and some tour operators, it is apparent that ecotourism can damage the natural assets on which it depends (e.g. Kamauro, 1996; McLaren, 2003; Shepherd, 2002). The outcome according to Lindberg (1991: ix) depends a great deal on how it is managed. Thus the implications for management are enormous. Managers must find a way to 'capitalize on its potential without jeopardizing the special features of natural areas' (Boo, 1990: xiv).

In order for ecotourism organizations to become aware of their place and role in ecotourism, it is important for them to be made aware of the differing needs of local communities while also aligning the operations of their businesses with national conservation/development strategies. Ecotourism, like tourism generally, is made up of a variety of sectors including government, private enterprise, local communities and organizations, non-governmental conservation organizations, and international institutions. If each sector has an understanding of where it fits within the broader framework of the tourism and conservation sectors then there is a better chance of carefully designed tourism programs. These would take protected areas as a focus for fostering host communities' values while providing education for visitors in relation to both conservation issues and the local community itself (Kutay, 1990: 38).

The United Nations Capital Development Fund (UNCDF) provides investment capital, capacity building and technical advisory services to promote microfinance and local development in the least developed countries. Loans are provided based on the philosophy of 'participatory ecodevelopment' (Frueh and Pesce, 2000) which provides the means of confronting the deleterious effects of tourism. Participatory ecodevelopment encompasses cooperative, self-management (autogestion), co-management (cogestion) and solidarity (solidarism) elements. It is recognized by most in developing nations that the old economic models do not work and benefit only the developed nations who end up controlling the economy, there are however alternate models currently in operation in varying forms.

> *Sometimes the imperatives to respect nature, satisfy basic needs, and participate in self-government point in the same direction. Establishing a more just system of land tenure, pricing, credit, and technical assistance for small and poor farmers could reduce deforestation and environmentally unsound farming practices, as well as be a source of basic-needs satisfaction and communal self-determination. Santa Rosa National Park rightly prides itself on integrating the restoration of its dry tropical forest with the education and employment of local residents as 'eco-tour' guides, foresters, educators and researchers. A proposed Peace Park on the Costa Rican–Nicaraguan border can protect the fragile regional peace as well as an endangered tropical ecosystem. (Encel and Encel, 1991: 159)*

Originally, in both ecotourism and biodiversity debates, conservation issues were foremost and the local community element was neglected. However, it has become increasingly obvious that biodiversity cannot be conserved without the involvement of local resident communities. While it is necessary to recognize national parks and protected areas as integral to biodiversity and ecotourism, ecotourism must also stress the importance of local human populations and tourist experiences (Goodwin, 2002).

CASE STUDY: Partnerships, National Parks and Native People

The Sitka National Historical Park comprises 106 acres of spectacular scenery bordered by the mouth of the Indian River, Alaska. The park is said to embody one of the most successful partnerships between the native population and national park authorities. In the park, Native American cultures are central to the interpretive experience of visitors and the Tlingit Indians operate the Southeast Alaska Indian Cultural Centre in association with the National Park Service (NPS). Native artists practice their skills, with a focus on 'elders' and the cultural traditions they represent. 'Bringing them [the elders] together is insurance for where we Tlingit are going in the future'.

Such partnerships are evident in Glacier National Park, where native programs include Slaish, Kootenai and Black-feet (Indian) lecturers, drummers and dancers. Glacier's

programs began in 1980, funded by the Glacier Natural History Association and other private sources. Although it was initially difficult to find native interpreters there are enough natives participating to run a program almost each day in July and August, and employ Blackfeet natives as summer rangers. Glacier's chief of interpretation stated 'This needed to be native Americans interpreting their own culture...when we romanticize about a native culture; we lose sight that it's a growing, living culture, not an artefact.'

An appreciation for living culture is evident in Canyon de Chelly National Monument in Arizona, where the Navajo still own the 83,840 acres. Except for walking the trail to White House Ruin, and following the north and south rim drives, no visitor enters Canyon de Chelly without a Navajo guide. One young guide (Hunter) began his employment in the park in construction before moving into interpretation, the switch a natural progression for him. Hunter states 'My grandmother said, "It's not your mouth you learn with, but your other senses. That's why we have two of everything else – ears, eyes, nostrils, hands. Your mouth is for sharing, everything else you learn with." She never used the word "teach". It's sharing.'

The Navajo guides are living history themselves, from families that continue to pasture sheep and goats in the canyon after 500 years. The canyons provided Hunter with this metaphor to describe the interplay of visiting and native cultures:'People talk about bridging. But with a bridge, two cultures come half way and then pull. A river [however] comes from all directions, comes together and slows together. No pulling, but weaving. Naturally. We people come in all different colours. Look at a finished rug, how beautiful it is. We just have to weave our threads' (Bowman, 1998).

In a groundbreaking arrangement, the Alaska Native Brotherhood assumed control of the demonstration program and established its focus on Southeast Alaska Native cultural arts in 1969; the Southeast Alaska Indian Cultural Centre celebrated its 30th anniversary in January, 2000. Many of the remarkable Tlingit artefacts in the collection were loaned or donated by local clans under agreements designed to ensure ongoing, traditional users.

Tourism and tourism based on natural areas do not take place in isolation from local people. Tourism requires infrastructure and access, all of which impact on local communities. In many cases the natural environment is used by the local people for sustaining their livelihood (e.g. Goodman, 2002). With the introduction of ecotourism it is found that there is a better basis for conservation of the natural resource as there are direct benefits to be gained from an intact environment. These benefits can be seen by local communities thereby encouraging an awareness of the need to conserve within an economic framework. However, if development is dictated by forces outside these communities it is common to see overdevelopment and excessive economic leakage followed by high social impact. Resentment can also build causing blatant harvesting or destruction of so-called protected natural resources.

FURTHER READING

Sofield, T.H.B. (2003) *Empowerment for Sustainable Tourism Development.* Pergamon, Amsterdam.

Sofield's text explores the relationship between tourism, sustainable development and community empowerment in South Pacific island nations.

van Egmond, T. (2007). Planning for the 'right' tourists. In *Understanding Western Tourists in Developing Countries* (T. van Egmond, ed.). CAB International, Wallingford, UK, pp. 144–73.

van Egmond's chapter provides a critical analysis of international tourism discourse by arguing that terms such as ecotourism, sustainable tourism, 'dark green' environmentalism, ethnic tourism and the search for authenticity are actually Western Protestant middle-class concepts. Thereby raising the question of whether or not developing countries can implement these Western concepts and Western tourist practices.

Special edition of *Current Issues in Tourism* (2002) (Global ecotourism policies and case studies: perspectives and Constraints) volume 5, issue 3.

CHAPTER 7

Ecotourism Case Studies

CASE STUDY 1. TREKKING ON THE KOKODA TRACK, PAPUA NEW GUINEA: ENHANCING DECISION-MAKING CAPACITY FOR KOKODA COMMUNITIES

INTRODUCTION

The Kokoda Track is a walking track that runs through the Owen Stanley Range in Papua New Guinea (PNG). Starting from Owen's Corner, about 50 kilometers east of the capital Port Moresby, it winds its way up and down for 96 kilometers north across rugged terrain to the village of Kokoda in Oro Province. The Kokoda Track has become an icon in Australia's military history as it was the site of a major World War II battle which was pivotal in repelling invading Japanese troops in 1942. The track also symbolizes the links between Australia and PNG as villagers along the track provided vital support for the Australian soldiers. Walking the Kokoda Track is for many a testament to the bravery and character of the soldiers who fought along it in extremely arduous conditions *(see Fig. 7.1)*.

Today the track represents PNG's premier land-based tourist attraction with a number of tour companies organizing 10-day treks for mostly Australian tourists. The number of trekkers has been growing rapidly over the last decade and is expected to reach 6000 (accompanied by 8000 guides and support staff) by the end of 2008. This has led to the development of a trekking industry on the Kokoda Track, which provides an example of how ecotourism can enhance the involvement and decision-making capacity of locals. Work has taken place to ensure the sustainability of this burgeoning industry from a social, environmental and economic perspective. For example, efforts are currently underway to ensure that tourism

CONTENTS

Case Study 1. Trekking on the Kokoda Track, Papua New Guinea: Enhancing Decision-Making Capacity for Kokoda Communities

Introduction

History

Tourism and Papua New Guinea (png)

Trekking and Host Community Involvement

Trekking Strategy

Planning for Trekking Development

Case Study 2. Porters and the Trekking Industry of Nepal

Introduction

Nepalese Porters

Porter

137

Representations
in Tourism
Marketing

Implications
for Ecotourism

Discussion and
Conclusion

Case Study 3.
Surfing Tourism
in Indonesia's
Mentawai Islands
by Jess Ponting

Introduction

The Mentawai
Islands and
People

Tourism in the
Mentawai Islands

Surfing Tourism

Why are the
Mentawai Islands
so Good for
Surfing?

Surfing Tourism
in the Mentawai

Recreational
Carrying Capacity
Management

The Land Issue

Solutions?

Further Reading

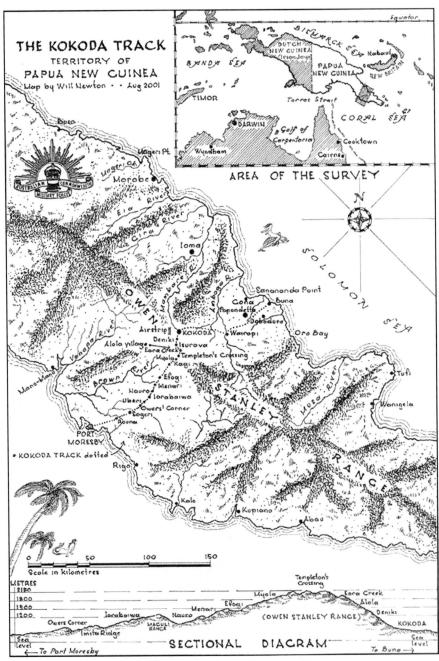

FIGURE 7.1 *Kokoda Track. Photo by Kokoda Track Authority.*

receipts are equally distributed among the local communities situated along the track and that trekkers are educated about minimal impact practices.

HISTORY

The Kokoda Track (or Kokoda Trail, as it is otherwise known) came into existence in 1904, when it was established by the administration of what was then British New Guinea. The track was the official overland mail route linking Port Moresby with the northern goldfields beyond the village of Kokoda. Prior to that time, all that existed was a series of disconnected 'forest pads' (cleared areas in the rainforest used for village settlement) between the scattered communities along the otherwise impenetrable Owen Stanley Range.

In 1942 during the Second World War the Japanese selected it as the axis for their advance on Port Moresby from Buna and Gona. The Kokoda Track then became a household name in Australia and PNG. A small band (approximately 400) of poorly equipped and inexperienced Australian soldiers (later reinforced by soldiers who had fought with the British in the Middle East and North Africa), were sent over the Track to Kokoda, where they faced a force of some 10,000 well-equipped Japanese troops highly trained and experienced in jungle warfare. After many months of bitter fighting and horrific casualties, and aided by the legendary Papua New Guinean carriers, or 'Fuzzy Wuzzy Angels' as they were fondly known, the Australian army succeeded in preventing the fall of Port Moresby. Thus the Kokoda Track was the scene of some of the most difficult fighting the Australian troops encountered in the Pacific theater, and the name became synonymous in Australia with courage, sacrifice, mateship and endurance *(see Fig. 7.2)*.

FIGURE 7.2 *Kokoda Track from the air. Photo by Stephen Wearing.*

TOURISM AND PAPUA NEW GUINEA (PNG)

Tourism to PNG has always been modest; however, it rapidly declined from a peak of 80,000 international arrivals in 1999, a decline that was triggered by political unrest and negative perceptions of safety for visitors *(see Fig. 7.3)*.

Whilst overall numbers have increased, the number of leisure and recreation tourists (as opposed to business travelers) has yet to recover to 1999 levels *(see Fig. 7.4)*. Further, levels of leisure travel are unusually low for the pacific. Leisure travel in PNG's neighboring Pacific states generally accounts for 80% of international arrivals whilst in PNG, 2005 figures were just 26% (as outlined in *Fig. 7.2*).

Over the past 3 years it has been PNG's niche markets which have led to the growth in the leisure tourism market particularly trekking on the Kokoda Track. Trekking permits issued for the Kokoda Track from 2001 to 2006 have grown from 75 in 2001 to over 2000 in 2006; estimates for 2007 have been placed in the realm of 5000 trekkers, and 6000 are expected to walk the track in 2008.

The existing Kokoda Track Reserve covers only 10 meters on either side of the Track. With the surrounding environment under threat from unsustainable logging practices and mining, groups concerned with natural and cultural heritage conservation are pressing for the protection of a much wider area to be protected under law. The United Nations Educational, Scientific and Cultural Organization's (UNESCO) World Heritage list is an increasingly sought after designation for the world's

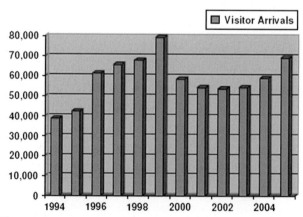

FIGURE 7.3   *International visitor arrivals to PNG, 1994–2005 (Trip Consultants, 2006: 24).*

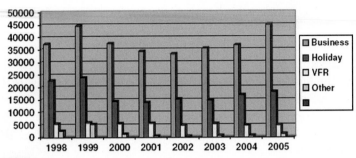

FIGURE 7.4 *PNG visitor arrivals by purpose of visit, 1994–2005 (Trip Consultants, 2006: 24).*

most valuable natural and cultural assets as it can serve to raise awareness and funding to ensure the conservation of these assets for perpetuity. As such the Kokoda Track Foundation, a body comprising concerned individuals, trek operators, Non-Government Organizations (NGOs) and academics concerned with conserving the heritage and natural values of the Kokoda Track region and the well-being of its landowning communities, and the World Wide Fund for Nature (WWF) are leading the push for the track and the surrounding Owen Stanley Ranges to be ratified and inscribed upon the World Heritage List.

TREKKING AND HOST COMMUNITY INVOLVEMENT

The Orokaiva and Koiari people who live along the Track lead a subsistence livelihood, clearing land to grow crops and raising animals for consumption. The only source of income, apart from tourism, is from the limited sale of produce to markets in Port Moresby. This livelihood, already under threat from a shortage of labor, is not one that the majority of the younger generation wish to pursue in the future. Tourism-related employment can help stem the outflow of young people and increase their education and future earning capacity through vocational training, such as basic tourism business management skills.

Relationships with the land are at the very core of the identity and cultural values of the people of PNG. Over 97% of the land area is under customary tenure, which is subject to ongoing relationships and negotiations between different groups. Boundaries can therefore reflect changes in power and authority. Being able to deal with the current landowners is important, and often difficult. Land issues are a common source of tension among the people along the track and negotiations can be highly complicated. It is vital that effective mechanisms be established for negotiation and dispute resolution if tourism in the area is to become sustainable.

In 2003, a strategy for the development of a sustainable tourism industry based on trekking along the Kokoda Track was identified as the highest priority for the Kokoda region, as it would provide a process to ensure that the primary source of income from trekking was able to support the planned socio-economic initiatives for villagers and their members along the track. The intention was to empower the host communities, enabling them to pursue their goals.

As a result of the rapid increase in the number of trekkers on the Kokoda Track and disputes among landowners regarding the distribution of benefits from tourism, the Kokoda Track Foundation successfully lobbied the PNG government to establish a Kokoda Track Special Purpose Authority (KTA) with representation from clan leaders, landowners, provincial and local-level government authorities, the Tourism Promotion Authority, the National Cultural Commission, community organizations and tour operators. On 9 December 2004, KTA was proclaimed by the PNG National Government as a statutory body of the Koiari and Kokoda local-level governments.

TREKKING STRATEGY

The establishment of the KTA and the preparation of community development/action plans were the first steps in empowering the local people to optimize the benefits from tourism and enable them to take a role in their own development. Through a strong partnership with the local government representatives, the intention was to allow the KTA to take control of planning, decision-making and funding allocations to the host communities, which was previously not carried out in any systematic manner and where locals relied on 'handouts' from tour operators.

As a part of this process the communities developed a 5-year Trekking Strategy drafted during workshops held at Port Moresby, Efogi and Kokoda *(see Fig 7.5)*. The plan was to create self-sufficiency through revenues generated from trekking fees, accommodation, food production and associated activities. The strategy focused on the environmental, economic, social and cultural aspects of sustainable development.

Land tenure along the Kokoda Track rests with each of the communities who carry out work on the track to ensure it remains open. They have established bridges, crossings, campsites and other infrastructure to support trekking. These communities have also managed to ensure, through the Trekking Strategy and the KTA, that they are represented in a collective way

FIGURE 7.5   *Efogi village workshop. Photo by Stephen Wearing.*

to outside organizations such as tour operators. Prior to the process of developing the Trekking Strategy the Kokoda communities struggled to make progress due to internal conflict. This led to individual negotiations with tour operators and the closure of the track by those who felt they were not getting a fair return from trekking.

Communities saw, what they considered 'well off' tourists spending very little in their villagers. What transpired was a highly skewed distribution of wealth where operators, and those with 'arrangements' with them, organized porters and accommodation for the trekkers increasing the wealth of those with connections and in a position to negotiate, while leaving many others on the track to miss out. The introduction of the KTA and the process of producing a Trekking Strategy saw a breakdown in the almost total control of the industry by tourism operators who often oscillated between the utilization and avoidance of 'people participation' where and when it suited them. For example, the industry relied on local porters to work within the labor conditions set out according to traditional and exploitative traditions. However, in discussions in both the Efogi and Kokoda workshops, most village groups were dissatisfied with this arrangement as conditions such as pay rates, loads, equipment supplied and general treatment, varied widely. The workshops enabled arrangements for minimum standards to be set, including only porters from the Kokoda group of villages.

To mobilize the Trekking Strategy four workshops were conducted for the villagers along the track. The second workshop in Efogi village gathered together representatives from all the villages on the Kokoda Track for the first time in living memory. Planes were used to fly in participants for a 3-day workshop.

One of the major problems with the workshops is that they tended to mobilize the elites only, which often meant that women were excluded. Most male 'advisors' focused their groups' discussions on what would advantage them without considering that the trekking industry was fundamentally supported and run within communities, including women. Moreover, males accounted for nearly all the participants representing the communities. Due to their disadvantaged standing, women were precluded from deciding their involvement and discussing what they might need to assist them in gaining from the trekking industry and the wider strategy. The paternalistic attitude prevailing among men created a situation where the women in the community engaged in a separate process that allowed them to clearly enunciate what they would like to see happen in the future with tourism. On the request of the Efogi women a single workshop with the women of Efogi village was held in conjunction, this had the effect of giving a voice to the women in the village who also wanted to benefit from the growing industry. In this way, women subtly and unobtrusively ensured that their collective voice was added to that of the male elites. The outcome was that the women were able to enunciate their interest in selling food to the trekkers. In order to do this the women had to gather information on what types of food trekkers might buy and then to organize themselves to prepare and sell this food along the entire length of the Kokoda Track. Previously, operators had not encouraged this and had supplied their own rations to trekkers.

PLANNING FOR TREKKING DEVELOPMENT

A key approach to manage the Kokoda Track has been to employ methodologies which encourage local communities to mobilize their own knowledge and ideas in the management of their resources. Participatory Rural Appraisal (PRA) is one such research tool which has been used successfully in aiding communities to make management decisions about their resources. The PRA approach was chosen in order to generate data concerning the lifestyle of communities on the Kokoda Track, their expectations of trekking and what changes could be made to enable them to benefit more completely from trekking. Research participants collected data by themselves with minimal assistance from the various researchers attached to the project. This enabled participants to take responsibility and assume accountability for their own knowledge and contributions with a view of enhancing self-confidence, independence and an awareness of each individual's potential.

Any form of trekking tourism depends on the support and use of the host community's available facilities such as accommodation, ancillary services and infrastructure such as medical, transport and labor. PRA was employed to help facilitate local communities (via various representatives) and to make decisions about the provision of such resources for tourist use. The technique also facilitated the development of a cooperative and coordinated regional approach to tourism development between all landowning clans along the track.

A regional/track wide approach to the development of the Kokoda was essential in ensuring that trekkers would be able to traverse the entirety of the track and pass through 16 different land owning clans. This approach brings increased levels of complexity in the logistics of participatory planning and management as it takes far longer, requires the collation of far more information, requires a great deal more compromise on the part of the villagers and involves many more difficulties to engage with the entire region rather than individual land owning units. Additionally issues can arise stemming from different levels of resistance, commitment and economic benefit between different participating communities. Despite these challenges, regional coordination is vital to the sustainability of the trekking industry on the Kokoda Track as it can lead to a number of benefits. These were found to include

1. Greater cooperation between stakeholders, creating economies of scale for marketing and training exercises.

2. The selection of appropriate sites along the track for camping in order to minimize impacts from trekking and to mobilize more people to become involved in trekking activities.

3. The development of a wider array of attractions in order to capture a wider ecotourism market.

Despite significant headway being made in the participatory planning of trekking in the region, challenges to the conservation of the wider area still remain. The conservation of natural resources in PNG must always be balanced against the community's desire for development and the reality that often their ability to achieve development is a product of the ability to derive a cash income from their natural resources.

Whilst much progress has been made in terms of participatory planning for the ongoing development of trekking along the Kokoda track, the conservation of the natural and cultural heritage of the wider area remains under threat. Despite the global significance of the Owen Stanley Range as a habitat for a broad range of endemic and endangered fauna, as home to 16 unique living cultures, and the highly significant heritage value of the region to Australia and PNG in terms of its military history, extractive resource exploitation, specifically logging and mining threatens the area with environmental devastation. In spite of the headway made with villagers in terms of cooperative agreements for track operation, the Kodu villagers have signed agreements with Frontier Resources (a multinational mining company) to develop a major copper mine which would require the re-routing of the Kokoda Track reducing its cultural authenticity and heritage value. Further, the Kodu group have threatened to close down their section of the track (approximately 10%), if there is a political interference with their plans. Trekking on the Kokoda Track is a good example of real life implementation of best practice community-based tourism development practices and the equally real multiplicity of forces which support and undermine it.

CASE STUDY 2. PORTERS AND THE TREKKING INDUSTRY OF NEPAL

INTRODUCTION

Since Nepal opened up its borders to tourists in the mid-twentieth century the country has become one of the world's most popular trekking destinations. Lured by the world's highest mountains, such as Sagarmatha (Mt Everest), tourists visit Nepal to experience unparalleled natural beauty, friendly locals and a highly developed trekking industry. The industry is made up of hundreds of organizations that offer a range of relatively cheap package walking holidays that last anywhere from 3 to 30 days. These include gentle excursions into the foothills, to major expeditions into remote areas crossing passes over 5000 meters high. The treks are usually highly organized and everything is taken care of by local guides, cooks and porters.

It is the porters who are the backbone of the industry as they ferry loads of food, water, fuel, tents and trekkers' personal belongings over some of the most rugged terrain in the world. However, the tourism industry in Nepal has tended to either deliberately or inadvertently ignore the conditions experienced by porters in the Himalayas. The perpetuation in some cases of a romanticized notion of the strength of the Himalayan Sherpa is a useful selling point for tourism providers. With the assistance of local porters, tourism providers are able to market tourism experiences based around mental relaxation and calmness in what would otherwise be a very challenging environment to negotiate.

NEPALESE PORTERS

In Nepal there are three broad categories of mountain porters (International Porter Protection Group (IPPG), 2003). They include

- Traditional porters

- High altitude climbing porters

- Trekking porters

The first group of porters are the traditional porters who work for local people. Their job does not pay very well and the loads are heavy, but it is not dangerous because it is usually carried out between villages at a lower altitude (although this has been changing with more hotels and restaurants being built at higher altitudes) (International Porter Protection Group, 2003). The second category of porters is the high altitude climbing porter. This is a small elite group, often consisting of Sherpas, who carry loads above base camp (usually over 4500 meters) for climbing expeditions. While their job is risky and fatalities are not uncommon, they are equipped with the latest western mountaineering equipment and well paid (International Porter Protection Group, 2003).

The third category is the trekking porter. There are around 100,000 trekking porters working in Nepal in a good trekking season. The majority come from the lower altitude middle hills and consist typically of poor farmers looking to earn an additional income. For many, being a porter is the only option for employment so it has become essential for the local Nepalese to undertake additional activities to generate income in order to survive (Ayers, 2003; van Klaveren, 2000). For example, it has been estimated that during peak tourist season, 65,000 trekkers in the Annapurna region provide more than 50,000 people with seasonal employment (Nepal, 2002). Porting is one of the few economic activities that provide an opportunity to gain additional income, albeit in the two trekking seasons (March–May and September–November) (van Klaveren, 2000). Infrastructure-related construction work (e.g. home maintenance) is common in lean tourism periods with porters used to transport logs and other materials from forested areas (Gelzen, 2002). The development of illegal markets for wood supply

FIGURE 7.6 *Nepalese porters carrying loads for a trekking group. Photo by World Expeditions.*

and the sustainability of Nepal's forests can therefore be directly connected to issues of appropriate wage allotment and tourism seasonality.

A common image of Sherpa porters is one of sturdiness and reliability (Spaltenberger, 2003). Porters are typically able to carry large and heavy loads (from 20 to 50 kg) and rarely succumb to altitude sickness or hypothermia even with inadequate clothing and footwear. This consequently supports the representation of a sustainable tourism industry. In reality, Sherpas are seldom trekking porters and are one of the most affluent ethnic groups in Nepali society. Sherpas are now owners and managers of lodges or trekking agencies or even living abroad (Nepal, 2002; Spaltenberger, 2003). Contrary to popular belief, Tamang not Sherpas are the main ethnic group portering for trekking tourists (van Klaveren, 2000) *(see Fig. 7.6)*.

The centrality of the Tamang ethnic group to the trekking industry is illustrated in the existence of a Kathmandu-based trekking outfit named Tamang Expeditions. Often other societal subgroups including children (i.e. those under 18 years) are also employed in porter roles, an issue that with the growth in global concern over child labor creates issues with respect to tourism industry sustainability (Kumar et al., 2001).

PORTER REPRESENTATIONS IN TOURISM MARKETING

The treatment of porters in the trekking sector is a complex issue. According to McKinlay (2003) trekking is a valuable industry that provides people in one of the world's most poverty-stricken countries with employment. While porters frequently operate in harsh and rugged conditions, articles in foreign media often perpetuate a romantic image of porters and their activities. Whilst not based on an exhaustive search, it is our view that articles such as *Why the*

Sherpas of Nepal would leave our fittest soldiers standing (Henderson, 2005) are reflective of much of the existing publication base. Such articles take a romantic view of porters, albeit couched in reputable scientific research. What appears to be reported on less are figures from groups such as Tourism Concern (2002, 2008) who note that porters suffer four times the number of accidents and illnesses than western trekkers, while earning between US$2 and US$5 per day. Through interviewing porters it has been revealed that they consider the conditions (hot and cold weather, steep trails, heavy loads, high altitude) and underpayment the major disadvantages of their work (van Klaveren, 2000). However, as the International Porter Protection Group (2003) reports, they are also granted the chance to learn English, make friends with foreigners and can therefore improve their conditions (for example, several trekking companies are owned by ex-porters). Similarly, porters themselves declare their contact with tourists and other porters and their allowances and potential tips as perks of the job.

Nevertheless, the amount of money earned by porters does vary in accordance to the type of trek undertaken (van Klaveren, 2000). Aside from the three categories of porters mentioned above, there is also an important distinction between porters who work for companies and temporary porters. The situation for porters who work for companies has improved substantially (McKinlay, 2003). As Ayers (2003) observes, tour operators in Nepal are beginning to understand that it is good business practice to look after the interests of porters. No doubt this has been aided by campaigns and initiatives by Tourism Concern and the Himalayan Rescue Association Nepal who, in 2005, sponsored a mountain safety training workshop for porters (Himalayan Rescue Association Nepal, 2006). A review by Tourism Concern of 81 United Kingdom-based trekking operators found that 40 now have policies to ensure that porters are provided with essential protection, fair pay and humane working conditions (Tourism Concern, 2002).

The Shangri-La image of the Himalayas has gradually been transformed to that of a cheap, rugged and dirty destination (Nepal, 2002). As a result, it is important to be aware of the images that are being used to portray trekking in Nepal. For example, images of porters carrying huge loads are romanticized based on the original Sherpas and the climbing industry. The reality, however, is often quite different with a variety of ailments including fever, backaches, chest pains, snow blindness and diarrhea suffered by many long-distance porters in Nepal (Kumar et al., 2001). There are also other long-term implications of such work including arthritis and chronic back, leg and neck pain.

Recent attempts to move toward sustainable practices have seen this romanticized portrayal of trekking in Nepal contrasted with media representations of accidents and maltreatment of porters. The *Nepali Times* has featured a variety of articles over recent years, focusing on the maltreatment of porters and the necessity of recognizing the value that porters play in Nepalese life, not just to its tourism industry. Subedi (2000) in a piece entitled *Celebrating the Porters* describes the treatment of porters in terms of the sort of treatment that would be ascribed to mules and donkeys. Samacharparta (2002) draws a direct connection between the use of children in porter roles and their later indoctrination into the ranks as child soldiers supporting rebel groups such as the Maoists. Ayres (2003) recounts horror stories of trek rescue helicopters refusing to airlift porters to safety, in spite of the presence of spare seats. These and other reports are distributed around the world, and at the same time contested by others. Images of porters with kerosene burns or frost bitten feet that are portrayed in the BBC video *Carrying the Burden* or on Tourism Concern's web site create an image of porters working under conditions, once described by a Pakistani tour operator, as tantamount to slavery (McKinlay, 2003).

IMPLICATIONS FOR ECOTOURISM

There has been a tendency amongst much of Nepal's trekking industry to use sustainability and ecotourism as a mechanism to present an idealized image of Nepal as a tourism destination. This creates sustainability challenges in that true integrated sustainability requires consideration of the ways in which local industries interact with their host societies (Clarke, 1997; Hunter, 2002; Weaver, 2006). Tourism in Nepal has much to gain by adopting sustainability ideologies. Concern for local stakeholders aside; 'the natural link between tourism and the environment provides an obvious self-interest for tourism to protect its environment' (McKercher, 1991a: 135). To date, however, it is fair to say that the adoption of sustainability principles in the Nepalese tourism sector has been limited. In developing a sustainable tourism industry in Nepal that is considerate of porters and other local groups, it is our view that three interrelated lines of action exist. These are the need for:

1. More emphasis on frameworks that prioritize the environment and cultural lives of host communities.

2. Further engagement with local economies.

3. Long-term coordinated planning efforts that recognize limits to growth and incorporate community organizations and government.

Complexities of development

The concealing of unsustainable economic growth under the guise of sustainable development has become a commonplace practice all around the world (Khan, 2002). In the case of tourism, western business models are often adopted in the rush to establish the tourism industry. A range of studies have shown that such models often result in high levels of revenue leakage from the destination region back to the foreign financiers, and the intrusion on local populations through unwanted social and environmental changes (Brohman, 1996; Fennell, 2003; Mahapatra, 1998; Marfut, 1999; Orams, 2001; Wearing and Wearing, 1999; Weaver, 1998).

We maintain that the pre-existing state of Nepali communities deserves greater consideration when examining the trekking industry in Nepal. This is relevant in the cases of several pro-poor tourism development initiatives in Nepal (Allcock, 2003; Hummel, 2004; Saville, 2001). Local people, such as porters and the community, generally represent one relatively powerless entity. It has been found that they are usually the last to benefit from development in the form of economic neoliberalism (Mahapatra, 1998; Smith, 2000; Timothy and Tosun, 2003). This idea is supported in the social impact assessment literature where it is noted that the social impacts of development (e.g. tourism) are primarily felt by individuals at a local scale, while economic benefits are accrued by more distant regional stakeholders (Howitt, 2002). A body of sustainable tourism literature and case examples suggest that success requires the broad spectrum of stakeholders to be involved in the consideration of destination areas (e.g. Bramwell and Sharman, 2000; Hall, 2000; Johnston, 2003; Pope et al., 2004; Timothy, 2001; Timothy and Tosun, 2003; Vanclay, 2003, Van der Duim et al., 2005; Wearing and McDonald, 2002).

In order to introduce a retreat from the polarized views presented in the western marketing media, we must assert that the limits of colonial discourse may be transcended by understanding the range of subjectivities involved (Bhabha, 1994). This can be achieved through frameworks, which prioritize the environmental and cultural lives of host communities (e.g. Mahapatra, 1998; Peet, 1999; Telfer, 2002, 2003; Timothy and Tosun, 2003; Wearing and McDonald, 2002; Wearing et al., 2005) *(see Table 7.1)*. In the case of Nepal, we suggest that the principles of ecotourism represent best practice in small-scale community-based tourism development (Blamey, 2001; Horn and Simmons, 2002; Koster and Randall, 2005; Ross and Wall, 1999), therefore offering a potential way forward.

Table 7.1 Ideals of Ecotourism and Trekking Realities (Holden, 2007)	
Ideals of Ecotourism	**Realities of Trekking Industry**
Should not degrade resources, development and should conform to ecologically sustainable best practice	Tourism is driven by commercial symbols. Increasingly attention is paid to environmental consequences of trekking as the long-term viability of profits is threatened
Should provide long-term social, economic and environmental benefits to local community	Being a porter is an important source of additional income. Adequate economic links with Nepalese communities still need to be further developed
Should recognize limits to growth and necessity of supply-oriented management	Being a porter is a seasonal occupation. Large numbers of temporary porters are in search of work
Should prepare travelers to minimize negative impacts through education, maintenance of small groups, minimal resource use and avoiding sensitive areas	Campaign by Tourism Concern and poster campaign of the IPPG and WWF along the main trails in Nepal
Should provide cross-cultural training for appropriate staff	Organizations like the Trekking Agents Association of Nepal (TAAN) and Kathmandu Environmental Education Project (KEEP) train mountain guides
Should involve education of and understanding between all stakeholders and recognition of the intrinsic resource value and encourage ethical responsibility toward the natural and cultural environments	In several tourist trekking destinations Sustainable Tourism Development Committees and Conservation Development Committees have been initiated. The trekking industry is cooperating with these committees; however, power is still weighted in favor of tourism operators
Is sensitive to and carefully interprets indigenous cultures	Operators are increasingly engaged in informed interpretation of the indigenous people
Marketing is accurate	Marketing becomes more and more accurate, moving away from the 'perfect space', images of 'Shrangila' and the superhuman power of porters

Complexities of local economies

The economies of developing countries are often structured around historical imperial domination over trading links and governance. This often results in unequal relationships with the developing and developed world (Lea, 1993). Tourism when viewed from a neo-colonialist perspective is often assumed to perpetuate this inequality, as companies based in the western liberal regimes possess the capital and expertise to invest in, and subsequently control developing nations' tourism interests. In many cases, a developing country's engagement with tourism is assumed to simply confirm its dependent, subordinate position in relation to the advanced capitalist societies; tourism then becomes a form of neo-colonialism (Britton, 1980; Brohman, 1996). As discussed above, portering is an important source of additional income for the poor, as well as being a source of additional finances for villages alongside trekking routes. Nepal (2002) reports that in 1 year at Sagarmatha National Park, the arrival of 17,000 trekkers resulted in the employment of 14,000 porters, 2500 guides and staff, 2800 yak owners and 14,000 merchandise porters carrying goods for lodge owners and other traders in the tourist region. According to Shrestha (2001), in the remote Manaslu area, one type of income received by the villagers is from the single dollar that they charge for each pitched tent at the campsites along the way.

Another type of income is the earning porters' expenditure along the way. They eat in the teashops or at villagers' houses along the way and when possible also sleep there. However, while each trekker pays US$75–90 for a permit to trek the region for 1 week, none of this goes directly to the area's development (Shrestha, 2001).

Gaining the community's perspective

In order to pursue sustainable tourism and development and a view of trekking beyond one that is literally borne on the back of the porters, the trekking industry must be able to incorporate a range of stakeholder subjectivities. In Nepal various initiatives attempt to improve the working conditions of porters. Some non-governmental organizations such as the Centre for Community Development and Research (CCODER), SNV Nepal, TMI and WWF Nepal regard portering as an important income generating activity for poor marginalized people. They focus on developing strategies to improve the access of portering for the poor and portering conditions. Other organizations like the IPPG, KEEP and TAAN are all directed toward the well-being of porters at a national level (van Klaveren, 2000). For example, in 1992 KEEP began their awareness program on trekking in Nepal to foreign tour operators. One area of attention was to increase awareness among these tour operators to improve the working conditions of their porters. A few years later the NGO started trekking guide training courses in which the situation of porters was discussed with trained guides. In another example the Mountain Institute – an INGO based in the USA – sold calendars to raise funds from their supporters. Through this they were depicting the plight of the porter and demonstrating the organization's efforts to improve the situation of the porters in Nepal. The same organization, together with the IPPG, WWF and KEEP developed a poster for tourists to raise awareness on how to improve the working conditions for their porters. This poster was distributed in the main trekking areas of Nepal. Moreover, the IPPG supports the interests of porters. All trekking companies now require health insurance to be taken out for their porters. Unfortunately, health insurance in Nepal is poorly organized and barely substantial. This is true for all people; particularly employees/labourers in the country and porters are no exception. In Nepal, protected areas like in the Annapurna Conservation Area are the most visited trekking destinations in the country (more than 60% of the trekkers to Nepal visit this area). As a result, private or public porter shelters have been constructed to accommodate porters in these places, considering local accommodation is otherwise unavailable. In several trekking areas of Nepal a specific support industry has emerged to cater for porters. For example, there are hotels and restaurants in Sagarmatha National Park where luxury and western food for foreign tourists is served. Nevertheless, Sagarmatha National Park also caters for porters with its smaller and inexpensive eateries.

A large number of changes have taken place during the last decade in relation to porters including an increase in media attention and an improvement in labor conditions. Many necessary improvements still remain.

DISCUSSION AND CONCLUSION

The trekking industry in Nepal has historically polarized opinion with respect to the degree to which integrative sustainability principles can be observed in its operations. On the one hand there are the global tourism industries, which are purporting the existence of a sustainable industry, which by its very nature is integrative and involving of local populations. The fact that mountaineering and other nature-based activities are at the heart of the Nepalese trekking industry (Musa, 2005) has aided the case of the ecotourism proponents. In contrast to this position, which is often built on neo-colonialist tourism marketing strategies, one also has other commentators who are bemoaning the poor conditions experienced by local workers in the trekking industry.

The fact that child labor and oppressive conditions are rife in Nepal (Kumar et al., 2001) makes it difficult for many of these commentators to attach ecotourism tags to the industry, particularly given the centrality of intergenerational equity principles to many sustainability ideologies. How does one therefore move forward in the sustainable development of the Nepalese trekking industry? The first task is to accept that the commonly held view regarding how the industry treats local people is often idealized.

The next task is then to consider by what means the trekking industry can promote the principles of ecotourism in their operations. Wearing and McDonald (2002) advocate the use of 'participatory research' as a precursor to any form of tourism planning and community development. Reference has already been made to the global nature of the tourism industry in Nepal. Ensuring sustainability for this industry requires broad stakeholder participation. Musa (2005) refers to the situation in the Annapurna region of Nepal where the success of national park development is said to be dependent upon the involvement of local people. Wearing and McDonald (2002: 194) note that participatory research 'requires participation from host communities by actively taking part in shaping the research (defining their own standards, symbols and ways of representation and interpretation)'. In the case of porters in Nepal, participatory research is a precondition not only for deconstructing existing myths, but also for correctly moving the trekking industry toward a sustainability goal. Attention needs to be given to how local people may move from being the backdrop for trekking tourism, to being a driving force in the development and management of the industry in their area.

This recommendation of participatory approaches to tourism development is, however, made with caution. It could easily be argued that it is unrealistic, and even unfair, to expect the rural, uneducated people to suddenly become the driving force of the tourism industry in the region, given the degree of professionalism required for people to work effectively in tourism-related industries. It is our view that successful tourism development requires cooperation between local people and tourism planners. What is needed for Nepal is a realization amongst planners of the role that local people may play in development initiatives. Techniques must be developed that allow the community voice, including the voice of often marginalized people such as women to be heard in a manner which is reflective of community circumstance. The role of women is becoming more important in Nepal. For example, in the Langtang Ecotourism Project women are recognized as 'the keepers of cultural traditions and knowledge' because men are often drawn away from their local area to find work in trekking industries' (Scheyvens, 2007: 194). Ongoing work into community-based tourism on the Kokoda Track in PNG is showing how a participatory approach to sustainable tourism may be achieved in some rural areas in developing countries (Wearing and Chatterton, 2007).

Himalayan trekking companies must consider a variety of conflicting issues when determining the nature of their operations in Nepal and other developed countries. In the first instance they must be conscious of the fact that predominantly it is the area's scenic beauty that draws visitors to Nepal. This, in a sense demands the perpetuation of neo-colonialist marketing strategies for the region. The provision of experiences that are acceptable to foreign tourists has led to a concern regarding the health of porters amongst non-governmental agencies such as the Kathmandu Environmental and Education Project and Himalayan Trust (Musa, 2005). Significantly many of these groups including the Himalayan Trust and Global Volunteer's Network have also been at the forefront of projects to assist the plight of local indigenous workers (The Himalayan Trust UK, 2006; Global Volunteer's Network, 2006).

Concern for the conditions of local populations is increasingly becoming the concern of local ecotourism operators. A variety of individual ecotourism organizations have instituted initiatives to improve conditions for porters and other local population groups. The 3 Sisters Adventure Trekking (2006) group in Nepal has been heavily involved in the Empowerment of the Women of Nepal project. Initiatives have also been put in place by individual trekking companies in developed countries, e.g. Paddy Palin and Falls Creek Ski Lifts in Australia. In conjunction with Porter's Progress, Paddy Palin is currently running a sale for purchasing of hiking boots, if you return your old hiking boots they will give you a 50% discount on a new pair – the usable boots are then donated to porters in Nepal (Robinson, 2006). Connections between trekking companies and porter groups may be developed through 'community-focused institutes' as a form of relational innovation that enables constructive dialog between disparate groups (Gergen, 2001).

If a range of tourism companies do as Paddy Palin have done there is a potential for real change through this mechanism. Falls Creek Ski Lifts is similarly donating warm weather clothing to the porters of Nepal through the Porter's Progress Association (Worrall, 2005). We believe that these types of initiatives by various elements in the tourism industry create a move toward a more sustainable tourism industry. What is needed, however, is a broader acceptance of the need for industry involvement in such activities. It is conceivable that the development of groups such as the Trekking Agents Association of Nepal could be a means of unification in this regard.

CASE STUDY 3. SURFING TOURISM IN INDONESIA'S MENTAWAI ISLANDS BY JESS PONTING

INTRODUCTION

Indonesia's Mentawai archipelago consists of four main islands and scores of smaller islands approximately 130 kilometers off the coast of central west Sumatra (Persoon and van Beek, 1998). The largest and most northerly

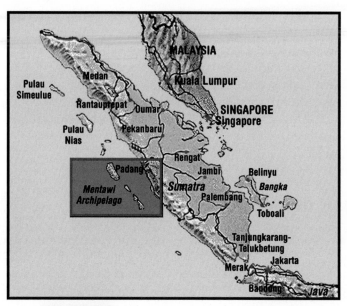

FIGURE 7.7   *Location of the Mentawai archipelago.*

island is Siberut. To the south is Sipora, and, further south again are North and South Pagai (Bakker, 1999; Persoon, 2003; Persoon and van Beek, 1998; Reeves, 2000).

Living conditions for the locals are highly impoverished and marked by periodic epidemics of preventable disease and infant mortality rates as high as 60% (Surf Aid International, 2005). Tourism visitation had been very small scale until the arrival of commercial surfing tourism in 1991. Within 5 years of the first commercial exploitation of the surf resources of the Mentawai, the global surf media had discursively transformed this depressed region into the most filmed, photographed, written about and desired surfing tourism destination on earth (Ponting, in press). Seventeen years and three attempts at industry regulation later, local communities have still not significantly benefited from most surfing tourism activities *(see Fig. 7.7)*.

THE MENTAWAI ISLANDS AND PEOPLE

Traditionally, Mentawaians lived along the fringes of forest watercourses, hunting and gathering, domesticating chickens and pigs and practicing shifting cultivation (Persoon, 2003). An average family income from harvesting copra in the Mentawai is in the realm of US$10 per month (Barilotti, 2003; Ponting, 2008).

The Mentawai archipelago has been ecologically isolated from mainland Sumatra since the mid-Pleistocene period resulting in high levels of endemism. Twenty fauna species are known to be endemic to the Mentawais, including four primate species. The islands are covered with primary dipterocarp and mixed forest. Despite possessing high conservation value the islands have been subjected to unsustainable logging practices since the 1970s (Kramer et al., 1997; Persoon, 1997).

TOURISM IN THE MENTAWAI ISLANDS

Historically, tourism was virtually unheard of in the Mentawais and halted completely between the Second World War and 1969 (Bakker, 1999). As Indonesia opened itself to tourism, visitation to the Mentawai Islands increased slowly. Guides from Bukittinggi, a popular tourism destination in the West Sumatran highlands, organized 'jungle adventure' tours that offered tourists a chance to see a 'stone age culture' on Siberut Island (Persoon, 2003). Appearing in the *Lonely Planet* guide as an 'adventure destination' ensured that by the mid-1990s several thousand tourists had visited Siberut (Bakker, 1999; Sills, 1998).

The last decade has presented Indonesia with a range of tourism challenges beginning with the Indonesian forest fires of 1997–1998, the downfall of the Suharto regime, the Asian financial crisis in 1997, the September 11, 2001 terrorist attacks in the USA and the resulting US led 'war on terror' in Afghanistan and Iraq, SARS, Birdflu, multiple bombings in Bali and Jakarta, the December 26, 2004 Indian Ocean earthquake and tsunami, the March 2005 Nias earthquake, the London bombings, and the series of earthquakes centered around Sumatra and the Mentawai Islands in 2007. Despite all this, jungle adventure tourism to Siberut survives on a small scale. It is surfing tourism, however, that has not only survived, but grown to become the dominant form of tourism in the region.

SURFING TOURISM

Surfing tourism began over one thousand years ago when indigenous Hawaiian surfers traveled in search of new surf breaks (George, 2008; Ponting, 2008). In the twenty-first century, slick marketing campaigns of multibillion dollar surf corporations depicting empty, perfect waves breaking in exotic locations have driven surfing tourism to virtually every surfable coast on every continent in the world (Ponting, 2008).

Commercial surfing tours began in the late 1970s and proliferated through the world's surf-rich tropical regions during the 1980s and 1990s (Barilotti, 2002; Buckley, 2002a; George, 2000; Lovett, 1998, 2005; Lueras and Lueras, 1997; Ponting, 2008a; Ponting et al., 2005; Warshaw, 2004). Over the last decade and a half, surf-industry marketing has blended a nostalgic discourse of early independent surf exploration with contemporary packaged travel styles (Brown, 1997; Hammerscmidt, 2004; Lanagan, 2002; Ponting et al., 2005). The result has been a rapidly expanding niche targeting 'cash-rich, time-poor' surfers with 'business-class' surf holidays involving direct flights, prompt and comfortable transfers, luxurious surf charter yachts and resorts, and in some cases, exclusive access to world class surf breaks (Bartholomew and Baker, 1996; Buckley, 2002a, 2002b; Carroll, 2000; Ponting, 2007; Verrender, 2000).

WHY ARE THE MENTAWAI ISLANDS SO GOOD FOR SURFING?

The Mentawai Islands arguably contain the best areas for surfing in the world. This is due to a complex combination of swell, local wind conditions and favorably shaped reefs *(see Fig. 7.8)*.

FIGURE 7.8 *Perfect waves, like this one off the village of Katiet, are unusually frequent in the Mentawais. Photo by Jess Ponting.*

Swell

The Mentawais have an exceptionally large 'swell window' being open to swell from virtually anywhere in the 39 million square kilometers of Indian Ocean between the west coast of Australia and the east coast of the African continent all the way south to Antarctica (Surfline, 2005; WaveHunters, 2005). During the 'swell season' between May and October, average swell heights are 2 meters or greater (Ponting, 2008) and multiple swell generating storm systems in the southern Indian Ocean create significant swell heights for weeks at a time *(see Fig. 7.9)*.

Wind

The Mentawais are located in the Inter Tropical Convergence Zone (ITCZ), known to sailors as 'the doldrums' due to long periods of shifting light winds. By contrast many of Indonesia's (and other tropical countries') surf-rich regions are subjected to strong south easterly 'trade winds', which greatly reduce the number of breaks which can be surfed. In the Mentawais, a wide variety of surf breaks open up as wind directions shift.

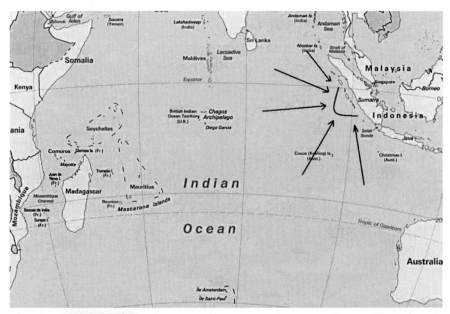

FIGURE 7.9 *The huge 'swell window' of the Mentawai Islands.*

Reef

The Mentawai Islands house thousands of bays, estuary mouths, reef passes and points. Of these, a small proportion are suitable for surfing. Generally, this will involve a regular edge of reef, rock or sand which presents at an angle to (rather than parallel with) oncoming swells. Given the relative abundance of favorably shaped reefs facing in all directions in the Mentawais, and the ability of long-distance swells to refract into bays and around islands, if there is swell moving through the Mentawais, it is likely that there will be a number of surf breaks experiencing favorable wind conditions and producing high-quality waves.

SURFING TOURISM IN THE MENTAWAI

A group of Australians first explored the Mentawais for surf in 1980 (Warshaw, 2004). A second wave of explorers moved through the Mentawais in 1990, one of whom led a commercial charter through the islands in 1991. In 1993, he arranged more surfing charters for professional surfers and surfing's corporate elite (Daley, 2005). In 1994, competition arrived in the form of two Australian-owned companies, the already established Surf Travel Company and newcomer Great Breaks International (Daley, 2005). They were joined the following year by US owned Good Sumatran Surf Charters, and subsequently operator numbers grew rapidly (Earnest Egan, personal communication, 2003).

A struggle for control of surfing tourism in the Mentawais began in the mid-1990s (and continues today) when in September 1996 the Governor of West Sumatra gave Australian tour company Great Breaks International and local partner organization Mentawai Wisata Bahari the right to control visitation to the islands (Dahlan, 1997). The surfing tourism industry refused to comply amid allegations of threats and corruption. Just over 2 years after the agreement was reached, a newly appointed Governor revoked it arguing that private sector companies had been given duties that were rightly those of official government agencies and had used this power to implement undesirable monopolistic practices. Mentawai Wisata Bahari took legal action against the Governor but the revocation was upheld in December 1999.

Meanwhile, the Mentawai islands were gazetted as a political 'regency' in their own right in 2000. Under the jurisdiction of the new regency, Mentawai Wisata Bahari (with Great Breaks International) applied for, and was granted, almost identical management rights to those revoked by the provincial

Governor just months earlier (Rick Cameron, personal communication, 2001). Again the industry refused to comply, rendering the system ineffective and unworkable (Slater, 2001).

Meanwhile, the surf media had become saturated with imagery of perfect waves breaking in the Mentawais, and the islands captured the imagination of the global surfing fraternity (Ponting, 2008). During the 2000 season, local home-stay facilities, a foreign/local joint-venture resort and a surf charter fleet of over 30 live-aboard boats accommodated more than 3000 surfing tourists in the islands *(see Fig. 7.10)*.

The political landscape of the Mentawai surfing tourism industry changed again in 2003 with the announcement of new regency level legislation known as 'Perdah 16'. Perdah 16 is strikingly similar to the previous attempts at provincial level legislation. Theoretically, it provides tour operators with exclusive management rights to surf breaks adjacent to surf resorts. Despite being introduced to operators in the 2003 season with a 12-month socialization period, Perdah 16 has still not been effectively implemented and enforced. The key points for the surfing tourism industry are summarized in *Table 7.2*.

In order to comply with Perdah 16, the surfing tourism industry will have to restructure and increasingly base its business operations in the islands rather than solely on mainland Sumatra as has been the case historically. Perdah 16 limits the Mentawai charter fleet to 30 boats with a maximum

FIGURE 7.10 *Four boats of the Mentawai charter fleet anchored off Katiet. Photo by Jess Ponting.*

capacity of 250 guests at any one time, this represents a 50% reduction in the size of the 2008–2009 charter fleet (Ponting, 2008). Assuming that licence holders will build resorts close to breaks with the most commercial value to secure 'support territories', charter operators will also need cooperative arrangements with various license holders in order to provide guests with access to Mentawai breaks subject to exclusive management by competing operators.

One license holder has already completed a resort near Silabu village within 1000 meters of the premier Mentawai break Macaronis. Another resort has been built within a potential buffer zone area of famous Mentawai break Lance's Right (also known as Hollow Trees or HTs) at the village of Katiet. Another is close to the highly popular waves Rifles and Kandui at the southern end of Siberut. Theoretically, a license will allow resort owners to control access to these breaks.

There are growing numbers of locally run accommodation operations targeting time-rich, cash-poor surfers through the islands. Aside from handicraft sellers in the village of Katiet who sell directly to tourists onboard their charter boats from dugout canoes, this is the only direct input from surfing tourism to the economy of local communities. Perdah 16 would force

Table 7.2   Summary of the Main Issues for Surfing Tourism Operations Arising from Perdah 16
• Only maritime tourism companies will be permitted to operate
• Holders must own a representative office and a location to run a business, have undertaken an environmental impact statement for their proposal, have at least 2 and no more than 6 passenger vessels taking a maximum of 50 guests, and have submitted plans for development and management of tourism business in the Mentawai
• A 'license' is valid for up to 15 years and can be renewed; license may be canceled if companies do not commence tourism activities within 12 months
• Resorts are to be granted exclusive 'support territories'. Capacity of more than 25 guests receives a support territory radius of 1000 m from resort site, less than 25 are given 750 m radius. Companies permitted to build on resort support territory will have a 250 m radius support territory of their own
• Tourism companies are obliged to preserve the natural environment
• Tourists are obliged to stay at a licensed hotel or charter vessel
• Tourists must respect the values and culture of residents
• Locally and foreign owned charter boats must operate under the 'license' of a tourism company issued by Mentawai regency government and may only operate in a resort support territory if a cooperation agreement has been entered into with resort owners.

Source: Regency of Mentawai Islands Verdict No. 35, 2003 Tourism Retribution and Attractions; Regional Regulations of Mentawai Islands No. 16 2002.

FIGURE 7.11 *Katiet handicraft sellers have to use canoes to access charter tourists who do not make landfall. Photo by Jess Ponting.*

these 'unlicensed' local operators out of the market in favor of high-end foreign owned developments *(see Fig. 7.11)*.

RECREATIONAL CARRYING CAPACITY MANAGEMENT

Arguments in favor of capacity capping and private sector surf resource management are couched in terms of preserving the sustainability of the surfing tourism industry (Buckley, 2002b). Two basic arguments are put forward based upon the ramifications of the alternative to capacity management: low-cost high-density surfing tourism.

The crowding of surf breaks makes them dangerous, only with tightly controlled capacity caps can the safety of surfers be assured. Unsafe conditions will deter visitation by high-end tourists.

Crowding will ultimately lead to the decline of the destination, or at best a shift toward lower-cost, higher-density surf tourism which will lead to a downscaling of profitability of the destination and environmental degradation.

On closer inspection, however, these arguments seem to prioritize the needs of surfers and the surfing tourism industry. Buckley (2002b) explores recreational carrying capacity in the Mentawais in light of models used to control river rafting in the United States and mountain gorilla tours in

Uganda. Recreational capacity management is positioned as the only way to ensure the economic success of the Mentawai surfing tourism industry, lest it becomes another overcrowded "crime-ridden tourist trap" like Bali (Buckley, 2002a: 432).

The definition of success in this line of thinking is immediately problematic. In the case of surfing tourism in the Mentawais, the industry – considered by many to be an economic success in its current form – is completely dominated by foreign investors who, by their own admission, put almost nothing back into the economy of the islands. The following excerpt from an interview with a Mentawai tour operator demonstrates.

> *People in the villages near the surf breaks don't much like that they're dying from tuberculosis and malaria and can't get supplies and good education for their kids while millionaires are playing on their beaches and all they get is the trash dumped in the coconut trees or washed up on the beaches. That's the reality of what's gone down and we are as guilty as anyone else. (Paul, Surf Tour Operator)*

Examining the underlying power relations behind the assumption that the economic success of this model should be protected by privately controlled capacity capping suggests that the economic success in question is that of foreign tour operators rather than traditional custodians of the surfing resources of the Mentawai Islands.

Indeed, indigenous Mentawaians are becoming increasingly outraged by the juxtaposition of the business-class Mentawai surfing tourism product (which is to be further encouraged by Perdah 16) and the lack of engagement and consultation of the surfing tourism industry with local resource owners in the first instance, and the ongoing lack of engagement with local people and their economy. The following extracts from interviews with Mentawaian stakeholders demonstrate this point.

> *If you count economically there is no business between the locals and tourism. But if you see this social/moral dilemma you have to be concerned about that because you use the resource and involve the locals if they like it or if they don't like it. In this way you cannot pass by while the people are sick. You stop where the people are supposed to fish. You anchor where the people go and come from the beach. Because you are joining the circulation of this environmental circumstances you must adjust yourself by involving the new circumstances where the local also exists. (Dede, Mentawaian Participant)*

If they keep going like this the local people won't trust them [the surfing tourism industry]… Maybe someday they will drive you away from the Mentawai. It's not a threat, but many of the Mentawais already know that they only exploit without handing over some benefit. (Andi, Mentawaian Participant)

From a local perspective, the industry could not be any less successful than in its current form. By enforcing the system of high-yield (and high leakage) luxury surfing tourism outlined in Perdah 16 and advocated by supporters of capacity capping for recreational amenity purposes, the barriers of entry to the market for local entrepreneurs become insurmountable in practical terms.

The argument that crowding will lead to the decline of a destination is also flawed if examined from outside the dominant Western discourse. Many of the world's best surf breaks are crowded and no longer represent 'nirvanic' surfing tourist space in its purest form, yet the quality of the waves still draws huge numbers of surfing tourists. The world famous surf of the Hawaiian Island Oahu is open to free public access and as a result is often crowded in terms of recreational amenity. Despite this, visitation by surfing tourists remains very high. On Australia's Gold Coast a huge sand bank, dubbed 'The Superbank' has formed from sand dredged from the mouth of the Tweed River. The Superbank produces waves of very high quality and length (occasionally approaching 2 kilometers), and with crowds of 500 reported in the water, it may be the world's most crowded break. Despite this, the quality of the break remains an international tourist attraction for surfers and non-surfers alike and continues to draw large numbers of international and domestic surfing tourists (Reuters, 2007). To suggest that crowding will lead to a decline in visitation ignores the enduring appeal of famous, yet crowded, breaks around the world.

If a surf break is genuinely worldclass (there are a number of genuinely worldclass breaks in the Mentawais) and relatively accessible, it will continue to draw surfing tourists well beyond the recreational carrying capacity required to sustain a small foreign-controlled boutique industry. This may not be the best result for the recreational amenity of visiting surfers, the profit margins of foreign investors and those ideologically invested in the much-hyped dream of uncrowded perfect surf. Nevertheless, the time has come to question the assumptions which underpin the discourse of capacity management in the Mentawais and introduce the perspective of local stakeholders; most of who could not care less if the surf is crowded.

THE LAND ISSUE

According to Perdah 16, foreign investors seeking a marine tourism licence in the Mentawai must first own land upon which to build a resort. Land ownership is a complex matter in the Mentawais and has proven problematic for foreign investors and undesirable for local stakeholders. Family members collectively own particular areas of land and boundaries are often contested. While one group may own land, an entirely different group may own the coconut trees planted upon it. Additionally, indigenous Mentawaians are fearful of land acquisitions. Firstly there is a sense that the tourism industry is pressuring locals into selling their land.

> *I don't think it's a good idea to buy the land. If you buy the local land, where will the locals stay? They have their assets at the islands. Coconut trees. This is their business before the surfers come, they sell this to the traders. They have changed their traditions, their old business… Actually they don't want to sell their land but the surf companies push them to sell the land. (Andi, Mentawaian Participant)*

Secondly, Mentawaians fear that the tour companies buying up land will deny future generations their heritage.

> *Local people need money too. Sometimes when you offer money to them, because they are not well-educated about our world they are just looking to the money. But to me the land is good to their grand children. Now they can sell their land and enjoy the money but when the money is gone, the land is gone, the grandchild asks: 'The land belongs to who? Not us anymore because we already sold it', and the grandchild will not think they are at home anymore. (John, Mentawaian Participant)*

Thirdly, there is a concern that in selling their land to the surfing tourism industry, local communities are surrendering governance and being tricked into accepting neo-colonial tourism practices and business models which do not serve their best interests.

> *Look what's happening in the Mentawai. They lose their land, they lose their governance… They cannot harvest the coconut, because the land has been sold to surfing activities…I feel bad because they sell the Mentawaian. They sell me. How much goes to the Mentawaian? That is neo-colonialism. Make them understand that. Make them agree to address their activities…The local people, they*

loose their land, they loose their rights because they do not know the trick of business… Is it helping the community? NO! You kill the community because you take their land away where their life depends on it. You take the coconuts where they're supposed to make copra so you take away their life. You kill the locals. So surfing tourism is not actually helping the people, tourism kills the locals. (Dede, Mentawaian Participant)

A Sumatran Minangkabau participant also recognized the importance of retaining land ownership in light of her observations of tourism development in Bali. She advocated Mentawaians building their capacity to eventually own and control their tourism industry themselves.

If the land belonged to me I don't like to sell, I think you can work together with a contract but not to buy. To buy can be jealousy for next time. The natural reality like in Bali where no-one from Bali have anything in Bali, they just work there. The owner of the big hotels and big restaurants are from outside Bali. For next twenty years, twenty five years it will be like that. Jealousy and demonstrations, this is the true reality in Bali. I hope the Mentawai cannot be like that, maybe they can limit it. Ten years or something like that is OK. After the local people watching that, learning how to work, how to handle people maybe they can do on their own after that. But to sell, I think that is not a good idea. (Rickie, Minangkabau Participant)

SOLUTIONS?

Sustainable management of surfing tourism in the Mentawai Islands requires a severing of ties with conventional modes of thinking. An alternative perspective might ask, for example, 'within limits of acceptable change (defined by local resource owners), how can the most value be appropriately extracted from the tourism resource in a manner which maximizes benefits to local communities?' This may turn out to be a high-yield capacity controlled solution, or, it may turn out to be a less capital intensive model able to be controlled by local interests. Regardless of the outcome, what is important to note in the planning process is the type of questions being asked and by whom, the assumptions underlying them and the stakeholders who are empowered to answer them.

Most surfing tourism operators claim to be seeking the same outcome – a profitable, environmentally, socially and economically sustainable surfing tourism industry, which provides real benefits to local communities. Despite significant goodwill, the industry's delivery of this outcome has been poor. The Mentawai Islands represent a tourism resource of immense value. There are numerous sites suitable for the development of a land-based surfing tourism industry that could be developed in lease hold partnerships and joint ventures with local resource owners. There is enormous potential for the development of a unique and sustainable surfing tourism destination offering both yacht-based and land-based products.

Perdah 16's insistence upon high-end tourism may, however, serve to further marginalize local communities. What is needed is an effort on the part of the private and public sectors to work with local communities to develop local capacity, to develop economic linkages with the existing industry and to enter the industry themselves. There are also many opportunities and potential industry niches which are yet to be filled, which could develop backward linkages into local transport, retail and agricultural sectors. The Mentawai government and surfing tourism industry could also usefully look for existing holiday yacht charter operations around the world, for example, the types of new businesses which may be possible to develop in support of the charter industry.

Surfing tourism in the Mentawai Islands is a case in which legislation and regulation have failed, and where conventional models of sustainable tourism planning based on capacity management threaten to further marginalize local communities from the tourism economy. Solutions require thinking outside the standard tourism development box to prioritize the needs of resource owners rather than continuing to elaborately justify and protect a failed status quo model in the name of sustainability.

FURTHER READING

Mowforth, M., & Munt, I. (2008) *Tourism and Sustainability: Development, Globalization and New Tourism in the Third World*, third ed. Routledge, London.

Now in its third edition Mowforth and Munt's text assesses the impact and potential of new forms of tourism in providing a route towards sustainable development. In a range of examples from developing countries they show that tourism driven development is often problematic providing little benefit for many communities who invest in it for their futures.

Butcher, J. (2007) *Ecotourism, NGO's and Development: A Critical Analysis*. Routledge, London.

Butcher's text investigates ecotourism as a strategy for combining development with conservation in the developing world and the advocacy role that NGOs play in this process.

Sharpley, R., & Telfer, D. (eds) (2002) *Tourism and Development: Concepts and Issues*. Channel View Publications, Clevedon, UK.

This edited collection brings together tourism studies with development studies in a basic easy to understand style. Chapters are devoted to tourism and development theories, economic, community and environmental relationships and the barriers to tourism development.

CHAPTER 8

Marketing Ecotourism: Meeting and Shaping Expectations and Demands

This chapter seeks to explore the relationship between ecotourism and marketing, both conceptually and practically. It examines the structure and nature of the tourism industry and the implications of ecotourism's worldwide growth. Fundamental to understanding and evaluating the connection between ecotourism and marketing is the issue of supply versus demand-driven marketing which we will examine in-depth in moving toward an analysis of the strengths, weaknesses, opportunities and threats to ecotourism.

Pivotal to understanding the marketing relationship to ecotourism are the implications for protected areas, conservation and local communities. Ecotourism marketing has been surrounded by much confusion and controversy as it attempts to take into account the dual objectives of protected areas and local communities on the one hand and those of the tourism industry on the other. The marketing of tourism products is generally still associated by many people with a commercial enterprise selling the maximum level of product for short-term profit. However, social marketing and ecological marketing are now being acknowledged as important elements of a more holistic marketing perspective. These perspectives significantly challenge the somewhat archaic belief that all marketing must be demand-led (e.g. Middleton, 1998).

CONTENTS

Ecotourism's Place in the Tourism industry

Marketing Ecotourism: Supplying Demand or Demanding Supply?

Marketing Ecotourism

Ecological and Social Marketing

The 'Greening' Market

Strengths in Marketing Ecotourism

Threats in Marketing Ecotourism

Opportunities in Marketing Ecotourism

Weaknesses in Marketing Ecotourism

Further Reading

ECOTOURISM'S PLACE IN THE TOURISM INDUSTRY

Any definition or range of definitions of ecotourism must have relevance to its practical implementation, its working context – the tourism industry. What then is this thing called the 'tourism industry' and what are its characteristics? Stear et al. (1988) provide us with an initial definition:

[a] collection of all collaborating firms and organizations which perform specific activities directed at satisfying leisure, pleasure and recreational needs. (1988: 1)

CASE STUDY: Kruger National Park, South Africa

Kruger National Park is one of the top ten National Parks in the world and is reportedly the most biodiverse Game Reserve on Earth. It provides a destination site and services for tourists interested in the parks remarkable ecosystem, comprising more than 2000 different forms of plant life, 146 different types of mammals, more than 490 species of birds, 114 species of reptiles and 49 types of fish and innumerable other forms of life (Middleton, 1998: 202). This park is of interest to a specific type of tourist who is catered for by a group of travel agents who will generally specialize in the area of nature-based tourism.

The tourism industry does not produce close substitute products, as does the manufacturing industry, but it comprises sectors, each of which produces closely substitutable products. The tourism industry sectors include accommodation, attractions, carrier, coordination, promotion and distribution, tour operators, wholesalers and miscellaneous groups (Stear et al., 1988). Conceptualizing ecotourism as an amalgam of products incorporating a particular *style* of tourism allows its relationship with the tourism industry to be understood. In this way ecotourism is not an industry per se but it does draw from products produced by the many sectors of the tourism industry.

CASE STUDY: Cradle Mountain Huts, Cradle Mountain-Lake St Claire National Park, Tasmania, Australia

Cradle Mountain Huts provides accommodation for hikers as they trek the Overland Track. Individual hikers, however, utilize products not only from the accommodation sector, but also air and coach travel from the carrier sector, natural areas from the attractions sector, rangers and tour guides from the tour operator sector and so on. It is these different products that are packaged together to form an ecotourism product *(see Fig. 8.1).*

FIGURE 8.1 *Cradle Mountain in Winter. Photo by Ted Bugg.*

MARKETING ECOTOURISM: SUPPLYING DEMAND OR DEMANDING SUPPLY?

Underpinning this widespread support for ecotourism is the assumption that tourists themselves are demanding more responsible, environmentally-appropriate forms of tourism yet, there is little evidence to suggest that the growth in ecotourism has been demand led. (Sharpley, 2006)

In order to gain an understanding of the market for ecotourism, it is important to examine exactly what marketing is. Marketing is neither a precise science nor is it an art but is chiefly 'concerned with research which is the foundation for organized planning'. It is primarily 'concerned with production and pricing and promotion and not least profits' (Jefferson and Lickorish, 1988: 27). Marketing is a component in a system of business activities designed to plan, price, promote and distribute – satisfying products, services and ideas for the benefit of the target market – including household consumers or industrial users, to achieve the organization's objectives (Stanton et al., 1992: 6).

The term 'organization's objectives' is critical here as it leads us to the heart of the marketing and ecotourism debate. What should the primary objective of an ecotourism operator be – sustaining the environment or profitability? Can the two objectives be pursued successfully and simultaneously?

The tourism industry has been swift to capitalize on new forms of tourism and in some cases the principles and philosophy of ecotourism we have discussed have been lost in the rush to profit (e.g. McLaren, 2003). Naturally both private enterprise and governments are supportive of the tourism industry because of its present and potential economic benefits in the form of individual profit for firms which accrue to nation states in the form of Gross National Product (GNP).

There are numerous striking examples of opportunistic market responses to ecotourism. The Environmental Management Industry Association of Australia (EMIAA), 1994 International Conference on Environmental Management and Technology for a Sustainable Tourism Industry, called on professionals, scientists and academics worldwide to submit and present papers at its conference titled 'Tourism Ecodollars'. In an attempt to entice potential delegates to attend, the EMIAA brochure advertising the event stated 'Tourism Ecodollars 94 will give you more ground-breaking, money-making insights into tourism towards 2000 than you could obtain form any other source'. Another example includes Valentine's (1991) account of his attendance at the 'Ecotourism and Small Business in the Pacific', conference held in Pohnpei, in the Federated States of Micronesia and staged by the US Department of Commerce, Economic Development Administration (EDA):

> There were more bankers speaking than ecologists; [as] there were
> more developers... architects...Governors... administrators...
> and...bureaucrats than ecologists... Despite the encouraging prospect
> of bankers speaking about 'ecotourism' in glowing terms, I came away
> with a distinct impression that there is an urgent need to put the
> ecology back into ecotourism. (1991a: 2)

MARKETING ECOTOURISM

Traditionally marketing can be defined as 'the development of products/ services which are consistent with client needs, pricing, promoting and distributing these products/services effectively' (National Park Service, 1984: 3). As indicated in the above definition, marketing is based on the 'four Ps' of product, place, price and promotion, with the emphasis on attracting, maintaining and expanding a customer base.

Theoretically, markets are places where buyers and sellers meet to engage in exchange. In the process of exchange prices are determined and quantities produced and this process hinges on the amount of demand for a particular product. Economists generally view demand as the desire and ability to consume certain quantities of goods at various prices over a certain period of time. The law of demand states that the quantity of a good or service is negatively related to its price. In other words, if everything is held constant consumers will purchase more of a good or service at a lower price than at a higher price. Tourism is no different in this respect. Tourism marketing is demand-led, that is to say if there is a demand for a certain product or service by consumers, it will be supplied and marketed by profit-maximizing organizations. This demand orientation determines that the 'requirements of the tourists are given highest priority and the destination area seeks to provide services to meet those requirements' (Ashworth and Goodall, 1990: 227). Examples of this can be seen in sectors such as transport and accommodation where new services are provided as a result of increased tourism demand for a destination. Supply on the other hand refers to what firms are actually willing and able to produce and offer for sale at various prices over a period of time. The law of supply is concerned with the fact that the quantity supplied of a good or service is usually a positive function of price. With all else held constant, suppliers usually will supply less of a good or service at a lower price. As we shall see, with the limited number of ecotourism 'destinations' prices will play an important role in controlling demand.

Supply-driven tourism places considerations other than profit at the centre of tourism products. Considerations such as the social impact of the tourism product on destination sites, the needs and wants of destination communities and the natural resource management of the supplier country and destination sites become central. The supply side nature of ecotourism means that the 'impact on the local natural resource base is more easily controlled than is the case with demand side tourism...dangers of overload and cultural submersion and tourists exceeding biological carrying capacities may be thus minimized' (Lillywhite and Lillywhite, 1990: 92). This is imperative for ecotourism. To establish the best methods for marketing an ecotourism destination it is important to stress the necessity of marketing to be a holistic enterprise, working with community groups, indigenous and other private voluntary organization programs.

CASE STUDY: Catlins Wildlife Trackers, Dunedin, South Island, New Zealand

Catlins Wildlife trackers is a small-scale tour operation, offering 2–3-day in-depth guided tours of the Catlins area. The mission statement for the venture covers three areas for the operators: Personal – 'We see this venture as an opportunity to provide us as a family, with an income in an environment and doing activities that we enjoy, and allowing personal growth by mixing and sharing with others', for others – 'We wish to offer a recreational and educational service to people, particularly those interested in active involvement with the natural, aesthetic, historic and human environment of the south-east coast and Catlins Area and conservation – 'We wish to highlight and share environmental values and to make a positive contribution to the protection of those values'.

The quality of the experience is assessed by the response from visitors who take up the tour. The experience itself is unique, with key aspects of the operation illustrating this fact. Management relies on home grown and home made foods, produced with only organic pesticides, rain water is collected on the roof of the 'home-stay' facility, solar heating panels supply hot water, all organic matter is recycled and, when necessary, local produce is used as much as possible. Visitors themselves are actively encouraged to collect litter seen during day excursions, weed certain areas (under the direction of the guide), count bird numbers and record sightings – small, but significant contributions to the improvement and sustainability of the natural environment. In 1991 visitation rates were relatively small, at 100 visitors. In 1994, this number had increased to 274. Although this rise had no visible and discernible effects on the environment, management needed to consider an alternate strategy in order to prevent increased demand from having detrimental effects on the physical environment. Since the quality of experience is not determined by rates of visitation, but by feedback from participants, operators chose to offer a 3-day excursion. Originally, all tours offered were on a 2-day basis. The introduction of 3-day tours provided potential consumers with an alternative and has thus far been successful at limiting numbers based on supply (Catlins Wildlife Trackers, 2007).

ECOLOGICAL AND SOCIAL MARKETING

Developed in the 1990s, ecological marketing is defined as an:

> *approach to highlight products and production methods that improve environmental performance, further ecological causes, or solve environmental problems. Marketing products and services on these effects is growing but not all environmental claims are accurate. Some might be examples of green-washing. (Dictionary of Sustainable Management, 2008)*

Ecological marketing then differs from traditional marketing as it relates to the marketing of ecotourism as it involves the promotion of products and services with positive ecological outcomes to environmentally concerned consumers. It would be naive to suggest that those organizations practicing ecological marketing are not motivated by making a profit, but this is not their sole measure of success. Quantifiable and unquantifiable outcomes are equally pursued, such as long-term environmental protection and customer satisfaction. Profit determines the level of products viability, but is not the only measure of success.

It has been suggested that, for ecological marketing 'the relationship between demand and supply' is the prime issue (Henion and Kinnear, 1976: 1). Ecological marketing questions the role of demand stimulation: if the product is environmentally harmful, demand stimulation is strongly discouraged (Henion and Kinnear, 1976). This is of fundamental importance to ecotourism: as a result of ecotourism growing at a much faster rate than mass tourism, more and more members of the traveling public are opting out of the traditional 'lie around the pool/beach' holiday and are instead choosing a more experiential ecotourism product: 'These people are going to create a demand and this demand is going to be met as usual by supply' (Richardson, 1991: 245). The danger is that supply may be met, not by the small, environmentally concerned operators, but by mass tourism operators with little understanding, or concern about the environment.

Related to ecotourism and ecological marketing is social marketing. Social marketing is defined generally as the design, implementation and control of programs which are able to influence the acceptability of social ideas and involving considerations of product planning, pricing, communication and market research. According to Drejerska social marketing:

> *is practiced mostly by government agencies and non-governmental organizations but, as an element of commercial marketing, is also used for the creation of positive image of a firm, brand or product. (2005: 27)*

Social marketing has great potential but is a little explored concept or practice within the area of ecotourism or within leisure and tourism services generally. Its dual focus on consumer satisfaction and community welfare should be of particular interest to ecotourism which seeks to improve the social, environmental and economic conditions of destination communities. In practice a social marketing approach to ecotourism would seek to mediate the preferences of the tourist with the long-term interests of the destination community (Kaczynski, 2008: 257).

With these dimensions in mind, we would like to suggest a definition of ecotourism marketing:

> *The development of ecologically sustainable tourism products and the pricing, promotion and distribution of these products, so impact on the physical and cultural environments is minimised, while maintaining some level of profit commensurate with these objectives.*

THE 'GREENING' MARKET

There is no doubt that the tourism marketplace is becoming 'greener'. Increasing concern for the environment and conservation issues is evidenced by the growing membership of environmental organizations such as

Greenpeace, the World Wildlife Fund for Nature (WWF) and the Wilderness Society in Australia. Indeed, many people in the world now rank the environment as the number one public issue. A poll conducted by the Australian National University found that Australians ranked the environment as the most important issue facing the country and the globe (Leigh, 2008). In a similar poll conducted by Ipsos-Mori in 13 countries environmental issues, including global warming, pollution and resource depletion, were ranked the 3rd most pressing issue facing the world in 1996, whereas in 2001 it was ranked number 1 (IPSOS-Mori, 2002). Therefore it is becoming increasingly difficult to dismiss the 'greening' of the market place as a fad (Honey, 1999). With the increasing range and proliferation of new products in most markets, consumers are becoming more discerning about what they want and they are far more independent as well as curious about what is on offer to them. According to Jon Hutchinson, the Australian Tourism Commission's managing director, this is due to a backlash against the 1980s when 'people bought regardless of quality and regardless of standards. People are more interested in gaining value from what they do than in gathering status symbols. There seems to be a psychological change in tourists' (Collins, 1993: 7).

Ecotourism is still very much in the growth stage of its business cycle and its popularity will continue to increase as 'issues associated with urban congestion and crowding, atmospheric pollution, increased leisure time, more flexible work options, work-related stress and concern for the environment continue to develop' (Carter and Moore, 1991: 141). Not only are people increasingly receiving messages through the media about the fragility of our environment and the daunting prospect of climate change, but also about its beauty and uniqueness and the importance of keeping areas as pristine and unspoilt as possible for now and for generations to come.

The incorporation of environmental principles and responsible behavior codes in developing sustainable ecotourism establishments and other ecotourism ventures is indicative of an increasing consumer challenge to traditional ethics, in a search for new alternatives to traditional tourism activity (Weaver, 2001b; Wight, 1993). As we have seen in Chapter 3, codes of practice have emerged to integrate the concepts of sustainability and stewardship for appropriate behavior relative to site visitation. These, however, are most often in the form of 'Codes of Ethics' which concentrate on the activities of the consumer/ecotourist, rather than on the operators themselves (Wight, 1993).

As the importance placed on environmental issues by the public at large continues to grow, and with the demand for consumer products and services that protect the environment, many organizations are attempting to capture these changes in preferences in order to sell their products, whether or not their businesses contribute to a more sustainable future or not. This has led to a problem that has come to be known as 'greenwashing'.

> *Greenwashing is a term merging the concepts of green (environmentally sound) and whitewashing (to conceal or gloss over wrongdoing). Greenwashing is any form of marketing or public relations that links a corporate, political, religious or nonprofit organization to a positive association with environmental issues for an unsustainable product, service, or practice. In some cases, an organization may truly offer a green product, service or practice. However, through marketing and public relations, one is wrongly led to believe this green value system is ubiquitous throughout the entire organization. (Dictionary of Sustainable Management, 2008)*

A good example of this was a report released in July 2002 by WWF – UK, which accused Green Globe (a tourism environmental certification system) of misleading practices. 'In particular, Green Globe was accused of permitting hundreds of businesses to use their logo simply by paying a fee and signing an agreement to move towards environmentally friendly practices' (Honey, 2002: 150). This problem is underlined by a survey carried out on domestic and international tourists in New Zealand which found that the majority of respondents report high levels of trust for such ecolabels (Schott, 2006). In one sense Schott's results are heartening in that the public is not yet cynical of ecolabels, yet on the other it poses a problem in that such systems rely on a critical market to ensure that businesses are living up to the environmental claims they make.

Marketing by ecotourism operators based on a less than committed approach to a sustainable future in the hunt for maximum demand and short-term profitability is defeatist. By exceeding the deemed carrying capacity of the venue, failing to reconcile facility management strategies with those of the adjacent natural environment or attracting a clientele with little regard for the preservation and conservation of the environment, risks degrading the resource on which visitation is founded. For many ecotourism operators, particularly those with a fixed asset (such as accommodation establishments) there is an incentive to plan, develop and operate their business with ethical consideration for not only their venture, but also for the surrounding areas which are subject to impacts from ecotourists. High capital investment in facilities and its associated risk is an incentive to provide a quality experience for prospective visitors, translated into long-term cash flow and profitability based on heightened satisfaction (Middleton and Hawkins, 1998).

Given the growth and changing nature of ecotourism it would appear that in order to market successfully operators will have to refocus their approaches to planning and communication strategies. That is, success cannot be measured by the number of people who visit the operation, but consideration must be given as to the customer's levels of satisfaction and their likelihood of returning. The total experience, including the emotional wants of the guests, must be considered: not just their functional require-ments. Methods to do this often take the form of feedback from clients through surveys and questionnaires or just by talking to them, which can give some indication as to the emotional benefits they gained from the experience.

Sustainability is a critical element of managing all aspects of the ecotourism venture. It is derived not only from repeat patronage, but pres-ervation of the physical and social environments of the region utilized on which education and interpretation of the environment are dependent. Just as feedback from ecotourists themselves is essential in determining the success of the business (in terms other than monetary), impacts of the business venture itself must be ascertained. This is frequently carried out as an environmental impact assessment in the initial phases of development which provides a 'snapshot' of likely environmental effects and thus the planning of management regimes created to combat them.

Best Practice (as discussed in Chapter 3) goes beyond appreciation of the natural environment and its associated flora, fauna, geography and ecology to encompass an understanding of social activities, economic impacts on the facilities and region and spatial expression of community values. This may be achieved through a marketing audit and an associated statement of strengths, weaknesses, opportunities and threats (SWOT). A marketing audit of relevant internal and external environments that potentially affect business is the first step toward making marketing efforts sustainable for ecotourism organizations.

The SWOT is an effective way to analyze the current status of ecotourism marketing and project the future threats and opportunities likely to impact the ecotourism suppliers and managers and ecotourists themselves. We will now discuss the product, pricing, promotion and distribution issues and the role they play in shaping consumer expectations and demands. It will be presented as a SWOT analysis and developed into a discussion of marketing issues as they relate to management and suggest ways to capitalize from existing trends and opportunities.

STRENGTHS IN MARKETING ECOTOURISM

Effective market segmentation is a key to defining an appropriate user group for ecotourism (e.g. Chafe, 2007). To market a genuine ecotourism venture, it is important to ensure the validity and legitimacy of the experience. Obtaining accurate statistics and a demographic and psychographic profile may go some way to doing this, by aligning perceived user wants with the product/service produced (see Chapter 9). Thus, promotion of the operation can utilize presently the existing data on likely user groups and align this with the orientation of the organization, removing some uncertainty from the need to match consumer with producer.

Ecotourism is based on visitation and appreciation of the natural attributes of a region. Although this dictates a degree of stewardship in order to preserve the resource, it provides a low-cost attraction on which ecotourism products may be developed and molded. As a marketer of a potential product/service, the natural attributes of the area are important to consider, including the geography, geology and the flora and fauna. The unique and varied nature of many protected natural areas provides an excellent basis for the development of specialized services focusing on a limited geographic zone, which can be translated to an appropriate advertising campaign and areas for sustainable competitive advantage.

Ecotourists are very discerning and take time to educate themselves about a destination prior to departure. Therefore an active knowledge base is a major factor in the tourist's decision-making process. There are strong correlations between involvement and information sourcing, and receptivity to promotional stimuli. This means that careful market research into the form of advertising most likely to attract the consumer by heightened involvement is liable to have a profound effect in achieving a response, and therefore producing a decision based on the characteristics of the target market.

THREATS IN MARKETING ECOTOURISM

In the last few years, ecotourism has become a marketing buzzword and has been used to sell any number of products, the 'eco' tag as mentioned previously in relation to greenwashing does not necessarily provide any indication of the quality of the product on offer. There has been a substantial increase in the quantity of products in this vein, a multitude of references abound to the 'ecotour', 'ecosafari' and 'ecotravel'. One reason for the increasing proliferation of the 'ecotourism' label is because of the general lack of understanding as to what ecotourism is. Some of the products being marketed are totally unrelated to ecotourism, yet it is this label which is being used to sell them.[21] As a result many of the problems or negative trends which make ecotourism unsustainable, relate to the fact that 'principles fundamental to ecotourism are not being incorporated into the conception, planning, design, development, operation or marketing of the product' (Wight 1993). For example, Lai and Shafer (2005) conducted a study investigating the ways in which the Internet is used by ecolodges in Latin America and the Caribbean to market and promote their services. A content analysis of the online marketing messages of these ecolodge websites – all of which were listed on *The International Ecotourism Society's* website – indicated that most of them were only partially aligned with ecotourism principles.

Wight suggests that some of the issues and challenges facing the ecotourism industry include

> *inadequate information service technologies, lack of suitable trained staff and guides, difficulties branding for ecotourism, lack of product transferability between marketplaces, air access problems and costs, financing, seasonality, competition for land, traditional consumptive product resistance to repositioning, lack of government assistance, and lack of national industry organization. (2002: 28)*

There is also the problem of inappropriate developments related to ecotourism, many of which are taking place in sensitive locations and many private operators and sometimes even government agencies are latching onto the short-term economic benefits of ecotourism 'without giving due regard to the underlying principles of ecotourism' (Wight 1993: 55). The International Ecotourism Society summed up the problem by warning customers of dubious claims of eager travel marketers who exploit the trend toward integrating environmental values into holiday choices.

Demand factors have been primarily focused on by ecotourism suppliers – either the government or industry – and they seem to be particularly interested in developing supply in response to the demand-driven market (e.g. Wight, 1997). As with other tourism segments, 'demand information is viewed as enabling greater numbers of visitors to be attracted,' as well as enabling more effective marketing (Wight 1993: 56). However, this orientation is not compatible with ecotourism and is largely due to general confusion about what ecotourism actually is, due in large part to ecotourism's

---

[21] Sharpley (2006) goes as far to argue that the ecotour and ecotourist label have become increasingly irrelevant as there is little distinction between mainstream tourism and most ecotourism ventures.

'varying mix of so many different activities and experiences' (Wight 1993: 57).

Rather than defining ecotourism in terms of products, it is more valuable to recognize that within ecotourism there are a number of experiences which may be supplied and demanded (Wight 1993). These may vary according to the following supply and demand factors:

Supply factors

■ the nature and resilience of the resource

■ the cultural or local community preferences

■ the types of accommodation, facilities and programs (Wight, 1993)

Demand factors

■ the types of activities and experiences encountered

■ degree of interest in natural or cultural resources

■ the degree of physical effort (Wight, 1993)

Negative consumer opinion may result from a product offering that does not satisfy the ecotourists' needs and expectations and simultaneously assumes the 'cover' of environmental responsibility. Additionally, an unethical operator may exceed carrying capacities to bolster revenue through attracting increasing numbers of consumers at a reduced price. Accreditation within the industry may go some way toward reducing instances of this scenario.

OPPORTUNITIES IN MARKETING ECOTOURISM

There are numerous opportunities available to marketers of ecotourism products/services that allow the goals of sustainability and profitability to be met simultaneously.

The proliferation of interest groups, particularly nature-based organizations provides an opportunity for direct marketing. Targeting specific age groups and nature-based groups such as adventure seekers, educational institutions, bushwalkers, canyoners and scientific groups is a very effective method of attracting users with an ecocentric orientation. Advertising in publications accessed by these groups, directly mailing promotional material to such organizations and cause-related marketing are methods of utilizing the communication channels of most benefit to the ecotourism operator. Remember 'ecotourism should not be geared toward the masses, but to smaller groups of discerning visitors who will pay more for an authentic value-for-money experience' (Kerr, 1991: 250).

An important area of competitive advantage for ecotour operators according to Price (2003, 2004) is the ecotourist's desire for high-quality environmental education experiences. However, a content analysis of current advertising material of ecotourism operators in the state of Victoria, Australia, found that many of these ventures place little emphasis on environmental learning in their marketing materials. Price argues that this is a substantial weakness in many operator's strategic marketing, indicating that the provision of environmental education in more ecotourism programs could provide an increased potential for more customers.

In order to ensure the sustainability of the venture, and the area on which ecotourism is based, the managerial philosophy adopted should be holistic. Ecotourism operators aligning their managerial plans with those existing and carried out by reserve/protected area/wilderness area management is an example. The recognition of the similarities that exist between the impacts that tourism generates and those produced through recreational use of specific environments facilitates a transfer of managerial strategies which mitigate the effects that visitors may have on any facility or surrounding region (Mercer, 1995). This can only result in an improvement in the product itself, possible cost advantages and the opportunity to promote the nature of this strategy to entice 'hard core' ecotourists.

The utilization of an Ecotourism Opportunity Spectrum (similar to the Recreation Opportunity Spectrum (ROS) discussed in Chapter 4) presents a long-term opportunity to further segment the ecotourism market based on the degree of authenticity of the ecotourism experience desired by the potential client.

The pattern of growth in ecotourism markets is both a challenge and an opportunity. The opportunity involves 'understanding and responding to market needs, preferences and expectations: the challenge is in keeping foremost the supply-oriented management perspective' (Wight, 1993: 62). Therefore matching the markets to products (supply), 'both with respect to type and location is imperative...otherwise resource capability can become secondary to actual or perceived market demand' (Wight, 1993: 63).

WEAKNESSES IN MARKETING ECOTOURISM

Ecotourism marketing, as a relatively new form of promoting nature-based activity displays a range of developmental weaknesses.

Ecotourism product marketing can be significantly improved through increasing analysis and study of carrying capacities and host communities prior to operation establishment; improved education and interpretive material and a greater focus on providing a quality experience. Khan's (2003) study on the service quality expectations of ecotourists found that they place an emphasis upon facilities that are appropriate to the environment, practices that minimize degradation and an assurance that they will be provided with the necessary information and that guides are available and have the knowledge to answer questions. Whereas other factors such as providing local entertainment, employees wearing local attire and the use of materials that are visually appealing scored much lower.

In a supply-led industry, carrying capacities must first be determined and then marketing strategies decided on, so these levels are reached, but not exceeded. This level must be developed in conjunction with local communities, as the socially responsible and environmentally viable goals of ecotourism 'cannot be fostered without a dialogue constructed and controlled along indigenous needs and in indigenous terms' (Craik, 1991: 80).

As we have seen in Chapter 5 and previously in this chapter, education and interpretive material is a critical element of the ecotourism product. Ecotourists express a strong desire to learn about nature on ecotours. An effective way to satisfy this desire to learn is through the use of interpretation. Unfortunately, a satisfactory level of interpretive material is rarely provided for participants. As a result, marketers miss out on being able to emphasize one of the key factors differentiating ecotourism from mass tourism – the educative component – and their marketing activities lose much of their appeal (e.g. Price, 2003, 2004).

A high-quality educative experience in limited supply does, by marketing standards, imply a high price. Price in marketing can be defined as the cost that the buyer must accept in order to obtain the product and includes money costs, opportunity costs, energy costs and psychic costs (e.g. Kotler and Armstrong, 2004). The main issue, then, is to formulate a price so that ecotourism remains supply rather than demand driven.

There are three primary ways for ecotourism to grow and remain profitable:

1. increasing the size of groups on an ecotour

2. the establishment of more ecotourism destinations

3. charging higher prices (Merschen, 1992)

The first two options impact negatively on the environment and host communities, as well as being demand-rather than supply-driven. However, price manipulation is an effective means of decreasing demand to a level that does not exceed the carrying capacity of a region. Increasing prices is not necessarily negative as 'consumers may impute high quality to a high-priced product and low quality to a low priced product' (Henion, 1975: 233), and the fact that ecotourism is a prestigious product can be emphasized in marketing activities. Ferraro et al. (2005) also argue that the price premium approach is likely to be more effective at achieving conservation and development objectives.

If demand is still greater than supply after prices have been increased, other non-price measures, such as requiring consumers to attend pre-trip lectures, would further limit demand. Another system which could be used is 'the ballot system' whereby names are either drawn out of a hat or potential visitors placed on a waiting list. This system is currently working effectively at a number of national parks in the United States.

If prices are to be increased, ecotour operators should donate some of this additional revenue to environmental causes or social causes, such as the improvement of host community living conditions. Drawing the consumer's attention to this strategy would also benefit the operator as tourists traveling with ecotour operators appear to be 'especially satisfied that a certain percentage of their tour cost is being donated to conservation' (Boo, 1990: 41). This already occurs in Costa Rica, where money donated by tour operators is put back into rainforest preservation programs (Masson, 1991).

Ecotourism marketing can also be improved significantly in the area of promotion. Promotion is the communication persuasion strategy and tactics that will make the product more familiar, acceptable and even desirable to the audience (Kotler and Armstrong, 2004). Central promotional issues that need to be addressed by ecotourism operators are

- the selection of target markets or 'niches'

- joint marketing

- effective selection of promotional methods such as direct mail and special interest magazines

Many marketing theorists have emphasized the importance of a highly targeted marketing campaign as opposed to a strategy that attempts to appeal to a broad sweep of consumers. This involves obtaining data, such as demographic and psychographic profiles of the potential market segments (Chapter 9) and aligning operations with the identified consumer group that corresponds best with the ideals of the specific venture.

Ecotourists are known to utilize a wide range of media to gain accurate in-depth information on a destination or area of interest to them. Information distributed in special interest magazines, direct mail and the Internet rather than newspapers and radio advertising may be one method of reaching a target market. Direct mail offers a particularly effective strategy to promote ecotourism (Durst and Ingram 1989; Ingram and Durst, 1989). Direct mail involves a selected person receiving promotional material about a product. Where ecotourism is concerned, direct mail is particularly effective for keeping in touch with previous customers and encouraging them to take another tour with the ecotourism operator. Overall it is probably the most effective medium out there for ecotourism organizations (Merschen 1992).

Joint marketing strategies by groups of two or more ecotourism operators also offer an effective means to market an ecotourism product due to the efficient use of resources that may already be strained by the small size of ecotourism ventures as joint marketing is more cost efficient and enables greater numbers of a target audience to be reached (e.g. Gould, 1999). Vertical joint marketing is particularly effective, for example, where a tour operator, accommodation establishment and carrier join promotional efforts and link their services. Additionally, if ecotour operator's work together in marketing, chances are they will work together in other areas, such as carrying capacity determination, which would produce beneficial effects for the environment and local populations impacted upon by ecotourism.

The final broad area where ecotourism marketing can be improved is in distribution or 'place' where the customer is able to purchase an ecotour from. The poor results of many social campaigns can be attributed in part to their failure to suggest clear action outlets for those motivated to acquire the product (Andreasen & Kotler, 2003). This is a regular occurrence with ecotourism: consumers motivated enough to inquire about ecotours at retail travel agents are often persuaded by these agents to choose a conventional tourism product (Richardson 1991). In a supply-led industry, however, this restriction in demand may not be entirely negative.

Ecotourism operators should not distribute their tours through general travel agents. The tours should only be sold at travel agents specializing in ecotourism (Boo 1990), or directly by the operators themselves. This will thereby restrict supply and also increase the efficiency of the ecotourism operators' marketing efforts, as they will no longer have to waste time in their mostly futile bids to convince travel agents to market their tours. This will also enable the operators to exercise more control over the type of tourists who participate in a tour with the company ensuring, where possible, that tourists motivated by environmental concerns make up the majority of the group.

From the above SWOT analysis of the strengths, weaknesses, opportunities and threats to ecotourism, it is apparent that numerous aspects of its development need to be ensured to produce sound marketing and sustainable resource management in order to shape demand and expectations appropriately:

- Ecotourism requires sensitively developed tourist infrastructure. The tourism industry therefore, must accept integrated planning and regulation. To date, tourism development has occurred incidentally to the urban, rural and foreshore development, as in many countries there is no specific tourism zoning. Economic development demands increasingly stringent environmental assessment techniques and reports to be included in applications for development, especially in countries where economic imperatives may take precedent over more qualitative aspects such as environmental, social and cultural significance of development.

- Ecotourism requires a supply-led tourism industry. For this to become a reality the industry must firstly define itself holistically and, secondly, agree to cooperate with and support a coordinating body or authority to make decisions about: number of operators, operating licenses, ceiling numbers for tours, price structures and so forth. Structural considerations such as pricing, economics of scale, price yield management, and all other financial tools will have to be modified accordingly. The very philosophy of ecotourism calls on low volume tourism with high ticket prices per head. This tactic also negates the business philosophy of competitive pricing to win new customers either from the latent market or from competitors.

- The body responsible for making these decisions and policing industry activities needs to be a third party to the tourism industry. However, care must be taken in appointing a government department or commission to adopt such a role, as even the government is not impartial to its interests in tourism growth, because of the short-term revenue that tourism can create for a region, state or country, especially where foreign currency is concerned.

- Ecotourism requires the establishment of carrying capacities and strict monitoring of these. It is a task that no profit motivated organization in the industry sees as its responsibility. The establishment of carrying capacities requires a comprehensive knowledge and expertise in the field of environmental, social and cultural assessments. The latter two are very difficult to measure, but a commendable starting point is with the host community, by identifying, in partnership with each community, what is of social and cultural importance. This task in itself requires a great deal of time to be invested in living with and learning from the community in order to establish these social and cultural carrying capacities. Monitoring is an essential component of carrying capacity management. It requires ongoing financial and human resource commitment to monitor and evaluate impacts and changing relationships.

■ Ecotourism relies on the environmentally sensitive behavior and operations of ecotour operators and tourists but the proponents of ecotourism may have placed undue faith in the notion that the behavior of tourists, developers and other industry operators can be modified through education and awareness programs (e.g. Duffy, 2002; Kamauro, 1996; McLaren, 2003). In the initial years of ecotourism development there was a flood of 'codes of ethics' of 'charters' released by a variety of tourism industry groups and environmental organizations ranging from conservation groups (e.g. World Wide Fund for Nature, Australian Conservation Foundation) to industry groups [e.g. Australia Tourism Industry Association (ATIA), Pacific Asia Travel Association (PATA)]. The benefits of raising awareness in this fashion have now been acknowledged but there are still many problems to overcome such as greenwashing (Honey, 2007).

■ The optimal method to market ecotourism involves taking components of traditional, social and ecological marketing. Ecotourism is certainly a product which fits under the aegis of ecological marketing, as it 'serves to provide a remedy for environmental problems' (Henion and Kinnear, 1976); and also social marketing, as it attempts to further the social cause of environmental quality. It is believed that the 'four Ps' of traditional marketing are still relevant to ecotourism marketing. This is, Andreasen and Kotler (2003) suggest, because the more conditions of a social campaign resembled those of a product campaign, the more successful the cause. Therefore, the marketing of ecotourism and thereby the marketing of environmental quality should utilize the key components of traditional marketing, specifically the 'four Ps'.

The most productive and cost-effective promotional method for ecotourism businesses is word of mouth and an up to date website (Mader, 1999; Owens, Patterson and Owens, 2007: 57–60).[22] If an ecotourist is satisfied with their ecotourism experience they will effectively become an 'ambassador for the

---

[22] Research indicates that a website is now vital for any tourism business. For example, 67% of US travelers in 2003 used the Internet for researching, planning and purchasing travel (Travel Industry Association, 2004).

company', spreading the good word very effectively. Asking tour participants to list the names and addresses of friends whom they think would be interested in participating in an ecotour with the company is a means of networking through word of mouth. Also, if a tourist is satisfied with their ecotourism experience, they are more likely to go on a tour with the company again, thereby ensuring an appropriate user group mentality and reducing the need for the company to conduct additional promotion.

The primary marketing factors which may be assessed and altered to fit with the environmental objectives in marketing for ecotourism organizations are

1. The target markets – the group of people at whom an agency specifically aims its marketing effort

2. Positioning statements – how you want your target markets to view your agency and its 'product'

3. Company objectives

4. Marketing mix – Product
   – Place (distribution)
   – Promotion
   – Price

Target marketing is an important procedure in marketing ecotourism. Because ecotourism is specific in its philosophies, it is important to select target markets that are compatible with organizational goals and objectives. A small group of potential customers may be targeted who share one or more similar characteristics and who have certain similar ideas as to what they want from the ecotourism experience. Some of these preferences would be the desire to travel to relatively remote areas, for the purpose of studying a natural area and its culture, having minimum impact on the environment and with the expectation of gaining educational gratification, with the knowledge that they will return something to the local community.

When considering the target market a number of things need to be considered. Firstly, socio-demographic characteristics, which include such things as age, sex, income, education, occupation and memberships. Secondly, it is necessary to consider behavioral characteristics. This is a very important stage in selecting target markets for ecotourism as it enables marketers to decide what characteristics they will select people on. It includes considerations of

■ the benefits sought

■ the consumer's motivations; perceptions of the ecotourism 'product'

- the level of skill – is it necessary for targets to have some basic levels of skill before embarking on an ecotourism experience?

- psychographic profiles – a concept that explains consumers' attitudes, opinions and lifestyles

- behavioral characteristics, which are especially important in choosing target markets because they can later be used as criteria in selecting people for specific 'ecotours'. As a marketer for an ecotourism destination it is important to be specific in selection as you want a certain type of person to participate who is compatible with agency goals and objectives

Positioning is an important consideration when marketing an ecotourism destination. Positioning is what the marketer 'wants the target market to think about the product, therefore positioning of the product must be consumer oriented' (Tonge and Myott 1989: 168). Ecotourism marketers need to differentiate their 'product' from mass tourism. Agency positioning

CASE STUDY: Belize, Central America

Belize is a Central American country with a tourism development policy focused on ecotourism. Although the country is well known for its outstanding barrier reef with unique diving opportunities, the attraction of natural and cultural assets to ecotourists is quite recent. With an array of attractions to tempt potential visitors, tourists and ecotourists have equally diverse expectations of the destination.

It is therefore important for ecotourism policy planners to define what is meant by ecotourism from a visitor perspective. Palacio and McCool (1997) attempted to achieve this aim by developing information about the tourism market based on a benefit segmentation assessment. The study found that within the category of nature-based visitors, there existed specific characteristics that distinguished four types of tourists as different from each other. These categories were 'Nature Escapists', 'Ecotourists', 'Comfortable Naturalists' and 'Passive Players'.

Nature Escapists and Ecotourists reported the highest activity percentages, followed by Comfortable Naturalists, then Passive Players. Ecotourists recorded the highest interest in a desire to escape, learn about nature, health-related activity participation and responded positively to the need for companionship and group cohesion.

The study noted that each segment required different facilities due to the different rates of recreation participation and differences in trip characteristics – perhaps with the exception of 'Nature Escapists' and 'Ecotourists', whose characteristics were very similar. Furthermore, promotional and product strategies for each segment would need to be altered slightly to align consumer preference with the product offering. The effective linking of environmental attributes to specific benefits for different nature-based tourists could be achieved through improved marketing efficiency. It may also help organizations determine the social, cultural and biophysical elements in greatest need of sustaining (Palacio and McCool, 1997).

objectives (for the area and product) would encompass everything that ecotourism stands for: sustainable development, minimal impact, local control, supply-driven, quality experiences, and so on (Nowaczek et al., 2007).

The marketing mix constitutes the core of an agency's marketing system. The identification of client groups and the marketing mix represents the combination of variables which the agency can control and manipulate to achieve desired outcomes. Once these decisions have been made the 'service' is offered in the dynamic environment of the community: 'The dynamic nature of this external environment comprises a host of variables such as political and legal forces, economic considerations, technology and competition' (Crompton and Howard 1980: 332). The agency cannot control these variables, therefore it must adapt to them.

At this point in determining the marketing mix, it could be suggested that the agency adopt a different strategy. Normally, the marketing mix activities are used to encourage potential customers to take advantage of the services offered or to increase their usage. Ecotourism, however, is one of those areas that is faced by the need to discourage demand for a service. For example, exceeding carrying capacities in a remote wilderness area may provide short-term satisfaction for some at the expense of overriding the ecotourism philosophy and maximizing public welfare and client group satisfaction over the long term. Because ecotourism is dealing with a 'scarce resource' the agency may use the marketing mix effectively for discouraging participation. This discouraging of demand has been termed 'demarketing': 'to emphasize that marketing may be used to decrease as well as increase the number of satisfied customers. Demarketing is not a negative concept…a decrease in numbers can lead to an increase in clientele satisfaction, through preserving a higher quality experience' (Crompton and Howard, 1980: 333).

Methods of demarketing may include

- Increasing prices, so they increase disproportionately as time spent in the ecotourism destination increases.

- Creating a queuing situation to increase the time and opportunity costs of the experience.

- Limiting the main promotional strategy to select and specialize media.

- Promoting the importance of the area through education of the public and the need to conserve the area through minimal impact and sustainable development.

- Promoting a range of alternative opportunities in surrounding areas which may satisfy needs and wants.

- Stressing the environmental degradation that could occur if too many people frequent the area.

- Stressing any restrictions or difficulties associated with travel to the area.

Product and distribution need to be looked at a little differently. In the case of ecotourism, the product is essentially an intangible which provides a set of want-satisfying benefits to a customer in an exchange. The ecotourism product is the place, region or area. Because an area is a non-renewable resource it is imperative that it be maintained in its original natural state. Ecotourism in its purest form aims to do this. Distribution is the 'channel structure' used to transfer products and services from an agency to its markets. Destination areas are usually remote and therefore less accessible. This part of the marketing mix, as with the 'product', is virtually impossible to alter.

Marketing is often seen as simply flogging a product to a mass market and therefore has negative connotations. From this discussion it is clear that through appropriate and stringent strategies, an agency can market a 'destination' in a way that complies with organizational goals and objectives and upholds the ecotourism philosophy. Through manipulation of the essential marketing mix factors, target markets, positioning statements and company objectives, marketing can be utilized as a tool for directing the future development of ecotourism within the boundaries of sustainable development. Effective promotion and communication strategies are one of the industry's best opportunities to shape consumer demand and expectations, so they are reconciled with the product offered.

Ideally, ecotourism is a small-scale, low-key tourism, so as to minimize the impacts which may occur on destination environments. Methods of achieving this may mean imposing ceiling numbers which in turn suggest economically that prices charged per person will be somewhat higher than 'mainstream tourism', where economies of scale and competition help determine pricing structures within and between organizations operating within one destination. These objectives, however, are unlikely to be reached in light of the nature and characteristics of the tourism industry in its present operations.

The initial objectives of ecotourism in a new destination may be to remain low-key and small scale but it is difficult to guarantee this once the tourism industry perceives a new product development opportunity and starts to market that opportunity (Griffin and Boele, 1993).

Suggested restrictions associated with sustainable development and ecotourism have included both qualitative and quantitative measures, including charging higher prices for access to tourist destinations and attractions. Indeed, restricting supply would automatically increase the price of tourism products, thereby reducing the opportunities for some prospective tourists. The question is whether this is consistent with the principle of equity, embodied in the concept of sustainability, one of the central tenets of ecotourism.

FURTHER READING

Andreasen, A., & Kotler, P. (2003) *Strategic Marketing for Non-profit Organizations,* sixth ed. Prentice Hall, Englewood-Cliffs, NJ.

Andreasen and Kotler's text now in its sixth edition provides a basic introduction to the marketing mix as applied to ethically driven organizations.

Middleton, V., & Hawkins, R. (1998) *Sustainable Tourism: A Marketing Perspective.* Butterworth-Heinemann, Oxford.

Although over 10 years old Middleton and Hawkins text gives examples of how the private and public sectors can work together to find solutions in day-to-day operations and marketing of sustainable tourism.

CHAPTER 9

Could the 'Real' Ecotourist Please Stand Up!

A new group of tourism clients have emerged who are demanding different activities, experiences and approaches to tourism from the industry: 'these are the ecotourists – people who require environmentally compatible recreational opportunities...where nature rather than humanity predominates' (Kerr 1991: 248). They are 'shrugging off the shackles of traditional tourism' in search of knowledge and experience. Their interest is not in 'lounging by hotel pools or hectic sightseeing schedules' (Collins 1993: 7). They are, however, 'interested in visiting wilderness, national parks, and tropical forests, and in viewing birds, mammals, trees and wildflowers', they want to 'experience new lifestyles and meet people with similar interests to themselves' and they want to see their traveling dollars contributing toward conservation and benefiting the local economy (Eagles, 1992).

So far we have explored many dimensions of ecotourism: a tourism product; a solution to planning; its relation to local, regional, national and international politics; a strategy for sustainable development. However, this has told us little of what ecotourists are actually like. As we have seen there are a diverse range of ecotourism experiences ranging from tourists wishing to learn about specific ecosystems or wildlife, those interested in experiencing indigenous cultures, some are adventure oriented and interested in more rigorously active experiences, while still others may wish to volunteer aid and community assistance in developing nations. Therefore, ecotourits are not a homogeneous group and are often difficult to pin down (Wight, 2001). Nevertheless, with current research we can develop a broad picture of the typical ecotourist.

This chapter explores the characteristics that differentiate ecotourists through an analysis of tourist motivation. We will examine demographic and psychographic characteristics, the needs of ecotourists, the images and attitudes ecotourists ascribe to a destination and the influence of social, cultural and physical environments. We will also address the managerial implications for ecotourism operators that we initially realized in the

CONTENTS

Building a Profile of the Ecotourist

Tourist Motivations

Tourism Interactions

Economic Differences

Further Reading

preceding chapter, particularly in attempting to align a preferred consumer group with a product offering. By understanding the nature of the target market, ecotourism operators can alter marketing mix components according to the needs of an environmentally conscious consumer.

Understanding what characteristics differentiate ecotourists also has significant implications for managers and protected area agencies. As any person visiting the environment will impact on it in some way, industry and park management agencies require knowledge of ecotourist characteristics in order to manage, influence and control impacts. However, due to the nature of ecotourism as an activity, with a focus on sustaining the environment and education and interpretation, ecotourists differ in their needs and attitudes relative to other travelers.

BUILDING A PROFILE OF THE ECOTOURIST

There are two primary groups of characteristics which will assist in exploring what features distinguish ecotourists. They are *demographic* and *psychographic* characteristics. Demographic segmentation involves defining the market by variables such as age, gender, life cycle stage, occupation, income and education. It is a quantitative analysis method whereas a psychographic profile is qualitative, analyzing in-depth data such as values, motivations and pre-established images of the ecotourist. Both forms of information are vital to ecotourism operators, not only as a one-off measurement, but as a continued body of information on the changing needs of their clients (Beeton, 1998).

Through the compilation of demographic characteristics we can initially begin to build up an image of ecotourists. Table 9.1 illustrates what the profile of the average ecotourist looks like.

Ecotourists can be generally characterized as having higher than average incomes, largely holding tertiary qualifications and there tend to be more female ecotourists than men.[23] According to The International Ecotourism Society (2008) ecotourists are experienced travelers who are more likely to have a college/university degree (compared with the general tourism market) and have a higher income bracket. Wight (1996a, 1996b) further refined the market profile of ecotourist characteristics, differentiating general consumers

---

[23] E.g. Blamey (1995a), Duff (1993), Galley and Clifton (2004), Holden and Sparrowhawk (2002), Loker-Murphy (1996), Niefer et al. (2002), Silverberg et al. (1996) and Wight (1996a).

Table 9.1	Ecotourist Profile			
Age	**Income**	**Education**	**Gender**	**Country of origin**
20–40 or 55+	$42,000–70,000	Generally possessing tertiary qualifications	Tends to be more females than males	United States, Canada, Germany, Sweden, Australia

interested in ecotourism and experienced ecotourism travelers. Experienced ecotourism respondents were very highly educated, more so than general tourists interested in ecotourism, and tended to travel as couples (61%), limited family (15%) and some singles (13%), compared to general tourists who predominantly traveled as couples (59%), with 26% traveling as a family. However, the most notable difference emerged in expenditure – experienced ecotourists are willing to spend more than general tourists.[24] Similarly in one study nature-based tourists who participated in challenging nature-based activities were found to be 'heavy spenders', whereas tourists who visited historic/cultural sites were classified as 'light spenders' (Mehmetoglu, 2007). '[Ecotourists] on average, would spend 8.5% more for services and products provided by environmentally responsible suppliers' (Wight, 1994: 41).

In terms of country of origin the majority of ecotourists are from relatively affluent Western nations such as the USA, Germany, Sweden, Canada and Australia. The rapidly aging populations of these nations and the shift of the 'baby boomers'[25] into late middle age are proving to be a substantial demographic trend for leisure and tourism as a significant proportion of these groups have significant levels of available leisure time allied with relatively high levels of disposable income to spend on leisure services.

Along with these socio-economic (demographic) characteristics are a range of attitudinal and behavioral patterns (psychographic characteristics) that significantly allow us to differentiate ecotourists.

Generally, ecotourists demonstrate the following eight psychographic characteristics:

1. Possession of an environmental ethic.

2. Willingness not to degrade the resource.

---

[24] In a survey by Pamela Wight on the differences in expenditure of the conventional tourist over an 'experienced ecotourist', she found that that the ecotourist was inclined to spend more than the conventional tourist (Wight, 1996a).

[25] The term used to refer to the generation born in the post-war boom between 1946 and 1964.

3. Focus on intrinsic rather than extrinsic motivation.

4. Biocentric rather than anthropocentric in orientation.

5. Aiming to benefit wildlife and the environment.

6. Striving for first-hand experience with the natural environment.

7. Possessing an expectation of education and appreciation.

8. High cognitive and affective dimensions (Ballantine and Eagles, 1994).

Ecotourists possess a preference for small groups and personalized service (Weaver, 2002: 21)[26] and tend to be outdoor enthusiasts and frequently travel as couples or individuals and are frequent and experienced travellers (e.g. Galley and Clifton, 2004; Wight, 1996). They are 'generally more accepting of conditions different from home than are other types of tourists' (Boo, 1991: 13). Luxury accommodation, food and nightlife are far less important to this group than living in local conditions, and sampling local customs and food. Due to their 'strong science orientation' and focus on study and learning, ecotourists are instead demanding of information and instruction on the destinations they visit (e.g. Galley and Clifton, 2004).

A study of Canadian ecotourists, for example, found that they were interested in tropical forests, birds, lakes and streams, trees and wildflowers, mammals, mountains and oceans. These physical features were highly ranked by ecotourists when asked about their motivations. The same group regarded gambling, amusement parks, nightlife, big cities, watching sport, doing nothing, indoor sports, shopping and resort areas as the least enjoyable activities and attractions to visit while on holiday. The study also found that while ecotourists are interested in nature in its own right they enjoy personal development through physical activity, experiencing new and simpler life-styles, meeting people of similar interests, seeing cultural activities and buying local crafts (Eagles 1992).

In this way ecotourism is more than a simple leisure activity. It is a style of travel that reflects and promotes a particular orientation to not only travel, but also to significant lifestyles, behaviors and philosophies:

---

[26] Weaver (2002) suggests that ecotourists can be placed along a spectrum of 'hard' at one end and 'soft' at the other. Hard ecotourists have a strong environmental commitment, seek out specialized trips that are conducted in small groups, are physically challenging and expect few or primitive services.

Ecotourists are expecting discovery and enlightenment from their ecotourism experience. Personal growth in emotional, spiritual, as well as intellectual terms appear to be expected outcomes from ecotourism travel for the majority of these travellers. (Williams 1990: 84)

In painting a picture of the ecotourist we will now broaden our brief brushstrokes by examining tourist motivations which help detail the differences that emerge for ecotourists as a specific market. Such an understanding assists tourism managers in making appropriate decisions that will lead to tourist satisfaction, maximization of positive experiences and minimization of negative experiences (Pearce, 2005). This analysis will be based on a model of tourist motivation developed by Small (1997) which illustrates the key factors of tourist motivation by pictorially demonstrating each factors relation to one another *(see Fig 9.1)*.

Tourist needs, images, attitudes, and the evaluation of needs and image are the primary focus of this model, with attention given to impacts of the physical, social and cultural environments. Reciprocal impacts exerted by the tourist (or ecotourist) on these same environments are indicated by the two-way flow arrow. The interplay of needs and images creates expectations, which differ for ecotourists relative to mainstream tourists. As sustainability is the focus of ecotourism, the impacts upon the environment will be critical in establishing whether ecotourism is viable with the present consumer base or whether operators need to define their market more stringently to achieve a match between environmental/social/cultural objectives, consumer needs/ wants and profitability.

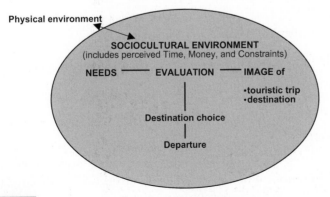

FIGURE 9.1   *A simple model of tourist motivation (adapted from Small, 1997).*

TOURIST MOTIVATIONS

One way we can identify particular forms and styles of tourism is through an examination of what factors motivate tourists. 'Motivation is aroused when individuals think of certain activities that are potentially satisfaction producing. Since people act to satisfy their needs, motivation is thought to be the ultimate driving force that governs travel behavior. Therefore, tourist's motivation should constitute the basis for marketing strategies' (Pyo et al., 1989: 277). Motivational research is based on the early works of Dann (1981), who identified that 'push' and 'pull' factors are central in motivating tourists. Push motives are internal to the individual while pull motives are aroused by the destination. Push factors establish the desire for travel and pull factors explain actual destination choice (Bello and Etzel, 1985).

Crompton (1979) modified the push/pull model in identifying tourist's desire for pleasure and the desire for a break from routine. He identified nine motives in determining causal factors resulting in a tourist's departure. 'Push' factors are motives concerned with the social and psychological status of the individual while 'Pull' factors, on the other hand, are 'motives aroused by the destination rather than emerging exclusively from the traveller himself' (Crompton, 1979: 410).

He found seven primary push motives and two pull motives:
Push motives

- escape from perceived mundane environment

- exploration and evaluation of self

- relaxation

- prestige

- regression

- enhancement of kinship relationships

- facilitation of social interaction

Pull motives

- novelty

- education

Crompton (1979) conceptualized motives as being located along a disequilibrium continuum. When disequilibrium arises due to a feeling of dissatisfaction in relation to one or more push factors, it can be rectified by a break in routine, thus restoring homeostasis (equilibrium), that is, through travel. For Crompton (1979) the destination site is merely a medium through which motives are satisfied.

Significantly, Iso-Ahola (1983) found that the individual possessed an inclination to travel primarily for intrinsic rewards. Intrinsically motivated activities are engaged in for their own sake, rather than any external remuneration. The connection between intrinsic motivations and push and pull factors was made by McGehee et al. (1996) who recognized that most of the push factors are intrinsic motivators. It is important here to note that satisfaction for the ecotourist may come not only from the experience itself but also from the external reward of having promoted environmentally sound travel and having made a contribution to the destination region.

Push factors are strongly related to Maslow's hierarchy of needs. For Maslow (1970) actualization is the central driving force of human personality but before it can be pursued lower order needs such as hunger, shelter and safety (to name a few) must be satisfied first. Maslow grouped these needs into five levels:

1. Physiological – hunger, thirst, shelter, sex, etc.

2. Safety – security, protection from physical and emotional harm

3. Social – affection, belonging, acceptance, friendship

4. Esteem: both internal (self respect, autonomy, achievement) and external (status, recognition, attention)

5. Self-actualization

A tourist motivation framework developed by Pearce (1988, 1993) and based on Maslow's hierarchy of needs provides an expansive framework to identify the needs that a tourist is fulfilling when traveling. A mainstream tourist is more concerned with fulfilling lower order needs of relationship, stimulation and relaxation where the ecotourist is more concerned with development and fulfillment, which includes self-education. If the focus of ecotourism is nature-based activity, often intrinsically aroused, with a degree of education and interpretation of the natural environment, it stands to reason that ecotourists are more focused on the self-actualization and higher level needs than basic needs identified at the base of Maslow's hierarchy, by the nature of the experience they seek (e.g. McDonald et al., in press). A good example of this can be seen in Harlow and Pomfret's (2007) qualitative study which investigated over time the personal development of seven ecotourists who undertook a 10-week nature-based volunteer project in Zambia. The research found that the participant's experienced strong spiritual emotions as a result of being in nature. Furthermore, their self-concept was enriched through both non-environmental and environmental events and they developed a range of new social skills as a result of the expedition experience.

Eagles (1992) also found that the motivations of an ecotourist and those of the general tourist differed in relation to intrinsic versus extrinsic motivations for travel. He found that the general tourist, in most cases liked to feel at home when away from home. The results from this study align strongly with the 'push' and 'pull' factors which influence tourist motivation. This is not to say that pull factors alone provide enough stimulation for a trip departure, because despite the fact that pull factors are paramount for ecotourists, push factors still do (to varying degrees) influence the departure decision. The application of Crompton's (1979) theory illustrates that pull factors are necessarily ranked higher for ecotourists than mainstream tourists, based on their psychographic characteristics.

However, accurately gauging the motivations of ecotourists is difficult. To begin with, defining tourist's motivations using the push and pull model is more complex when applied to a specific market niche such as ecotourists, rather than mainstream tourists. The internal push motives of discovery, enlightenment and personal growth are important to ecotourists but features of a natural destination are more than simply pull motives to this group, for ecotourists see physical locations as motivation in themselves (e.g. Chan and Baum, 2007). To describe this as a pull phenomenon is to overlook the importance of the natural environment as a motivator (Eagles, 1992).

The goals of ecotourism are to provide ecologically sound travel experiences that contribute to the natural, economic, social and cultural environments. The provision of tourism services is becoming central to local communities, particularly in a shift away from the dependence on extractive industries. A combination of ecotourist needs and the image they have of the destination pre-departure creates expectations that an ecotourist assumes will be satisfied. By understanding ecotourist motivations the local community will be in a better position to meet these needs and expectations (e.g. Holden and Sparrowhawk, 2002).

The tailoring of products using motivational research is important in any sector of tourism. Recognizing that motives of ecotourists differ from mainstream tourists is essential for tourism managers. Due to reduced numbers of tourists, the likelihood of reduced impacts and interest in an educative component, roles and rules for ecotourists may be redefined and shaped about the needs this market niche possesses, resulting in higher rates of satisfaction.

Research on visitor expectations was used in the ecologically sustainable management of whale shark tourism in Queensland. Swayed respondents felt regulations allowed divers to swim too near to whale sharks. Management used this research to modify guidelines, increasing the distance which enhanced protection of the species, while still offering a satisfying experience for ecotourists (Birtles et al., 1995). This demonstrates a differing managerial response to the market based on their unique needs and characteristics.[27]

Similarly, a United States survey found that '45% of US travelers felt that travel suppliers do not provide enough environmental protection training and support to employees'. Respondents also felt that companies offered little educational content on environmental awareness and protection during tours. Familiarity with ecotourist motivations will help prevent such dissatisfactions and bring added environmental protection advantages. The ability of ecotourism operators to meet ecotourist needs will determine 'whether or not the destination is ultimately regarded as a viable and worthwhile ecotourism destination' (Wight, 1994: 47).

TOURISM INTERACTIONS

Tourist behavior does not start at the time of travel, it exists before the tourist has left for the destination site and it is here that a major difference between ecotourists and mainstream tourists is evident, not only does this include motivation, but also when the tourist first decides which destination to visit.

Social interactions involving tourists can take the form of tourist–peer group interaction, tourist–tourist interaction or tourist–host interaction. The first of these – tourist–peer group interactions – has a significant effect on destination choice. Social groups exert four kinds of effect in destination selection:

- direct persuasion to visit a certain destination

- normative influence on a traveler's opinion of a destination

- long-term socialization leading to conventional wisdom about a destination

- social group members living in destination areas (Dann and Crompton cited in Crompton, 1981)

---

[27] Another example of this can be seen in Smith et al.'s (2006) study of Monkey Mia in Western Australia which investigates the way in which the state parks agency has managed the conflict between preservation and use with regards to the dolphin swimming at this popular resort.

Although each of these factors, to differing degrees, applies to the mainstream tourist, an ecotourist may not relate to any of these influences. For example, the ecotourist would be unlikely to visit a friend in a distant location and call it 'ecotourism'. In addition, the social group's opinion and persuasion is often of less significance for an ecotourist as they may well visit places that others do not necessarily know about.

Once a pre-departure decision has been made, the next significant 'phase' of social interaction is that which occurs at the destination site itself. For all people social interaction is fundamental: 'It has long been recognized that the interactive nature of social groups exerts a strong influence on an individual's behaviour' (Crompton, 1981: 551). In the case of mainstream tourists, the majority of social interaction occurs between members of the group of tourists. For ecotourism, however – with a reduced group size and an emphasis on destination attributes – the focus of interaction is between the tourist and those encountered at the destination (Wearing and Deane, 2003).

The ideal ecotourist is likely to actively seek immersion in the local environment, rather than enforcing an artificial barrier between themselves and the host community. Cohen (1972: 167) refers to this as the 'environmental bubble' whereby the tourist is demarcated from the destination environment – such as resort facilities where recreation opportunities are enclosed largely within the resort.

In determining the qualitative and quantitative differences in social interaction that differentiate mainstream tourists from ecotourists, Cohen's (1972) typology of tourists serves to demonstrate that differences in interaction can be the result of a willingness or otherwise to venture beyond a tourist's comfort zone. Cohen's (1972) typology identifies four different types of tourists:

- the organized mass tourist

- the individual mass tourist

- the explorer

- the drifter

Each of these tourist types embodies unique characteristics that influence their likelihood to immerse themselves with the host culture, or alternatively, remain within the confines of their touring companions, thus minimizing discomfort or culture shock. Organized mass tourists and individual mass tourists never fully immerse themselves into an environment as familiarity is a fundamental concern for them. They tend to 'look' at the host from within the relative security afforded by their traveling companions. The individual mass tourist differs slightly from the organized tourist type in that their tours are not entirely pre-planned, however, both descriptions fit closely with a particular mode of tourist behavior.

Explorers and drifters vary in the degree to which they communicate, immerse and learn from the host communities. The explorer is similar to the ecotourist in that they both travel individually and get 'off the beaten track'. They do leave the 'environmental bubble' yet unlike the ecotourist, they often require comfortable accommodation with reliable transport. They travel primarily to interact with other cultures but again, unlike the ecotourist, they are not necessarily motivated by the desire to experience the natural environment.

Cohen's (1972) final tourist type is the drifter. This tourist ventures furthest off the beaten track and wholly immerses themselves into a community's customs and culture, where novelty is of utmost importance and all familiarity disappears. The levels of social interaction with the host culture and environment are maximized by this form of tourist, particularly in comparison to the mass tourist (Cohen, 1972). Again this tourist type is similar to the ecotourist in that they are motivated by a desire for 'experiences' but they are not necessarily traveling principally to experience natural areas scenery.

These differences in interaction between tourist types and the social environment can be contextualized broadly with reference to the notion of tourism 'authenticity'. MacCannell (1976) sees tourism as a modern functional substitute for the spiritual aspects of religion that have diminished in social significance as a result of the alienation of modern man from 'traditional' modes of life and therefore of perceiving the world. This shift from traditional institutional bonds has caused man to seek the 'real' life of others, that is, what are perceived as 'authentic' modes of life and cultures.

MacCannell proposed a continuum of tourist settings across six stages, each denoting a level of authenticity gained from specific tourist experiences. Stage One describes the social space that tourists attempt to overcome or penetrate, such as tourism facilities, institutional cultural sites, etc. This 'front stage' often suffices for organized mass tourists, as it is constructed specifically for their benefit: 'Tourists commonly take guided tours of social establishments because they provide easy access to areas of the establishment ordinarily closed to outsiders' (1976: 98). At the furthest end of the continuum is Stage Six which denotes the back region, where there is limited (if any) access to outsiders, a region where it is perceived that 'authentic' cultural representations take place (MacCannell, 1976).

Although MacCannell identifies that mainstream tourist's experience 'staged authenticity' as a general rule, he also recognizes that on occasion's mainstream tourists do have intimate involvement with the social environment. Nevertheless, he also recognizes that often these authentic experiences happen by accident: 'The tourist is passive; he [sic] expects interesting things to happen to him' (Boorstin cited in MacCannell, 1976: 104).

The constructed nature of the 'authentic' experience is often facilitated by the tour guide's instruction, mediated through the perceptions and choice of information conveyed. Boorstin recognizes the importance of the guide in influencing a tourist stating that 'a good guide, working in the correct context, provides a relatively safe and secure milieu for the tourist to collect those authentic experiences which fulfil the individual's motivation for travelling' (Pearce, 1984: 136). Periera (2005: 1) adds 'given the intangibility of the ecotourism product...the guide defines the quality of the product...drawing the tourist toward or away from sustainable practices, and significantly contributes to the success or failure of the ecotouristic venture'. Operators often underestimate the value that ecotourists place on knowledgeable guides who have the ability to interpret the environmental and cultural landscapes (Gardner and McArthur, 1995).

An ecotourist is generally likely to have obtained a detailed knowledge of the local environment pre-departure. However, ecotourists are not immune to inaccurate information given by the guide, as they also rely on the guide for this.

Not only is the information given by the guide important, but also whether the tourist remembers the information is also important, as it will affect the tourist's behavior: 'the tourist's own experience and knowledge; and the features of the setting at hand would appear to be a major requirement for promoting the tourist's memory and the recall of the setting' (Pearce, 1984: 143). This would imply that, in general, a heightened awareness of the environment for the ecotourist would result in a better retention of the information given by the guide regarding those environments. Therefore, the guide's role in influencing a tourist's behavior can be problematic. The mainstream tourist receives a 'mainstream' guide (by that it is meant that the guide elaborates in less detail about specific sites and caters to the sightseeing needs of the mainstream tourist) while the ecotourist receives a more descriptive and environmentally aware guide to cater for their inherent interest. In addition, the ecotourist retains more of the guide's information about the environment than the mainstream tourist does, as the ecotourist has traveled with a specific interest in the topic of environmental impact and interaction. Therefore, it seems inevitable that the ecotourist must behave differently to the mainstream tourist, as in general, they have access to better and more detailed information. This information allows them to act more environmentally consciously. The mainstream tourist does not have the same opportunity to behave more like the ecotourist, because the nature of the information they receive does not assist in guiding their behavior to be environmentally sensitive to the same degree.

Up to this point we have discussed the differences between the ecotourist and the mainstream tourist's interactions with their social and environmental surroundings. As we have seen, ecotourists generally have, and seek, an intimate understanding of the environment, which is not an essential factor for mainstream tourists. Therefore, it may seem obvious that the biggest differences between the behavior of the ecotourist and the mainstream tourist lie in their interaction with the physical environment.

From the perspective of the physical environment, ecotourism and mainstream tourism play very different roles. The ecotourist ideally enters a destination in the 'discovery and emergence' stage of the 'tourism destination product life cycle' (Prosser, 1994: 23). This means that an ecotourist is an 'explorer' or someone who seeks the wilderness, or unspoilt areas, for the natural and cultural assets contained within the region before others have the chance to make a noticeable impact (Chan and Baum, 2007). In contrast, the mainstream tourist would be involved in a destination in all of the stages of the life cycle after the initial discovery and emergence stage.[28] However, the logical conclusion of placing ecotourism within the tourism destination product life cycle is the inevitable saturation and decline of an area through the emergence of mainstream tourism to the region once it is 'discovered'. Does it really matter then if ecotourists and mainstream tourists behave differently if the eventual outcome of an ecotourist entering a site is the eventual invasion of mass tourism, hence the region's destruction?

A tourist's attitude relates significantly to their behavior toward the physical environment. It has been widely recognized that mainstream tourists generally tend to have a less environmentally conscious attitude when on holiday:

> *When on holiday…we may give little thought to whether such thought is socially or environmentally acceptable in our chosen destination, and indeed, if we are aware, we may rationalise that we have paid and they have taken our money, so we are entitled to take our holiday as we wish. (Prosser 1994: 32)*

---

[28] These successive stages include 'growing popularity and fashion', 'saturation', 'fading fashion' and 'decline'.

Ecotourists, as we have seen, actively seek to minimize the impacts that they have on a destination. However, while the individual ecotourist may independently minimize their impacts, the management of the natural area to which they are traveling determines whether the impacts are minimized overall: 'Trekking tourists in the Nepalese Himalayas would almost without exception declare themselves to be eco-conscious or green, yet they too are pushing against the carrying capacity and hence the sustainability of the regional environment' (Prosser, 1994: 33). Therefore, while the individual ecotourist may behave differently to the mainstream tourist in respect to the physical environment, ecotourists as a group, can potentially create similar impacts on the physical environment as a group of mainstream tourists. Holden and Sparrowhawk add with regards to trekking in the Nepalese Himalayas:

> The future of Annapurna should not be jeopardised by the old fashioned, yet still common notion, that success in tourism is measured by an increasing number of visitor arrivals. Instead ongoing strategic planning for the area is required, which as well as including land use and carrying capacity measures, needs to consider marketing and the type of tourist that is compatible with the environmental surroundings of the area. In this sense, the motivational research of tourists has a part to play not only in strategic business decisions, but also in strategic environmental decisions. (2002: 445)

As we have noted mainstream tourists tend to visit established destinations, places where the physical environment has been developed to a considerable degree and tourism infrastructure is in place. Ecotourism, however, is often associated with travel to more remote and environmentally sensitive locations. The common thread which ties ecotourists and mainstream tourists is the behavior of moving from one destination to another for new experiences. Mainstream tourists do not necessarily need to behave like an ecotourist in the respect of limiting impacts to the natural environment, as the physical environment is not as fragile as those areas often utilized by ecotourists (although the cultural and social environments may be as fragile).

One potential catalyst for the difference in the behavior of tourists is the perception that the individual has knowledge of what 'minimal impacts' actually are. Often people do not make changes to benefit the environment until they realize that it is damaged. However, the ecotourist is preventative in attempting to ameliorate impacts from the moment of initiating travel and by striving to leave the environment as they find it – an objective not always shared by mainstream tourists: 'For every traveller prepared to meet the wilderness on its own terms, there exists hundreds of others who demand that it be modified for their use with the provision of surfaced roads, cafeterias, toilets, parking, picnic facilities and a range of other amenities' (Todd, 1989). This alone exemplifies the major difference in the behavior of ecotourists and mainstream tourists toward the environment visited: ecotourist behavior is determined according to the environment while the mainstream tourist adapts the environment to suit his or her usual behavior.

ECONOMIC DIFFERENCES

Economic conditions are also fundamental to understanding the differences in behavior between the ecotourist and the mainstream tourist. Economic based analysis of the destination region results in identification of a number of key differences in impacts (both direct and indirect) by ecotourists relative to mainstream tourists. A balance of economic impacts in any tourism region is dependent on the characteristics of the economy (e.g. size, level of development and linkages), the type of goods and services demanded (or supplied in the case of ecotourism), the type of tourism and ownership of services, infrastructure and superstructure. Due to the fact that the levels of development for ecotourism in the destination region are likely to be reduced relative to mainstream tourism, goods and services are produced in limited supply, based on the carrying capacity of the region, and ownership is more likely to be local.

Mainstream tourism often occurs in cities and towns, whereas ecotourism most often involves villages or smaller communities. Destination regions benefit from ecotourism, as the ecotourist attempts to minimize cultural, social and physical impacts, while creating beneficial economic impacts, purchasing local goods and services. The ecotourist does not demand that local communities engage in extensive infrastructure development or changes in their normal cultural practices. Mainstream tourists, however, require that the products and services supplied 'must reach the required standards' of the tourist (Vellas and Becherel, 1995: 319). This is an example of the 'environmental bubble' whereby tourists need to recreate that which is found in their home country and determines the satisfaction of the tourism experience.

Similarly, the nature of ecotourism development – small scale with minimal social and environmental impacts – reduces the likelihood of economic leakages to external owners, operators and investors (e.g. Rinne and Saastamoinen, 2005). Leakages are likely to be high if:

- the economy is small with a limited range of domestically produced goods and services
- there is a high propensity to import goods and service provision
- there is a low level of local ownership of tourist facilities
- there is a high proportion of transient imported labor

These are often characteristics of developing countries, whose adoption of ecotourism in some instances has reversed the high leakages dictated by the previous structuring of their tourism industries. However, in some cases even ecotourism is not immune to the problems highlighted above (e.g. Mazibuko, 2007).

CASE STUDY: Ecuador

In Capirona, Ecuador, a community of 24 Quichua Indian families have chosen ecotourism as the most appropriate form of economic development. This community demonstrated a dependence on economic returns from crops (which had become insufficient), and sought ecotourism as a form of industry that directly benefits the community, whilst minimizing leakage. With the growth in visitor numbers to the Quichua communities, these new spin off ecotourism ventures have apparently achieved rapid financial success. The Rio Blanco Community Ecotourism Project, for example, was able to repay all of the loans used to finance construction and development costs, within its first year of operations. The community's intention is to increase the number of visitors to around 300 per year, but not more. According to reports, these Quichua communities have successfully established tourism ventures, which provide cash income from uncleared primary forests and make a significant, but not dominant contribution to a diversified economy, with relatively little negative social or environmental impacts associated specifically with tourism (Buckley, 2003: 146).

Individual's perception of the environment has a profound influence on how it is experienced: 'Both perceptual distortion and the expectations we bring to the environment effect the role we play in it. People develop selective and unique conceptions' (Ittelson et al., 1974: 14). The expectations of a tourist therefore play a large part in the way a tourist behaves. They also determine if a destination will satisfy the tourist's needs, i.e. if the expectations meet the experience. Considering that ecotourists and mainstream tourists are motivated to travel by different desires it is understandable that tourists will hold different expectations requiring the satisfaction of different experiences. An ecotourist is seeking education about a region along with the experience of both natural and cultural environments and may not be satisfied by the 'pseudo' events (Boorstin, 1972) that are dominating the tourist market. As we have seen, ecotourists will seek to educate themselves about the destination site prior to departure and will therefore have some knowledge about the destination. The mainstream tourist, however, 'seldom likes the authentic product of the foreign culture; he prefers his own provincial expectations' (Boorstin, 1972: 106). These expectations are often greater than the destination may provide and is often satisfied by a 'commodified' experience.

Service providers such as tour operators can manage the tourist and ensure satisfaction by providing a tour which fulfills the needs of the different tourist types. For a tour operator who is to provide the total ecotourist experience, the tour must enhance a genuine environmental experience whereby the tourist learns and communicates with the host environment.

The management of tourists is undertaken to control and influence tourist behavior, thus seeking to minimize the impacts of tourism on communities and on the environment. This chapter has shown that ecotourists and mainstream tourists differ in their behavior to an extent so it stands to reason the management systems implemented for these two types of tourists will be different: The difference in behavior between the ecotourist and the mainstream tourist relates directly to the fact that the attitude and motivation for traveling are very different between the two groups. Ecotourists travel to experience natural environments, to educate themselves about these areas. Mainstream tourists on the other hand travel to satisfy leisure, pleasure and recreational needs. Therefore differing customer perceptions, needs, attitudes, levels of environmental stewardship and likely impacts must be considered by operators – both managers and marketers – natural area managers, and local communities when considering this market segment.

FURTHER READING

Wight, P.A. (2000). Ecotourists: not a homogeneous market segment. In *The Encyclopedia of Ecotourism* (D.B. Weaver, ed.). CAB International, Wallingford, UK, pp. 37–62.

Wight's chapter provides a comprehensive overview of the market for ecotourism. Particular areas of focus include the identity of ecotourists, ecotourists and their trip characteristics, their origins and destinations, motivations and levels of satisfaction.

Holden, A., & Sparrowhawk, J. (2002) Understanding the motivations of ecotourists: the case of trekkers in Annapurna, Nepal. *International Journal of Tourism Research*, 4(6), 435–46.

Holden and Sparrowhawk investigate the intrinsic motivations of ecotourists visiting the Annapurna area of the Nepalese Himalaya's, providing a number of recommendations on how ecotourism destinations can be managed and how the success of such ventures should be measured.

CHAPTER 10

Ecotourism: A Model for Sustainable Development?

We currently live in a world dominated by neo-liberal political ideologies where market forces and their rationalist philosophies underpin our social and economic organization, where 'good' decisions are deemed to be those that are able to identify and provide a tangible and measurable balance of benefits, adjudicated by cost-benefit ratios and statistical quantification. However, as we have seen, little, if any, accord is given to the principles and values that underpin such evaluations. Whilst the western world aspires to increase the range of low-cost goods and efficiency of production and provision of services, it reaps instability in the global labor market, the financial markets and environmental degradation in the form of atmospheric pollution, biodiversity decline and land degradation (Beck, 1992) – all of which are leading to catastrophic climate change in the form of global warming.

Just as wilderness and natural areas are in marked decline, both in terms of quality and quantity, demand for tourism to these areas is increasing markedly. However, tourism as an industry deserves significant criticism, not least because in many cases it contributes to the decline of natural areas. Tourism is dominated by the developed western countries with tourist marketer's increasingly designing, planning and implementing tourism into developing countries. However, without inclusive processes that in the least utilize consultation with the host communities, or ideally where development of these projects is controlled by local communities, there is always the danger of imposing a cultural hegemony. Once established, cultural hegemony means that the values of the tourist culture not only encroach on and often destroy the host culture, but also reinforce the narrow perceptions and representations of these cultures through western eyes.[29]

CONTENTS

Developing Tourism
Partnerships

Sustainable Models
and Ecotourism

Climate Change and
Ecotourism

Volunteering and
Ecotourism

Impacts, Potentials
and Possibilities

Further Reading

---

[29] See, for example, Aitchison (2001), Edensor (1998), Favero (2007), van der Duim et al. (2005) and Wearing and Wearing (2006).

The tourism industry often does not acknowledge that 'explicitly or implicitly, every debate on policy is a debate about values' (Stretton, 1976: 3–18) and yet decisions are made on approaches, projects and practices without considering the effect of values, especially their own, on their work. The transfer of methods, techniques and practices from mass tourism approaches to ecotourism practices without reassessment of their relevance or appropriateness has been problematic.

The analysis and outcomes are therefore likely to perpetuate the mode of practice rather than find appropriate alternatives. Ecotourism has often been defined and debated from within this frame, often as little more than a 'niche market'. However, as we have seen ecotourism is one of many forms of 'alternative' tourism that are influenced by recent philosophic, social and environmental shifts. Indeed they are all oriented by a change in current value systems *(see Table 10.1)*.

Despite claims to the contrary, ecotourism has not simply allowed the tourism industry to significantly expand in market scope. Its significance lies in its ability to offer alternative approaches to the industry's operational practices. These 'alternative' paradigms make possible an increase in the breadth and depth of understanding of the industry. Specific philosophical approaches such as ecocentrism, ecofeminism and environmentalism as we have seen pose significant questions for the tourism industry in their challenge to the economic rationalist practices in tourism. From an ecocentrically informed perspective ecotourism is not just an 'industry' or an activity undertaken in the natural environment; it is intended to be an experience that an individual or group has that affects their attitudes, values and actions. Ecotourism then is as much about environmental education, the fostering of attitudes and behavior that is conducive to maintaining natural environments and empowerment of host communities as it is about fostering a sustainable industry. Ecotourism can therefore be said to have three primary objectives, as both an industry and as a form of tourist experience: sustainability, conservation and empowerment of host communities. The unifying concern is one living in harmony with nature and recognizing the intrinsic value in beings other than humans (Haywood, 1988). That is, it is concerned with the relationship between humanity and nature, with the intention of making that relationship more equitable.

In contrast to more conventional forms of tourism, ecotourism is unique in its ecocentric focus along with education, personal growth and other intrinsic values underlying travel motivation. Ecotourists tend to be highly focused on these intrinsic values and, unlike other tourist forms, they pursue these goals 'with high levels of physical and mental rigour' (Williams, 1990: 83). Many ecotourism activities combine physical activities such as trekking,

Table 10.1 Concerns of Mass Tourism and Alternative Paradigm (Ecotourism) Views (Maguire, 1987: 12)	
Mass Tourism	**Alternative Tourism**
1. Management of 'evolutionary' change (survival of the fittest) within a western neo-liberal rationalist approach based on free market economic principles	1. Radical change moving toward cooperatives and community-based approaches outside of the existing tourism industry
2. Maintaining social order, existing tourism systems unquestioned	2. Transforming social systems, analyzing structural conflicts and contradictions and including nature in the equation
3. Greater efficiency of current tourism systems, hence increased profitability	3. Creating more just and equitable systems that can step beyond the tourism system
4. Appearance of harmony, integration and cohesion of social groups involved in the tourism process	4. Contradictions between social ideals and reality, attempts to demonstrate this and alleviate it
5. Focus on ways to maintain cohesion and consensus	5. Ways to dismantle or change systems of domination
6. Solidarity	6. Emancipation and liberation
7. Identifying and meeting individual needs within existing social system	7. Current tourism systems incapable of equitably meeting basic human needs
8. Focused on actuality, discovering and understanding what is	8. Focused on potentiality: providing a vision of what could be

cycling and kayaking with environmental awareness raising pursuits. Experience of indigenous foods and customs occurs in close proximity to learning about native flora and fauna. Thus ecotourism activities focus on active appreciative endeavors (Swanson, 1992).

A feminist perspective will not be concerned with identifying the target market of ecotourism and their level of satisfaction; rather it will be concerned with understanding the range of experiences of all participants in ecotourism (host and guest) and explaining why these patterns of experience exist (Wearing and Wearing, 1999). It will also be concerned with identifying sites of oppression and possible processes to overcome such oppression. A feminist perspective is important here because ecotourism, like other elements of the tourism industry, has the potential to reflect a modernistic commodified paradigm where

> the environment and its inhabitants (human and non human) are dominated by scientific, industry and other interests that treat these primarily as means to an end, that is, instrumentally. (Jamal, Borges and Stronza, 2006: 145)

Feminism will look for and question male-defined concepts such as globalization and anthropocentrism, which will limit the interpretation to male-defined concepts. As such, feminism would examine the:

- ecotourist's experience

- access to ecotourism experiences

- access to power and decision-making in the management of ecotourism

- host's experience

In exploring ecotourism the question of who participates, who makes decisions and who controls the structure of the ecotourist experience will be pursued. A feminist paradigm would highlight and identify as one issue of concern, the narrow socio-economic group which constitutes the ecotourism 'market'. That is, feminism identifies the issue of equity of access. The issue is of concern not only because of the inherent imbalance of opportunity which reflects a system of oppression, but also because the issue needs to be addressed in order to fulfill the original agenda of ecotourism itself. Remember that ecotourism aspires to educate visitors about the value of natural environments, however, without considering the equity of access the current 'target market' will simply be 'preaching to the converted'. In addition, equity is an issue because ecotourism activities principally occur within publicly owned resources and according to current (but possibly changing) community views access should not be limited to elite groups (Swain and Swain, 2004). As we have seen ecotourism has great potential for its ability to be both a tool for conservation and sustainable development. Ecotourism appears to present us with one of the few activities where the link between economic development and conservation of natural areas is potentially clear and direct. However, these links have not led to the expected benefits for many communities or conservation groups, particularly because in many cases the dominance of short-term profit orientated goals becomes dominant. Clearly, where there has been innovation and new management practices which separate ecotourism from mass tourism, positive outcomes have occurred. Partnerships will be an important component of these innovations which can see ecotourism benefiting both parks and local communities. In a commodified market place ecotourism also cannot exist without government regulation or strong delegation of management authority to the regional or local levels, otherwise ecotourism in most places would not differ from mass tourism. The challenge for ecotourism planners will be to establish regulations and incentives so that socio-economic benefits are generated, and appropriately distributed, from activities which are culturally and ecologically sustainable (Sharpley and Telfer, 2002).

Unfortunately, however, government has also seen it as a panacea for development problems: a solution for lack of employment, foreign exchange and capital for infrastructure. In formulating projects a lack of thought and direction has resulted, in many cases ecotourism has not lived up to the expectations in terms of creating revenues for conservation or creating alternative income sources for communities. It is regarded by many social scientists, and many tourists themselves, with increasing skepticism given the increasing documentation of its environmental record, cultural impact and the quality of jobs it has created. In a majority of countries, ecotourism has been promoted by government or industry without an overall strategy, effective protected area management plans and without consultation or inclusion of local communities. While local communities do receive benefits from ecotourism, these benefits are most frequently in the form of seasonal or low-paying jobs. At the community level, ecotourism may generate increased revenues, provide for more infrastructures such as roads and electricity or proceeds from ecotourism may be directed to community projects such as school construction and health clinics, but this has to be clearly identified and specified in its development. Additionally, it has to be made clear to these local communities that these benefits may be offset by interference in their daily lives and resultant cultural changes. When outside control or profit oriented segments of the local community dominate the decision-making process often the low-impact scale of ecotourism is exceeded and it takes on the characteristics of mass tourism, with increased traffic, pollution, sequestering of profits by outsiders and rising local prices all becoming significant problems. This model of development parallels that of developing countries' economies when dominated by a developed nation's agenda and the World Bank.

The effectiveness of ecotourism in the future will ultimately depend on who will benefit, as well as where, when and how it can be appropriately implemented: all of which is dependent on a wide range of actions, all of which are underpinned by the philosophical approaches we have discussed in Chapter 2, particularly in relation to their implementation planning and management frameworks.

Underpinning this approach is a need for support from local communities, and to best investigate this support and involve these communities in an empowered way there is a need to use community development approaches. A community development approach advocates that change comes from within communities not outside, and that power and decision-making associated with that change should be community-driven and controlled. An initiative that would be relevant for ecotourism is community-based conservation (CBC) which arises from within the community (Davidson et al., 2006). A variety of terms have been used such as joint management (Hill and Press cited in Western and Wright, 1994: 499) and co-management (Brechin et al. cited in West and Brechin, 1991: 5), all of which can be operationalized by organizations like the World Bank and World Tourism Organization (WTO) if they are willing to embrace the alternative paradigms offered through ecotourism. Ecotourism, from this perspective, is therefore concerned that communities retain and exercise control in ecotourism development and implementation. That is, from a community development perspective one of the central issues is equity of power between community, state, individual and corporate enterprise.

DEVELOPING TOURISM PARTNERSHIPS

Ecotourism has facilitated a major change in the relationship between host communities and tourism development. Since its recognition, there has been a movement away from developing a site or region without any consultation between local residents and development bodies. Even now their needs and concerns are not always heard; however, ecotourism and other alternative forms of tourism have recognized that partnerships between local people, the private sector and government open up a range of opportunities that would not be available to any one group. Most of these partnership arrangements are of recent origin: most are accepted because they make good economic sense and benefit all partners.

Some partnerships will be born of necessity, for example, the need for local communities to market their destination to a wider audience with images that represent for them what they really are rather than what some marketers would like to sell them as.[30] Other linkages may result from a need for greater flexibility in management where areas of the natural environment are closed off to tourism only because of international conservation guidelines that have no relevance to that local community's situation. These sorts of conflicts have led to the development of partnerships between governments and Non-Government Organizations (NGOs) (or community-based organizations), where management is delegated to the NGO/community group who are often in a much better position to act with the community in their interest.

An example of this can be seen in Barkin and Bouchez's (2002) study of Bahias de Huatulco on the Pacific coast of Oaxaca, Mexico. In this example the indigenous communities of the area were suffering as a result of the degradation of their forests through logging and the various impacts of a mega international tourist resort on the areas' beaches. With the support of a local non-governmental organization (the Centre for Ecological Support) which was set up with the assistance of Oaxaca regional government, the local communities are now managing their forest more sustainably and have created a local wildlife reserve through the support and assistance of ecotourism ventures in the area. Examples such as these illustrate how NGOs might contribute to reconciling the competing interests over natural resources as well as recognizing the unique role that NGOs can play in facilitating community participation and involvement.

NGOs have been typically critical of tourism and have often campaigned against tourist resorts (or planned developments) that have led to environmental degradation, child prostitution and sex tourism generally, the exploitation of developing countries land and water resources and the flow of income from tourism into the hands of foreign developers as opposed to local communities whose resources tourism is often dependent (Holden and Mason, 2005). However, it is becoming more common to see NGOs becoming actively involved in sustainable tourism ventures such as the example above, the World Wildlife Fund for Nature in Greece (Svoronou and Holden, 2005), or the Zambezi Society in the Zambezi Bioregion (Sithole, 2005). It is argued that NGOs are uniquely placed to form partnerships with local communities to plan, fund, develop and operate sustainable tourism ventures because they prioritize sustainable development processes

---

[30] Cunningham's (2006) study provides an example of how 'social valuing' can be used as an alternative basis for communicating messages about the value of a destination.

(economic, environmental, social) and emphasize host–community interactions (Wearing et al., 2005).

New ways of looking at partnerships between the government and the private sector have allowed the private sector to manage operations and run concessions in places where the government lacked the resources, capacity and investment, such as accommodation in national parks (e.g. Darcy and Wearing, in press; MacKinnon et al., 1986). Interesting partnerships have started between governments and local people, such as at Uluru, in Australia, where joint management arrangements have created new approaches and more refined equitable ways of organizing tourism.

New mechanisms and arrangements are constantly being devised with an increasing number of partners, including many that are often not considered by more mainstream tourism organizations, and with the global recognition of ecotourism international industry donors have come to play a role. For example, United States Aid Programme (USAID) is promoting a tourism strategy called Low Impact Tourism (LIT). LIT focuses on establishing indigenous natural resource management through private sector initiatives and investment in rural village-based tourism business infrastructure. Rural communities would get a percentage of the tourism revenues, employment benefits and improved infrastructure (Lillywhite, 1992) while international donors can provide water turbines or other technology-based infrastructure to the markets that have not needed this before ecotourism came to these remote areas.

However, though bringing many partners to the table offers the strengths of the combined organizations, it can make coordination and decision-making quite cumbersome. In such cases, ecotourism development may seem akin to a large integrated development project, with many of the difficulties that these projects face. Projects with fewer partners may be more manageable, but may require high levels of coordination with other agencies. Ecotourism then provides the catalyst for the development of improving processes for decision-making while giving an initial framework that may allow attempts to reach partnership agreements based on a shared vision.

Ecotourism, for example, would suggest that for equity to be established in say national parks and other conservation areas which are used extensively for tourism there needs to be trust and respect between the traditional custodians of the land and the more recently arrived park management agencies. This respect and trust can only come through recognition within the tourism industry of other ways of practicing; this can lead to more equitable outcomes. For this to happen, both parties must understand the other's culture in order to come to terms with each other's interpretation and perceptual view of any given situation. This understanding requires facilitation across what is often a significant cultural divide. The role of culture in interpersonal dealings is more fully explained below:

> *cultural learning's influence the perception of other people. Developing crosscultural understanding involves perceiving members of other cultural groups positively. By understanding the basic principles of person perception, and the natural effects of one's own cultural experience and learning's on perceiving other people, unproductive explanations of crosscultural misunderstandings as prejudice or even just differences may be replaced with productive methods of avoiding misunderstandings and stimulating positive perceptions of other people. How we perceive other people affects how we behave towards them and how they, in turn, behave towards us. (Robinson, 1988: 49)*

Placing external definitions and ways of life (such as tourism) on people and communities can affect the lives of those people in far-reaching ways (Wearing and McDonald, 2002). Ecotourism tends to acknowledge when working with the marginalized sectors of society that may already be dealing with stereotypes and misconceptions placed upon them by the society in general (Eckermann and Dowd, 1988). It is thus desirable to work with flexible models that are more open to express individual characteristics of a subject group. For example, in telling a story about defining Aborigines, their lands and their cultures, Barlow makes four points:

> *Aborigines have never had to define themselves, their cultures or their lands – that definition was made in the time before time when the great ancestral creative beings brought into existence land, people, and Law. All other definitions have been made by people who are not Aborigines for their own reasons. People who are not Aborigines continue to define Aborigines, their cultures and their lands for their own reasons. These definitions are effectively imposed on Aborigines so that they are impelled to act in accordance with them. (Barlow, 1991: 57)*

It can be seen that the underlying philosophies of these paradigms are significant to the manner in which ecotourism is examined and interpreted, and that these approaches take into consideration the original driving philosophy of ecotourism. There is a danger of losing the principal ethical ideas that surround ecotourism without utilization of these paradigms.

In addition to influencing what we see in the world, paradigms map out expectations or operating norms within our respective disciplines. What is needed is a deconstructive approach to how we think, write and practice tourism, a reflexive analysis of both the desire that motivates theory and the presuppositions that structure knowledge. The very ambiguity of ecotourism lends itself to a theoretical and research approach that is itself about the movement of meaning and embodiment.

We believe that ecotourism can offer a clearly defined philosophical approach as shown in Chapter 2, and in doing this it has expanded the tourism paradigm beyond positivism and logocentrism, ecotourism is able to achieve environmental sustainability and its affiliated social goals. These goals include the minimization of damage to natural resources, education of ecotourists to conservation values, access of the tourism experience beyond a 'converted and elite' group and the distribution of the rewards to local communities.

Ecotourism represents an alternative approach to tourism. That, is the thinking around ecotourism is derived equally if not dominated by alternative paradigms which will allow ecotourism to be placed outside of the current dominant framework to challenge contemporary tourism practices.

Ecotourism generates benefits for biodiversity conservation and can often succeed in meeting conditions which cannot be met in other activities. It often allows partnership where sites are competitive and the protected area authorities have the capacity and jurisdictional mandates to design, implement and manage sustainable ecotourism consistent with their protected area objectives through having a workable framework in ecotourism. Fees can be levied that reflect the true cost of tourism and site protection. Finally, they have mechanisms where revenues from fees can be allocated to the parks and can be applied toward priorities in overall biodiversity conservation in the country. These frameworks have been difficult to establish prior to the recognition of ecotourism.

SUSTAINABLE MODELS AND ECOTOURISM

'Sustainable development' has been a much talked about model for development in a policy context, with conferences such as The United Nations Climate Change Conference 2007 in Bali, Indonesia and the Vth World Congress on National Parks and Protected Areas 2003 in Durban, South Africa. However, the mechanisms for local communities to participate in tourism only came about through the phenomenon of ecotourism. Local communities should learn about impacts, options and possibilities of ecotourism development, explore means for ownership of specific ecotourism ventures and consider strategies for ecotourism as compensation for restricted access to protected areas, including coordinated investments in local infrastructure and services that improve local quality of life and collection of local user fees from tourists which support local development initiatives.

Governments have found that it provides approaches to supplement ongoing activities by improving existing policy, including requiring the development of ecotourism strategies as components of government documents as well as clarifying the jurisdictional mandates and responsibilities of agencies involved in ecotourism planning and management. In addition, governments were able to justify developing pricing policies for use in protected area sites which reflect the social cost of operating and maintaining such areas and could decentralize responsibility for area-specific ecotourism, strategies and developments.

Additionally, many governments support the collection of user fees from tourists. However, in many cases these fees are often appropriated into general revenue rather than to maintain and improve the quality of parks and protected areas by the development of facilities which are environmentally and culturally appropriate in scale, construction and context. Similarly, broader principles also need to be adopted such as introducing sound environmental practices including waste reduction and recycling; and to explore joint ventures and partnerships with local communities, NGOs, and other organizations for ecotourism development.

NGOs and academic institutions who have supported the development of the tourism industry have found, in ecotourism, a mechanism with which to practice sustainability. In this context, they are able to have a clarified role in the industry, such as acting as intermediaries between the private sector and local interests in ecotourism development. Similarly, they can identify technologies and products that are produced or used locally and which are economically and environmentally sustainable in order to reduce waste, provide local groups with training, technical assistance and information necessary to participate in the benefits and employment opportunities from ecotourism. Lastly, they can collect information, monitor and evaluate ecotourism development.

CLIMATE CHANGE AND ECOTOURISM

Since the first edition of this book climate change has become the single biggest environmental issue to face the planet. As tourism of any sort – including ecotourism – involves the movement of people from one place to another it contributes to the growing emissions of greenhouse causing gases.

The most problematic form of transport in terms of global warming, and the one most readily associated with tourism, is flying. Of all forms of transport aircraft emit the highest amount of carbon per passenger, and they emit carbon at altitudes that are far more damaging than emissions produced at ground level. At present aircraft contribute to 5% of all carbon emissions and this percentage is expected to rise as the number of commercial passenger journeys increases from 200 million in 2003 to 470 million by 2030, representing the world's fastest growing source of greenhouse gases (Friends of the Earth, 2008). One solution to this problem is carbon trading, or carbon offsetting which is defined as:

> *any trading system designed to offset carbon emissions from one activity (such as burning fossil fuels in manufacturing, driving, or flying) with another (such as installing more efficient technologies, planting carbon-reducing plants, or establishing contracts with others not to partake in carbon-releasing activities). (Dictionary of Sustainable Management, 2008)*

Possibilities for offsetting carbon emissions include schemes such as 'Climate Care' which offer tour operators or holidaymakers the opportunity to pay a voluntary levy on air travel into a fund that supports renewable energy and forest sequestration projects (WWF, 2001: 1). Other options include choosing accommodation and destinations that make use of renewable forms of energy supply such as wind, biomass and solar, and which adhere to high efficiency standards. Where possible tourist transport destinations need to include buses, rail, walking and cycling. For travel to short-haul destinations rail and coach should be used as opposed to flying, as these two options emit far lower levels of carbon per passenger (WWF, 2001: 2–3).

Ecotourists are usually attracted to accommodation of the type mentioned above and typically undertake activities such as walking, cycling, kayaking and cross-country skiing as a part of viewing and enjoying nature, however, the issue of flying still remains and it is one in which ecotourists currently cause the same level of impact as mainstream tourists. While carbon trading or carbon offsetting provide a possible amelioration of carbon emissions, such a solution is highly problematic and it has virtually no support among the world's foremost environmental NGOs. At the moment carbon offsetting policies and procedures have yet to be agreed upon internationally and there is no national or international body that exists to monitor and enforce them.

Climate change is also having a dramatic effect on the environment of many ecotourism destinations. As ecotourists are primarily interested in visiting areas of scenic beauty and biological diversity, the success and sustainability of ecotourism are highly dependent on the health and well-being of these ecosystems. Global warming is already effecting ecotourism destinations around the world. These include coral reefs which are been bleached by increases in sea temperature and high irradiance, wildlife populations in many protected areas are moving or dying out, glaciers in mountain and arctic regions are receding and beaches and low lying islands are slowly disappearing due to rising sea levels. The supply then of ecotourism destinations is under threat, posing the single biggest challenge to the industry.

VOLUNTEERING AND ECOTOURISM

One area of ecotourism that has been growing rapidly over the last decade is 'volunteer tourism'. Like ecotourism, volunteer tourism emphasizes positive interactions between tourists and local communities based on travelers visiting a destination and taking part in some form of project that makes a positive difference to social, economic and/or environmental conditions of the area visited. Projects are commonly nature-based, people-based or involve the restoration of buildings and artefacts. Wearing defines volunteer tourists as those who:

> volunteer in an organised way to undertake holidays that may involve the aiding or alleviating the material poverty of some groups in society, the restoration of certain environments, or research into aspects of society or environment. (2001: 1)

Figures on volunteer tourism remain sketchy but market researchers Mintel valued the gap year at $5bn in 2005, predicting it to rise to $20bn by 2015. In the UK it is estimated that 200,000 people between the ages of 18 and 25 take time out to travel abroad each year for an extended period (usually 6–12 months), often undertaking some form of volunteer work as a part of their travels, and spending on average $9500 each (Bowes, 2005). The Travel Industry Association (TIA) in the United States indicates that up to 55 million Americans have taken some type of volunteer vacation at sometime in their lives (TIA, 2008).

In order to take advantage of this rising interest there has been a substantial growth in the number of organizations offering volunteer tourism programs (Brown and Morrison, 2003). Many travelers, particularly younger travelers, are looking for experiences that go beyond the traditional passive holiday. They want to become immersed in the local culture and contribute their time and expertise to something that makes a positive difference, not only for a local community but also for themselves. Mustonen (2005) suggests that volunteer tourism is closely related to modern backpacking tourism yet is motivated by a different set of values, most notably altruism. The focus on altruism 'giving something back' means that volunteer tourism is an ideal form of decommodified ecotourism as it overcomes the problems associated with tourism in general, and ecotourism specifically (Gray and Campbell, 2007).

Environmental volunteering, which is most closely associated with ecotourism, has become a popular activity. The nature of environmental projects often requires overnight travel to a destination situated in a remote and rural area. Gray and Campbell (2007) note that the UK Earthwatch Institute has sent more than 72,000 paying volunteers on scientific research expeditions since its founding in 1971. Other organizations such as Conservation Volunteers Australia and the British Trust for Conservation Volunteers have been growing rapidly in the last 20 years reflecting a similar interest and motivation for environmental volunteering. For the ecotourism industry volunteer tourism represents a new market with the potential for significant growth *(see Fig. 10.1)*.

Nevertheless, like all rapidly expanding industries volunteer tourism is experiencing a number of teething problems. The first and most widely publicized is the proliferation of unscrupulous organizations purporting to

FIGURE 10.1 *Volunteers working on an ecotourism project in Guatemala. Photo by Youth Challenge Australia.*

sell volunteer tourism packages to developing countries that are overpriced, poorly organized and turn out to be unfulfilling for the participant, and of little direct benefit to the local community where the project takes place. Worse still some volunteer tourism projects end up creating a new set of problems that did not exist previously. This often arises when volunteer tourists put their own needs ahead of the community's they work in (Klaushofer, 2007). For example, McGehee and Andercek (2008) found that many tourists and charitable organizations may have the best of intentions but lack an understanding of how their actions affect the dignity of local residents. The authors relate a case in Tijuana, Mexico where a US organization was interested in bringing a truckload of used clothing to a local charitable mission so that they could distribute it directly to local families. The local mission did not support any kind of free handouts of items and they offered to take the clothing then sell it at a very inexpensive price at their local thrift store; this way it would preserve the dignity of local residents and reduce dependency on outside sources. The response from the US organizer was that they wanted to set up a table with the truck and personally hand the clothing to the needy folks themselves (McGehee and Andercek, 2008).

IMPACTS, POTENTIALS AND POSSIBILITIES

This book has highlighted the complexity of using ecotourism as a tool for conservation and sustainable development. The explosion of interest in ecotourism as a funding source for conserving both biodiversity and cultural patrimony and as a strategy for generating socio-economic development has seen a mechanism for a movement of the tourism industry to become more aligned to the sustainable development models that underpin ecotourism. And with the demand for ecotourism steadily increasing, a trend that can be expected to continue its influence on the tourism industry and communities can only continue to promote sustainable models of development.

If ecotourism can influence mass tourism practices in incorporating principles of ecological and cultural sensitivity and the consideration of, and attempts to minimize negative impacts then it has made a major contribution to sustainability. This book has attempted to provide a means for the reader to evaluate how well ecotourism might live up to the expectation created for it. Case studies presented in the book cover a range of protected areas, cultures, types of ecotourism enterprises and management options and suggest that we are moving toward more sustainable models. Where these projects have not lived up to expectations in terms of creating revenues for conservation or in creating alternative income sources to take pressure off protected areas or for local communities, they have at least begun to develop mechanisms that can become a potential avenue for conservation through ecotourism.

In learning about the impacts, potentials and possibilities of ecotourism development enables the creation of mechanisms to allow for every stake-holder's involvement in ecotourism planning and development. Sustainable models of development are not inherently designed to restrict, rather they allow for new ways of thinking that can, and should, achieve a range of objectives guided by a common interest. Ecotourism, as a sustainable development practice, is a strategy for mapping and addressing new approaches to humanity's interaction with the environment for the twenty-first century.

FURTHER READING

Jamal, T., Borges, M., & Stronza, A. (2006) The institutionalisation of ecotourism: certification, cultural equity and praxis. *Journal of Ecotourism*, 5(3), 145–75.

Jamal, Borges and Stronza's paper critically evaluates some of the inequities that currently exist in ecotourism with a focus on cultural aspects such as human–ecological relationships. The authors argue that some elements of ecotourism have come to reflect the very values it seeks to transcend such as commodification and instrumentality.

Craig-Smith, S.J. (2004). Global warming and tourism in Oceania. In *Oceania: A Tourism Handbook* (C. Cooper, & C.M. Hall, eds). Channel View Publications, Clevedon, UK, pp. 353–61.

This chapter by Craig-Smith attempts to predict what may happen in the South Pacific as a result of global warming and its impact on the different tourism types in the area including urban tourism, ecotourism, winter-based tourism, ocean-based tourism and small island tourism.

Journal of Sustainable Tourism 2005, 13(5). This special edition of the journal investigates the creative contribution and partnerships that NGOs are playing in sustainable tourism operations around the world.

Glossary

Alternative tourism The common feature of 'alternative tourism' is the suggestion of an attitude diametrically opposed to what is characteristically viewed as mass tourism. Alternative tourism is often presented as existing in fundamental opposition by attempting to minimize the perceived negative environmental and socio-cultural impacts of people at leisure in the promotion of radically different approaches to tourism. Examples include ecotourism, green tourism, nature-oriented tourism, soft tourism, pro-poor tourism and defensive tourism.

Anthropocentric Focuses on the human and the instrumental value of nature, regards humans as the central fact of the universe and therefore interprets everything in terms of humans and their values.

Areas of high conservation value Areas important at a regional or national level for the conservation of native fauna, flora, natural features or systems or sites of cultural significance.

Baseline study Assessment of the present situation in order to measure changes in that environment over time.

Best practice Involves seeking excellence, keeping in touch with innovations, avoiding waste and focussing on outcomes which are in the community interest. It involves managing change and continual improvement and in this way it encompasses all levels of an organization.

Biocentric Focuses on living things (different species and genetic variability) as the central point to the development of value systems as opposed to anthropocentrism which focuses on the human and the instrumental value of nature. See also **Ecocentric**.

Biodiversity The variety of different species and genetic variability among individuals within each species.

Biological diversity The variety of all life forms, the different plants, animals and microorganisms, the genes they contain and the ecosystems they form. It is usually considered at three levels: genetic diversity, species diversity and ecosystem diversity.

Bioregion A territory defined by a combination of biological, social and geographic criteria rather than by geopolitical considerations; generally, a system of related interconnected ecosystems.

229

Built environment A reference to buildings, dwellings, structures, utilities, roads and services which enable people to live, work and play, circulate and communicate and fulfil a wide range of functions. The built environment of a place reveals its historical and spatial development, its past and present, and something of its social structure and conflicts.

Carbon offset Any trading system designed to offset carbon emissions from one activity (such as burning fossil fuels in manufacturing, driving or flying) with another (such as installing more efficient technologies, planting carbon-reducing plants or establishing contracts with others not to partake in carbon-releasing activities) (Dictionary of Sustainable Management, 2008).

Carrying capacity The level of visitor use an area can accommodate with high levels of satisfaction for visitors and few impacts on resources. Carrying capacity estimates are determined by many factors such as environmental, social and managerial.

Climate change Refers to significant long-term changes in average weather patterns for a particular region. Changes in climate are effected by myriad factors including solar radiation, the earth's orbit, ocean currents, tectonic plates and volcanoes. In recent years the term climate change has been used in conjunction with global warming, which scientists now agree is most likely caused by human influences attributed to the increase in CO_2 gases into the atmosphere. See also **Global warming**.

Code of conduct Guidelines for appropriate social, cultural and environmentally responsible behavior. Codes of conduct are in no way binding on the industry or the individual.

Commodification The production of commodities for exchange via the market as opposed to direct use by the producer. One form of commodified leisure today can be seen in specific forms of tourism, where travel to far distant and different places is marketed as 'paradise gained'. Tourism becomes a 'freely chosen' leisure activity to be consumed.

Community See Local community.

Community-based tourism (CBT) CBT is generally considered a privately offered set of hospitality services (and features), extended to visitors, by individuals, families or a local community. A key objective of CBT is to establish direct personal/cultural exchange between host and guest in a balanced manner that enables a mutual understanding, solidarity and equality for those involved.

Conservation The protection, maintenance, management, sustainable use, restoration and enhancement of the natural environment (ANZECC Task Force on Biological Diversity, 1993). The management of human use of the biosphere so that it may yield the greatest sustainable benefit to present generations while maintaining its potential to meet the needs and aspirations of future generations (National Conservation Strategy for Australia).

Conservationists People who believe that resources should be used, managed and protected so that they will not be degraded and unnecessarily wasted and will be available to present and future generations.

Constant attractions Attributes that are widespread or have an intangible quality about them (e.g. good weather, safety, etc.).

Creative thinking The act of redefining an issue by looking at it from a new perspective.

Decentralization A conscious policy of locating or relocating some parts or the whole of an organization in outlying regions away from metropolitan areas with concomitant developments of infrastructure coupled with extensions of existing residential areas or the establishment of new towns. The policy may aim at the strengthening of specified regional administrative centres.

Deep ecology The belief that the earth's resources should be sustained and protected not just for human beings but also for other species. People who believe in this philosophy tend to have a life-centered approach rather than a human-centered approach to managing and sustaining the earth's resources by working with nature, not wasting resources unnecessarily and interfering with non-human species to meet the needs of humans.

Demarketing The term is used to emphasize that marketing may be used to decrease as well as increase the number of satisfied customers. It is used to decrease numbers so that an increase in clientele satisfaction can be achieved, through preserving a higher quality experience.

Development The modification of the biosphere and the application of human, financial, living and non-living resources to satisfy human needs and improve the quality of human life (World Conservation Strategy). The application of human, financial and physical resources to satisfy human needs and improve the quality of life: inevitably development involves modification of the biosphere and some aspects of development may detract from the quality of life locally, regionally, nationally or globally.

Ecocentrism Focuses on the environment as the central point to the development of value systems as opposed to anthropocentrism which focuses on the human and the instrumental value of nature. See also **Biocentric.**

Ecologically sustainable development Using, conserving and enhancing the community's resources so that ecological processes, on which life depends, are maintained and the total quality of life, now and in the future, can be increased (Ecologically Sustainable Development Working Groups, 1991).

Ecologically sustainable tourism An activity that fosters environmental and cultural understanding, appreciation and conservation.

Ecosystem A dynamic complex of plant, animal, fungal and microorganism communities and the associated non-living environment interacting as an ecological unit.

Ecotourism There is no general definition currently in circulation but any conception of it must involve travel to relatively undisturbed or uncontaminated natural areas with the objective of studying, admiring and enjoying the natural environment of that area. An important point is that the person who practices ecotourism has the opportunity of immersing him or herself in nature in a way that most people cannot enjoy in their routine, urban existences. As there is no strict consensus on a specific definition of ecotourism it had been suggested that it also is responsible travel that conserves natural environments and sustains the well-being of local people.

Environmental impact assessment (EIA) A method of analysis which attempts to predict the likely repercussions of a proposed major development upon the social and physical environment of the surrounding area.

Endangered species Fauna and flora likely to become extinct due to direct exploitation by humans, intrusion into highly specialized habitats, threats from other species, interruption of the food chain, pollution or a combination of such factors.

Endemic tourism Broadly defined as tourism which recognizes that each individual locality or community has its special character, and that particular character or identity may well constitute its major attractiveness to tourists.

Environment All aspects of the surroundings of human beings as individuals or in social groups (Commonwealth Environmental Protection [OP] Amendment no. 12, 1967).

Environmental economics A recognized field of specialization in economic science. Environmental economics examines the costs and benefits of pollution control, and protection of the environment.

Environmental education A concept ranging from media coverage of environmental issues to formal environmental education, its aims ranging from raising awareness to formal training.

Environmentalists People who are primarily concerned with preventing pollution and degradation of the air, water and soil. See **Conservationists**.

Ethics What we believe to be right or wrong behavior.

Ethic of 'Nature' Holds that non-human entities are of equal value with the human species. It is broadly intrinsic and ecocentric.

Ethic of 'Use' This is the normative or dominant mode of how human beings relate to nature: where nature is viewed predominantly as a set of resources which humanity is free to employ for its own distinct ends. It is an instrumental and anthropocentric view.

Global warming Refers to the increase in temperature of the earth's lower atmosphere and oceans in the twentieth and twenty-first centuries. In recent years scientists all over the world have noticed a steady and slight increase in temperatures of 0.6 degrees since 1900. The Intergovernmental Panel on Climate Change indicates that observed increases in globally averaged temperatures since the mid-twentieth century is very likely due to man-made greenhouse gas concentrations. Scientists are predicting that if greenhouse causing gases are not reduced then average worldwide temperatures could increase by 5 °C by 2100. Increases in global temperatures will cause sea levels to rise and there will be an increase in severe weather events such as droughts, floods and storms. This will dramatically affect agricultural yields, lead to glacier retreats, species extinction and increase the range of diseases such as malaria (Porteous, 2000).

Greenwashing A term that merges the concepts of green (environmentally sound) and whitewashing (to conceal or gloss over wrongdoing). Greenwashing is any form of marketing or public relations that links a corporate, political, religious or non-profit organization to a positive association with environmental issues for an unsustainable product, service or practice. In some cases, an organization may truly offer a green product, service or practice. However, through marketing and public relations, one is wrongly led to believe that this green value system is ubiquitous throughout the entire organization (Dictionary of Sustainable Management, 2008).

Infrastructure The buildings or permanent installations associated with a site. Infrastructure for ecotourism is often developed in protected areas and usually involves a scaled down or minimal approach to physical development and change. Infrastructure such as boardwalks and viewing platforms can be used by resource managers to provide for visitor access to ecotourism destinations, while at the same time assisting the management of environmental impacts and the physical protection of natural resources.

Institutional planning Planning by institutional agencies and public bodies not central to the planning process, yet having significant implications for environmental planning. One of the functions of the central planning agency is to accommodate and coordinate proposals to enable the objectives of other agencies to be reconciled with overall planning objectives.

Integrated planning Planning process which takes into account the social and cultural priorities of host communities to shape tourism into a form appropriate for each locality.

Intergenerational equity Refers to a concept that the present generation should ensure that the health, diversity and productivity of the environment are maintained or enhanced for the benefit of future generations.

Internalization of environmental costs Internalization of environmental costs involves the creation of economic environments so that social and private views of economic efficiency coincide. It is concerned with structures, reporting mechanisms and tools to achieve this end.

Interpretation An educational activity which aims to reveal meanings and relationships through the use of original objects, first-hand experience and illustrative media, rather than simply by communicating factual information.

Intrinsic value Value that exists in its own right, for its own sake.

Land use zoning Land use zoning divides sections of land into areas based on their sensitivity and conservation values.

Limits of acceptable change (LAC) A model used to help establish the maximum 'damage' level for a resource that society is prepared to accept as custodian of resources for both present and future generations and to define the maximum level of use consistent with that damage level (RAC Coastal Zone Inquiry Information Paper no. 8, 1993).

Local community The concept of local community concerns a particularly constituted set of social relationships based on something which the individuals have in common – usually a common sense of identity (e.g. Marshall, 1994: 73–76).

Management plan The process of the coordination and preparation of a document and the realization of a set of goals, within a protected area or local community or organization that leads to some common directions.

Market demand How much of an economic good consumers are willing to buy at a particular price.

Market supply How much of an economic good consumers are willing and able to produce and sell at a particular price in a given period.

Mass tourism Mass tourism is generally seen as being an overarching term for tourism that is undertaken by the majority of travelers. This thesis, in exploring the specificity of a particular tourist experience in-depth, may contribute toward an understanding of not only the significant divergences and convergences that exist between both mass tourism and alternative tourism, but also the subtle nuances that subtend these tourist experiences. Therefore, it is not simply a matter of differentiating, in a binary fashion, between a general category of mass tourism and the derivation of niche elements within it. Semiotically, in its structural sense, the appellation of 'alternative' logically implies an antithesis. It arises as the contrary to that which is seen as negative or detrimental about conventional tourism, so it is always a semantic inversion, which is found at all levels of discourse. In the domain of logic, an alternative is based on a dialectical paradigm that offers only two possibilities. Two contemporaneous terms are placed in mutual exclusion, with an 'excluded middle', that leaves a conclusion that is either one or the other. Therefore the terminology of alternative and mass tourism is mutually interdependent, each relying on a series of value-laden judgements that themselves structure the definitional content of the terms.

Microsocial Macro- and microsocial are used in the context of sociology. The former generally examines the wider structures, interdependent social institutions, global and historical processes of social life, while the latter is more concerned with action, interaction and the construction of meaning. It is important, however, not to generalize too greatly as the relationship between social system and social actor is not always clearly distinguished (e.g. Marshall, 1994: 298).

Motivations The factors that determine a human's reasons for doing something, in the context of travel the reasons for someone to travel to a destination.

Multiple use Principle of managing public land such as a national forest so it is used for a variety of purposes, such as timbering, mining, recreation, grazing, wildlife preservation, and soil and water conservation.

Natural Existing in, or formed by nature, non-urban; also incorporates cultural aspects.

Performance standards Standards employed in environmental planning which specify desired results and do not in themselves specify the methods by which performance criteria should be met.

Philosophy The system of principles concerning all the conditions in which humans live and which influence their behavior and development.

Precautionary principle Where there are threats of serious or irreversible environmental damage, lack of full scientific certainty should not be used as a reason for postponing measures to prevent environmental degradation. In the application of the precautionary principle decisions should be guided by careful evaluation to avoid serious or irreversible damage to the environment and an assessment of the risk-weighted consequences of various options.

Pro-poor tourism A form of alternative tourism that attempts to reduce poverty by using tourism in poor communities to generate local employment and profits. Pro-poor tourism is not a specific product or sector of tourism, but an approach to the industry. Its strategies aim to unlock opportunities for the poor, whether for economic gain, other livelihood benefits, or participation in decision-making (Asley et al., 2000).

Protected areas Defined in Article 2 of the International Convention on Biological Diversity as a geographically defined area which is designated or regulated and managed to achieve specific conservation. Protected area system characteristics are *adequacy* – the ability of the reserve to maintain the ecological viability and integrity of populations, species and communities; *comprehensiveness* – the degree to which the full range of ecological communities and their biological diversity are incorporated within reserves; *representativeness* – the extent to which areas selected for inclusion in the national reserve system are capable of reflecting the known biological diversity and ecological patterns and processes of the ecological community or ecosystem concerned.

Recreation opportunity spectrum (ROS) The basic assumption of ROS is that a quality recreational experience is assured by providing a diverse range of recreational opportunities, catering for various tastes and user group preferences. The ROS focuses on the setting in which recreation occurs. A recreation opportunity setting is the combination of physical, biological, social and managerial conditions that give value to a place. ROS has been described as a framework for presenting carrying capacities and managing recreational impacts. The ROS provides a systematic framework for looking at the actual distribution of opportunities and a procedure for assessing possible management actions.

Social impact assessment (SIA) An assessment of the impact on people and society of major development projects: social impact assessment is often a weak point in environmental impact assessments. Social impacts are defined as those changes in social relations between members of a community, society or institution, resulting from external change.

Stewardship An approach to the care of nature through its dominance by humans relying on predominantly economic value systems and the pre-eminence of technology (backed up by enormous advances in scientific understanding).

Strategic planning A dynamic and issue-orientated process to help the individual/organization to take control of significant and desirable potential futures. Strategic planning is the process of deciding what the future of the operation should be, and what strategies should be followed in order to make that future happen.

Sustainable Able to be carried out without damaging the long-term health and integrity of natural and cultural environments.

Sustainability This is advanced through the magical transmutation of the term 'ecological sustainable development' into 'economically sustainable development' through the substitution of the letter E in the acronym 'ESD'. It is an indication of the latitude with which the concept of sustainability can be interpreted. Thus, the concept of sustainability is both contested and deployed, often, for profoundly different reasons.

Sustainable design Environmentally and culturally sensitive building design, where construction methods and materials have minimal impact on the environment.

Sustainable development Defined by the World Commission on Environment and Development (WCED) in 1987 as 'development that meets the needs of the present without compromising the ability of future generations to meet their own needs'. Environmental protection and management is central to sustainable development.

Sustainable yield The use of living resources at levels of harvesting and in ways that allow those resources to supply products and services indefinitely.

SWOT analysis SWOT is an assessment of the project/organization strengths and weaknesses and an analysis of the opportunities and threats that exist in the market place.

Technocentrism A belief system that supports the idea that the creation of new products and processes will be able to improve our chances of survival, comfort and quality of life before the depletion or destruction of renewable resources.

Tourism Optimization Management Model (TOMM) This model builds on the LAC system to incorporate a stronger political dimension and seeks to monitor and manage tourism in a way that seeks optimum sustainable performance, rather than maximum levels or carrying capacities. TOMM involves identifying strategic imperatives (such as policies and emerging issues), identifying community values, product characteristics, growth patterns, market trends and opportunities, positioning and branding and alternative scenarios for tourism in a region, while seeking optimum conditions, indicators, acceptable ranges, monitoring techniques, benchmarks, annual performance and predicted performance having done this it can examine poor performance, and explore cause/effect relationships.

Tourism industry The collection of all collaborating firms and organizations which perform specific activities directed at satisfying leisure, pleasure and recreational needs (Stear et al., 1988: 1).

Tourists All visitors traveling for whatever purpose involving at least an overnight stay 40 kilometers from their usual place of residence (World Tourism Organization).

User pays The principle that management and maintenance costs for individual parts should be borne (either partially or fully) by those using them.

Utilitarian A focus on the usefulness of nature in terms of human values rather than a focus on beauty or spirituality – practicality of nature's use by humans for material gain.

Visitor activity management process (VAMP) The visitor activity management process relates to interpretation and visitor services. This framework involves the development of activity profiles which connect activities with the social and demographic characteristics of the participants, the activity setting requirements and trends affecting the activity. The VAMP framework is designed to operate in parallel with the natural resource management process.

Visitor impact management (VIM) The visitor impact management process involves a combination of legislation/policy review and scientific problem identification (both social and natural). The principles of VIM are to identify unacceptable changes occurring as a result of visitor use and developing management strategies to keep visitor impacts within acceptable levels while integrating visitor impact management into existing agency planning, design and management processes. It attempts to do this based on the best scientific understanding and situational information available. While both LAC and VIM frameworks rely on indicators and standards as a means of defining impacts deemed unacceptable and place carrying capacities into a broader managerial context. VIM, however, makes reference to planning and policy and includes identifying the probable causes of impacts, whereas LAC places more emphasis on defining opportunity classes.

Volunteer tourism Volunteer tourism emphasizes positive interactions between tourists and local communities based on travelers visiting a destination and taking part in some form of project that makes a positive difference to social, economic and/or environmental conditions. Projects are commonly nature-based, people-based or involve the restoration of buildings and artifacts.

Wilderness Land that, together with its plant and animal communities, is in a state that has not been substantially modified by and is remote from the influences of European settlement or is capable of being restored to such a state, and is of sufficient size to make its maintenance in such a state feasible. A wilderness area is a large, substantially unmodified natural area (or capable of being restored to such a state). Such areas are managed to protect or enhance this relatively natural state, and also to provide opportunities for self-reliant recreation in a relatively unmodified natural environment.

Zone of opportunity A geographic area that ideally encompasses an endemic core resource, as well as particular resources/attractions.

A Guide to Ecotourism Agencies and Other Sustainable Tourism Resources

Centre on Ecotourism and Sustainable Development – www.ecotourismcesd.org

Climate Care – www.climatecare.org

Dictionary of Sustainable Management – www.sustainabilitydictionary.com

Ecotourism Association of Australia (EAA) – www.ecotourism.org.au

Ecotourism Laos – www. ecotourismlaos.com

Ethical Escape – www.ethicalescape.com

Friends of the Earth – www.foe.co.uk

Galapagos Conservation Trust – www.gct.org

Global Volunteers Network – www.volunteer.org.nz

Himalayan Trust UK – www.himalayantrust.co.uk

International Centre for Responsible Tourism – www. theinternationalcentreforresponsibletourism.org

International Ecotourism Association (IEA) – www.ecotourism.org

International Porter Protection Group – www.ippg.net

Interpretation Australia Association – www.interpretationaustralia.asn.au

International Union for Conservation of Nature (IUCN) – www.iucn.org

Journal of Ecotourism, Journal of Sustainable Tourism, Journal of International Volunteer Tourism and Social Development – www.multilingual-matters.com

Sustainable Arctic Tourism – www.arctictourism.net

National Geographic Centre for Sustainable Destinations – www. nationalgeographic.com/travel/sustainable

Sustainable Tourism Net – www.sustainabletourism.net

People and Planet – www.peopleandplanet.net

Pro-Poor Tourism – www.propoortourism.org.uk

Tourism Concern – www.tourismconcern.org.uk

Tourism Optimization Management Model – www.tomm.info

Vanuatu Cultural Centre – www.vanuatuculture.org

World Volunteer Web – www.worldvolunteerweb.org

World Tourism Organization (WTO) – www.world-tourism.org

World Wide Fund for Nature (WWF) – www.wwf.org.uk

References

Adam, D. (2007). US answer to global warming: smoke and giant space mirrors. *The Guardian Newspaper*, 27 January.

Ahn, B., Lee, B., & Shafer, C.S. (2002) Operationalizing sustainability in regional tourism planning: an application of the limits of acceptable change framework. *Tourism Management*, 23(1), 1–15.

Aitchison, C. (2001) Theorizing other discourses of tourism, gender and culture: can the subaltern speak (in tourism)? *Tourist Studies*, 1(2), 133–47.

Allcock, A. (2003) *Sustainable Tourism Development in Nepal, Vietnam and Lao PDR. Experiences of SNV and Partner Organisations*. SNV Netherlands Development Organisation, The Hague, Netherlands.

Allcock, A., Jones, B., Lane, S., & Grant, J. (1994) *National Ecotourism Strategy*. Australian Government Publishing Service, Canberra, Australia.

Almond, B. (1994) *Interpretation Strategy: Shelly Beach Marine Reserve*. Unpublished masters thesis, University of Technology, Sydney.

Andreasen, A., & Kotler, P. (2003) *Strategic Marketing for Non-profit Organizations*, sixth ed. Prentice Hall, Englewood-Cliffs, NJ.

Archer, B., Cooper, C., & Ruhanen, L. (2005). The positive and negative impacts of tourism. In *Global Tourism* (W.F. Theobald, ed.), third ed. Elsevier, Burlington, MA, pp. 79–102.

Ashley, C., Boyd, C., & Goodwin, H. (2000) Pro-poor tourism: putting poverty at the heart of the tourism agenda. *Natural Resource Perspectives*, 51, 1–6.

Ashley, C., Roe, D., & Goodwin, H. (2001) *Pro-poor Tourism Strategies: Making Tourism Work for the Poor – A Review of Experience*. Overseas Development Institute, London.

Ashworth, G., & Goodall, B. (1990) *Marketing in the Tourism Industry: The Promotion of Destination Regions*. Croom Helm, London.

Ayers, B. (2003). Carrying Nepal on their backs. *Nepali Times Newspaper*, 10–16 October.

Bakker, L. (1999) *Tiele! Turis! the Social and Ethnic Impact of Tourism in Siberut (Mentawai)*. Unpublished MA thesis, Leiden University, The Netherlands.

Ballantine, J., & Eagles, P. (1994) Defining ecotourists. *Journal of Sustainable Tourism*, 2(4), 210–4.

Barkin, D., & Bouchez, C.P. (2002) NGO-community collaboration for ecotourism: a strategy for sustainable regional development. *Current Issues in Tourism*, 5(3–4), 245–53.

Barilotti, S. (2002). Lost horizons: surfer colonialism in the 21st century. *The Surfer's Path*, Oct/Nov, pp. 30–9.

Barlow, A. (1992). Land and country: source, self and sustenance. In *Aboriginal Involvement in Parks and Protected Areas* (J. Birckhead, T. De Lacy, & L. Smith, eds). Aboriginal Studies Press, Canberra, Australia.

Bates, B. (1991). *Ecotourism: A Case Study of the Lodges in Papua New Guinea*. Paper presented at the PATA 40th Annual Conference, April 10–13, Nusa Indah Convention Centre Bali, Indonesia.

Bartholomew, W., & Baker, T. (1996) *Bustin Down the Door*. Harper Sports, Sydney.

Bauer, T. (2001) *Tourism in the Antarctic: Opportunities, Constraints and Future Prospects*. Haworth Hospitality Press, New York.

Beaumont, B. (1997) Perceived crowding as an evaluation standard for determining social carrying capacity in tourism recreation areas: the case of Green Island, North Queensland. In *Tourism Planning and Policy in Australia and New Zealand: Cases, Issues and Practice* (C.M. Hall, J. Jenkins, & G. Kearsley, Eds). Irwin Publishers, Sydney.

Beck, U. (1992) *Risk Society: Towards a New Modernity*. Sage, Thousand Oaks, CA.

Beckmann, E. (1991) *Environmental Interpretation for Education and Management in Australian National Parks and Other Protected Areas*. Unpublished PhD thesis, University of New England, Australia.

Beeton, S. (1999) *Ecotourism: A Practical Guide for Rural Communities*. Landlinks Press, Collingwood, Australia.

Bello, D.C., & Etzel, M.J. (1985) The role of novelty in the pleasure travel experience. *Journal of Travel Research*, 24(1), 20–6.

Belshaw, C. (2001) *Environmental Philosophy*. Acumen, Stocksfield, UK.

Bhabha, H. (1994) *The Location of Culture*. Routledge, New York.

Bıcak, H.A., Altınay, M., Aksugür, E., Günyaktı, A., & Katırcıoglu, S. (2006) Could yacht tourism be an alternative tourism potential in North Cyprus? *Tourism in Marine Environments*, 3(1), 49–57.

Biénabe, E., & Hearne, R.R. (2006). Public preferences for biodiversity conservation and scenic beauty within a framework of environmental services payments. *Forest Policy and Economics*, 9(4), 335–48.

Bilsen, F. (1987) Integrated tourism in Senegal: an alternative. *Tourism Recreation Research*, 13(1), 19–23.

Birch, C. (1991). A titanic on a collision course. *21 C*, Autumn.

Birtles, A., Cahill, M., Valentine, P., & Davis, D. (1995). Incorporating research on visitor experiences into ecologically sustainable management of whale shark tourism. In *Ecotourism and Nature-Based Tourism* (H. Richins, J. Richardson, & A. Crabtree, eds). Ecotourism Association of Australia, Brisbane, Australia, pp. 195–202.

Birtles, A., & Sofield, T. (1996). Taking the next step. In *Ecotourism and Nature-Based Tourism* (H. Richins, J. Richardson, & A. Crabtree, eds). Ecotourism Association of Australia, Brisbane, Australia, pp. 15–22.

Blamey, R. (1995) *The Nature of Ecotourism* (occasional paper no. 21). Bureau of Tourism Research, Canberra, Australia.

Blamey, R.K. (2001). Principles of ecotourism. In *The Encyclopedia of Ecotourism* (D.B. Weaver, ed.). CABI, New York, pp. 5–23.

Blangy, S., & Epler-Wood, M. (1992). *Developing and Implementing Ecotourism Guidelines for Wild Lands and Neighbouring Communities*. The Ecotourism Society, Burlington, VT.

Blangy, S., & Nielsen, T. (1993) Ecotourism and minimum impact policy. *Annals of Tourism Research*, 20(2), 357–60.

Boo, E. (1990) *Ecotourism: The Potentials and Pitfalls*, vols 1 and 2. World Wide Fund for Nature, Washington, DC.

Boo, E. (1991) Planning for ecotourism. *Parks*, 2(3), 4–8.

Boorstin, D.J. (1972) *The Image: A Guide to Pseudo-events in America*. Atheneum, New York.

Bowman, S. (1998). Parks in partnership. *National Parks*, January/February, pp. 30–3.

Bragg, L. (1990) Ecotourism: a working definition. *Forum*, 2(2), 7–12.

Brammer, N., Beech, J., & Burns, P. (2004) Use and abuse of tourism: the Goan experience. *Tourism Culture and Communication*, 5(1), 23–35.

Bramwell, B. (2005). Interventions and policy instruments for sustainable tourism. In *Global tourism*, third ed. (W.F. Theobald, ed.). Elsevier, New York, pp. 406–25.

Bramwell, B., & Sharman, A. (2000). Approaches to sustainable tourism planning and community participation: the case of the Hope Valley. In *Tourism and Sustainable Community Development* (G. Richards, & D. Hall, eds). Routledge, London, pp. 17–35.

Britton, S.G. (1980) The spatial organisation of tourism in a neo-colonial economy: a Fiji case study. *Pacific Viewpoint*, 21, 144–65.

Brohman, J. (1996) New directions for tourism in the third world. *Annals of Tourism Research*, 23, 48–70.

Brown, M. (Writer) (1997). Billion dollar breakers: the professional surfing world. *Radio National Background Briefing*. ABC Radio National Background Briefing 13th April, Sydney.

Brown, S., & Morrison, A.M. (2003) Expanding volunteer vacation participation: an exploratory study on the mini-mission concept. *Tourism Recreation Research*, 28, 73–82.

Bruggemann, J. (1997). National parks and protected area management in Costa Rica and Germany: a comparative analysis. In *Social Change and Conservation* (K. Ghimire, & M.P. Pimbert, eds) . Earthscan, London, pp. 71–96.

Brundtland Commission. (1987) *Our Common Future*. Oxford University Press, Oxford, UK.

Brunet, S., Bauer, J., de Lacy, T., & Tshering, K. (2001) Tourism development in Bhutan: tensions between tradition and modernity. *Journal of Sustainable Tourism*, 9(3), 243–63.

Buckley, R. (2002a) Surf tourism and sustainable development in Indo-Pacific islands. 1. The industry and the islands. *Journal of Sustainable Tourism*, 10(5), 405–24.

Buckley, R. (2002b) Surf tourism and sustainable development in Indo-Pacific islands. 2. Recreational capacity management and case study. *Journal of Sustainable Tourism*, 10(5), 425–42.

Buckley, R. (2003). Australia and New Zealand. In *Case Studies in Ecotourism* (R. Buckley, ed.). CAB International, Wallingford, UK, pp. 95–129.

Buckley, R. (2004) Partnerships in ecotourism: Australian political frameworks. *International Journal of Tourism Research*, 6(2), 75–83.

Buckley R., & Pannell, J (1990). Environmental impacts of tourism and recreation in national parks and conservation reserves. *Journal of Tourism Studies*, 1(1), 24–32.

Buckley, R., & King, N. (2003). Visitor-impact data in a land-management context. In *Nature-Based Tourism, Environment and Land Management* (R. Buckley, C. Pickering, & D.B. Weaver, eds)International Centre for Ecotourism Research, Griffith University, Southport, Australia, pp. 89–99.

Buckley, R., & Littlefair, C. (2007) Minimal-impact education can reduce actual impacts of park visitors. *Journal of Sustainable Tourism*, 15(3), 324–5.

Bunting, B. (1991, 12 April). *Nepal's Annapurna Conservation Area*. Paper presented at the PATA 91, 40th Annual Conference, Bali, Indonesia.

Burchett, C. (1992). *A New Direction in Travel: Aboriginal Tourism in Australia's Northern Territory*. Paper presented at Northern Territory Tourist Commission Environmental Conference – Expo 1992, Darwin, Australia.

Burke, A., & Vaisutis, J. (2007) *Lonely Planet Guide to Laos*. Lonely Planet, Footscray, Australia.

Busch, R. (1994, 7–10 November). *Ecotourism: Responsibilities of the Media*. Paper presented at 1994 World Congress on Adventure Travel and Ecotourism, Hobart, Australia.

Bushell, R. (2003). Balancing conservation and visitation in protected areas. In *Nature-Based Tourism, Environment and Land Management* (R. Buckley, C. Pickering, & D.B. Weaver, eds). International Centre for Ecotourism Research Griffith University, Southport, Australia. pp. 197–208.

Bushell, R., & Eagles, P. (eds) (2003) *Benefits Beyond Boundaries: Proceedings of the Vth IUCN World Parks Congress – Durban, South Africa, 8–17 September 2003*. CAB International, Wallingford, UK.

Butler, J.R. (1992, 10–12 February). *Ecotourism: Its Changing Face and Evolving Philosophy*. Paper presented at the International Union for Conservation of Nature and Natural Resources (IUCN), IVth World Congress on National Parks and Protected Areas, Caracas, Venezuela.

Butler, J.R., Hvenegaard, G.T., & Krystofiak, D.K. (1994). Economic values of bird-watching at Point Pelee National Park, Canada. In *Protected Area Economics and Policy: Linking Conservation and Sustainable Development* (M. Munasinghe, & J. McNeely, eds). World Bank, Washington, DC, pp. 253–62.

Butler, R.W. (1990) Alternative tourism: pious hope or Trojan horse? *Journal of Travel Research*, 3(1), 40–5.

Butler, R.W. (1991) Tourism, environment and sustainable development. *Environmental Conservation*, 18(3), 201–9.

Butler, R.W. (1999) Sustainable tourism: a state-of-the-art review. *Tourism Geographies*, 1(1), 7–25.

Buultjens, J., & Luckie, K. (2004) *Economic Impacts of Selected National Parks in North-eastern New South Wales*. Sustainable Tourism Cooperative Research Centre, Gold Coast, Australia.

Byers, A. (2005) Contemporary human impacts on alpine ecosystems in the Sagarmatha (Mt. Everest) National Park, Khumbu, Nepal. *Annals of the Association of American Geographers*, 95(1), 112–40.

Byrd, E.T. (2007) Stakeholders in sustainable tourism development and their roles: applying stakeholder theory to sustainable tourism development. *Tourism Review International*, 62(2), 6–13.

Catlins Wildlife Trackers (2007). Ecotours. Retrieved 21 May, 2007, from, www.catlins-ecotours.co.nz.

Calkin, J. (1997) *Sustainable Tourism Strategy for Tonga*. Calkin & Associates, Sydney.

Cameron-Smith, B. (1977) Educate or regulate? Interpretation in national park management. *Australian Parks and Recreation*, 34–7.

Cape Otway Centre (2008). Experiences. Retrieved 25 March, 2008, from, www.capeotwaycentre.com.au.

Capra, F. (1988) *The Turning Point: Science, Society, and the Rising Culture*. Flamingo, New York.

Capra, F. (1997) *The Web of Life: A New Synthesis of Mind and Matter*, New ed. Flamingo, New York.

Carroll, N. (2000). Defending the faith: a brief history of the secret spot. In *Nat Young Surf Rage: A Surfers Guide to Turning Negatives into Positives* (D. Kampion, C. Rielly, & T. Learner, eds). Nymboida Press, Angourie, Australia.

Carson, R. (1962) *Silent Spring*. Penguin, London.

Carter, F., & Moore, M. (1991, 25–27 September). *Ecotourism in the 21st Century*. Paper presented at First International Conference in Ecotourism, Brisbane, Australia.

Carter, R.W. (1979) *Interpretation: An Approach to the Conservation of the Natural and Cultural Heritage of Australia*. Queensland National Parks & Wildlife Service, Brisbane, Australia.

Carter, R.W., Whiley, D., & Knight, C. (2004) Improving environmental performance in the tourism accommodation sector. *Journal of Ecotourism*, 3(1), 46–68.

Cater, E. (1994). Introduction. In *Ecotourism: A Sustainable Option?* (E. Cater, & G. Lowman, eds). John Wiley & Sons, New York, pp. 3–17.

Cater, E. (2006) Ecotourism as a Western construct. *Journal of Ecotourism*, 5(1–2), 23–39.

Ceballos-Lascurain, H. (1990, 26–27 November). *Tourism, Ecotourism and Protected Areas*. Paper presented at the 34th Working Session of the Commission of National Parks and Protected Areas, Perth, Australia.

Ceballos-Lascurain, H. (1992, 10–12 February). *Tourism, Ecotourism and Protected areas: National Parks and Protected Areas*. Paper presented at International Union for Conservation of Nature and Natural Resources (IUCN) IVth World Congress on National Parks and Protected Areas, Caracas, Venezuela.

Ceballos-Lascurain, H. (1996) *Tourism, Ecotourism and Protected areas: The State of Nature-Based Tourism Around the World and Guidelines for its Development*. International Union for Conservation of Nature, Gland, Switzerland.

Ceballos-Lascurain, H. (n.d.) Faxed research notes from the author in 1987.

Cengiz, T. (2007) Tourism, an ecological approach in protected areas: Karagöl-Sahara National Park, Turkey. *International Journal of Sustainable Development and World Ecology*, 14(3), 260–7.

Chafe, Z. (2005) *Consumer Demand and Operator Support for Socially and Environmentally Responsible Tourism* (working paper no. 104). Centre on Ecotourism and Sustainable Development & The International Ecotourism Society, Washington, DC.

Chafe, Z. (2007). Consumer demand for quality in ecotourism. In *Quality Assurance and Certification in Ecotourism* (R. Black, & A. Crabtree, eds). Worldwatch Institute, Washington, DC, pp. 164–95.

Chan, K.L.J., & Baum, T. (2007) Motivation factors of ecotourists in ecolodge accommodation: the push and pull factors. *Asia Pacific Journal of Tourism Research*, 12(4), 349–64.

Chhabra, D., Healy, R., & Sills, E. (2003) Staged authenticity and heritage tourism. *Annals of Tourism Research*, 30(3), 702–19.

Choegyal, L. (1991, 10–13 April). *Ecotourism in National Parks and Wildlife Reserves*. Paper presented at PATA 40th Annual Conference, Bali, Indonesia.

Chok, S., Macbeth, J., & Warren, C. (2007) *Pro-poor Tourism: Who Benefits? Perspectives on Tourism and Poverty Reduction*. Channel View Publications, Clevedon, UK.

Church, P.A. (1994) *Protecting Biological Diversity: Jamaica Case Study* (USAID working paper 190). United States Agency for International Development, Washington, DC.

Clarke, J. (1997) A framework of approaches to sustainable tourism. *Journal of Sustainable Tourism*, 5(3), 224–33.

Clark, L., & Banford, D. (1991, 18–22 November). *Ecotourism Potentials and Pitfalls*. Paper presented at Regional Seminar on the Promotion of Sustainable Tourism Development in Pacific Island Countries, Suva, Fiji.

Clark, R., & Stankey, G. (1979) *The Recreation Opportunity Spectrum: A Framework for Planning, Management and Research* (General Technical Report). Pacific North–West Forest and Range Experiment Station, U.S. Department of Agriculture, Seattle, WA.

Cockrell, D.E., Bange, S., & Roggenbuck, J.W. (1984) Normative influence through interpretive communication. *Journal of Environmental Education*, 15(4), 20–6.

Cohen, E. (1972) Towards a sociology of international tourism. *Social Research*, 39(1), 164–82.

Cohen, J., & Richardson, J. (1995) Nature tourism vs. incompatible industries: megamarketing the ecological environment to ensure the economic future of nature tourism. *Travel and Tourism Marketing*, 4(2), 107–16.

Cole, D. (2000) Natural, wild, uncrowded, or free? *International Journal of Wilderness*, 6(2), 5–8.

Cole, D. (2001). Visitor use density and wilderness experiences: a historical review of research. In *Visitor Use Density and Wilderness Experience: Proceedings (RMRS-P-20)* (W.A. Ereimund, & D.N. Gole, eds). U.S. Department of Agriculture, Forest Service, Rocky Mountain Research Station, Ogden, UT.

Cole, S. (2007) Beyond authenticity and commodification. *Annals of Tourism Research*, 34(4), 943–60.

Collins, C. (1993). Wraps come off the new age traveller. *The Australian Newspaper*, 31 December.

Coppock S.T., & Rogers A.W. (1975) Too many Americans out in the wilderness. *Geographical Magazine* 47(8), 508–13.

Courtenay, J. (1996) Savannah Guides, Australia. *British Airways Tourism for Tomorrow Awards 1996 Pacific Region*, Unpublished paper.

Cox, J. (1985, 4–11 November). *The Resort Concept: the Good, the Bad and the Ugly*. Paper presented to National Conference on Tourism and Resort Development, Kuring-gai College of Advanced Education, Sydney.

Craik, J. (1991) *Resorting to Tourism: Cultural Policies for Tourist Development in Australia.* Allen & Unwin, Sydney.

Crompton, J.L. (1979) Motivations for pleasure vacations. *Annals of Tourism Research*, 3(1), 408–24.

Crompton, J.L. (1981) Dimensions of the social group role in pleasure vacations. *Annals of Tourism Research*, 8(4), 550–67.

Crompton, J.L., & Howard, D.R. (1980). Financing, managing and marketing. In *A Strategy for Tourism and Sustainable Developments* (L. Cronin, ed). Government of Canada, Ottawa, Canada, pp. 12–6.

Cunningham, P. (2006) Social valuing for Ogasawara as a place and space among ethnic host. *Tourism Management*, 27(3), 505–16.

Curtin, S., & Wilkes, K. (2005) British wildlife tourism operators: current issues and typologies. *Current Issues in Tourism*, 8(6), 455–78.

Cusack, D., & Dixon, L. (2006) Community-based ecotourism and sustainability: cases in Bocas del Toro Province, Panama and Talamanca, Costa Rica. *Journal of Sustainable Forestry*, 22(1–2), 157–82.

Dahlan, Y. (1997). Clarification from the Office of the Provincial Government of West Sumatera regarding development of tourism in the Mentawai Archipelago. Retrieved 11 April, 2000, from, www.greatbreaks.com.au/pemda. html.

Daley, M. (2005). Indies trader – history. Retrieved 5 July, 2005, from, www. indiestrader.com/history.html

Dann, G. (1981) Tourist motivation: an appraisal. *Annals of Tourism Research* 4, 184–94.

Darcy, S., & Wearing, S. (in press). Public–private partnerships and contested cultural heritage tourism in national parks: a case study of the stakeholder views of the North Head Quarantine Station (Sydney, Australia). *Journal of Cultural Heritage Studies*.

Davidson, A., Mufati, R., & Ndjavera, U. (2006) Community-managed tourism small enterprises in Namibia. *Participatory Learning and Action*, 55(1), 45–55.

Davies, J. (2002) Exploring open spaces and protecting natural places. *Journal of Ecotourism*, 1(2–3), 173–80.

Dear, C.E., & Myers, O.E. (2005) Conflicting understandings of wilderness and subsistence in Alaskan national parks. *Society and Natural Resources*, 18(9), 821–37.

de Jonge, E. (2004) *Spinoza and Deep Ecology: Challenging Traditional Approaches to Environmentalism*. Ashgate, Aldershot, UK.

Department of Tourism, Sport and Recreation (1994) *Ecotourism: Adding Value to Tourism in Natural Areas – A Discussion Book on Nature Based Tourism in Tasmania.* Department of Tourism, Sport and Recreation, Hobart, Australia.

Dernoi, L.A. (1988). Alternative or community based tourism. In *Tourism: A Vital Force for Peace* (L.D'. Amore, & J. Jafari, eds). L.D'. Amore, Montreal, Canada.

Diamantis, D. (2004) *Ecotourism: Management and Assessment*. Thompson Learning, Belmont, CA.

Dictionary of Sustainable Management (2008). www.sustainabilitydictionary.com.

Donagan, A. (1977) *The Theory of Morality*. Chicago University Press, Chicago, Ill.

Donohoe, H.M., & Needham, R.D. (2006) Ecotourism: the evolving contemporary definition. *Journal of Ecotourism*, 5(3), 192–210.

Dowling, R. (1991). An ecotourism planning model. In *Ecotourism: Incorporating the Global Classroom* (B. Weiler, ed.). Bureau of Tourism Research, Canberra, Australia, pp. 127–33.

Drejerska, N. (2005) The role of social marketing in tourism. *Acta Scientiarum Polonorum – Oeconomia*, 4, 27–34.

Driver, B., Brown, P.J., Stankey, G.H., & Gregorie, T.G. (1987). The ROS planning system: evolution, basic concepts and research needed. *Leisure Sciences*, 9(3), 201–12.

Duff, L. (1993) Ecotourism in national parks. *National Parks Journal*, 37(3), 18–20.

Duffy, R. (2002) *A trip too far: ecotourism, politics and exploitation*. Earthscan Publications, London.

Dunster, J., & Dunster, K. (1996) *Dictionary of Natural Resource Management*. CABI, Wallingford, UK.

Durst, P., & Ingram, C. (1989) Nature-orientated tourism promotion by developing countries. *Tourism Management*, 26, 39–43.

Ecotourism Association of Australia (EAA) (1996) *National Ecotourism Accreditation Program – Application Document*. Ecotourism Association of Australia, Brisbane, Australia.

Eagles, P.F. (1992). The motivation of Canadian ecotourists. In *Ecotourism: Incorporating the Global Classroom* (B. Weiler, ed.). Bureau of Tourism Research, Canberra, Australia.

Eagles, P.F.J., & McCool, S.F. (2004) *Tourism in National Parks and Protected Areas*. CABI, Wallingford, UK.

Eber, S. (ed.) (1992). *Beyond the Green Horizon: Principles for Sustainable Tourism*. World Wide Fund for Nature, Godalming, UK.

Eckermann, A.K., & Dowd, L.T. (1988) Structural violence and aboriginal organisations in rural–urban Australia. *The Journal of Legal Pluralism and Unofficial Law*, 27, 55–77.

Eckersley, R. (1992) *Environmentalism and Political Theory*. University College London Press, London.

Econsult Pty Ltd (1995) *National Ecotourism Strategy Business Development Program Report*. Commonwealth Department of Tourism, Melbourne, Australia.

Edensor, T. (1998) *Tourists at the Taj: Performance and Meaning at a Symbolic Site*. Routledge, London.

Edward, S. (1992). The rape of the Himalayas. *The Guardian Newspaper*, 4 June.

Edwards, G., & Prineas, T. (1995, 26 February–1 March). *Plans, Networks and Lines: Workshop on Planning for Networks of Regional Open Space*. Paper presented at the First International Urban Parks and Waterways Best Practice Conference, Melbourne, Australia.

Eidsvik, H.K. (1980) National parks and other protected areas: some reflections on the past and prescriptions for the future. *Environmental Conservation*, 7(3), 185–90.

Encel, J.R., & Encel, J.C. (1991) *Ethics of Environmental Development: Global Challenge and International Response*. University of Arizona Press, Tucson, AZ.

Ecologically Sustainable Development Steering Committee (ESDSC) (1992) *Draft National Strategy for Ecologically Sustainable Development: A Discussion Book*. Australian Government Publishing Service, Canberra, Australia.

Evans-Smith, D. (1994) *National Ecotourism Strategy*. Commonwealth Department of Tourism & Australian Government Printing Service, Canberra, Australia.

Farrell, T.A., & Marion, J.L. (2000). Camping impact management at Isle Royale National Park: an evaluation of visitor activity containment policies from the perspective of social conditions. In *Proceedings – Rocky Mountain Research Station, USDA Forest Service* (D.N. Cole, S.F. McCool, W.T. Borrie, & J. Loughlin, eds). Rocky Mountain Research Station, Fort Collins, CO, pp. 110–4.

Farsari, Y., Butler, R.W., & Prastacos, P. (2007) Sustainable tourism policy for Mediterranean destinations: issues and interrelationships. *International Journal of Tourism Policy*, 1(1), 58–78.

Favero, P. (2007) What a wonderful world! On the 'touristic ways of seeing', the knowledge and the politics of the 'culture industries of otherness'. *Tourist Studies*, 7(1), 51–81.

Fennell, D.A. (2001) A content analysis of ecotourism definitions. *Current Issues in Tourism*, 4(5), 403–21.

Fennell, D.A. (2002) *Ecotourism Programme Planning*. CABI, Oxford, UK.

Fennell, D.A. (2003) *Ecotourism: An Introduction*, second ed. Routledge, London.

Fennell, D.A., & Dowling, R.K. (Eds) (2003). *Ecotourism Policy and Planning*. CABI, Oxford, UK.

Ferraro, P.J., Uchida, T., & Conrad, J.M. (2005) Price premiums for eco-friendly commodities: are 'green' markets the best way to protect endangered ecosystems? *Environmental and Resource Economics*, 32(3), 419–38.

Font, X., & Wood, M.E. (2007). Sustainable tourism certification marketing and its contribution to SME market access. In *Quality Assurance and Certification in Ecotourism* (R. Black, & A. Crabtree, eds). CABI, Wallingford, UK, pp. 147–63.

Foran, B.D. (2007) Sifting the future from the past: a personal assessment of trends impacting the Australian rangelands. *Rangeland Journal*, 29(1), 3–11.

Forestell, P.H. (1990). Marine education and ocean tourism: replacing parasitism with symbiosis. In *Proceedings of the 1990 Congress on Coastal and Marine Tourism – A Symposium and Workshop on Balancing Conservation and Economic Development* (M.L. Miller, & J. Auyong, eds). National Coastal Resources Research and Development Institute, Newport, OR.

Forestry Tasmania (1994) *Tourism in Tasmania's State Forest: A Discussion Book*. Forestry Tasmania, Hobart, Australia.

Fox, W. (1990) *Towards a Transpersonal Ecology*. Shambhala, Boston, MA.

Friends of the Earth (2008). Aviation and global climate change. Retrieved 27 May, from, www.foe.co.uk.

Frueh, S., & Pesce, B. (2000). Participatory eco-development. Retrieved 25 March, from, www.uncdf.org.

Fuller, D., Caldicott, J., Cairncross, G., & Wilde, S. (2007) Poverty, indigenous culture and ecotourism in remote Australia. *Development*, 50(2), 141–8.

Gabor, M.T. (1997, 1–3 October). *A Millennium Vision for Tourism: A Government Perspective*. Paper presented at Australian Tourism Conference. Tourism Council Australia, Sydney.

Gajurel, D. (2004). Nepal engages local communities to conserve southern plains. Retrieved 15 December, 2007, from, www.ens-newswire.com/ens/aug2004/2004-08-18-02.asp.

Galapagos Conservation Trust (2008). Frequently asked questions (FAQ). Retrieved 15 July, 2008, from, www.gct.org/faq.

Galley, G., & Clifton, J. (2004) The motivational and demographic characteristics of research ecotourists: operation Wallacea volunteers in southeast Sulawesi, Indonesia. *Journal of Ecotourism*, 3(1), 69–82.

Gardner, T., & McArthur, S. (1995) Guided nature-based tourism in Tasmania's forests: trends, constraints and implications. *Tourism Recreation Research*, 22(1), 53–6.

Garrod, B. (2003) Local participation in the planning and management of ecotourism: a revised model approach. *Journal of Ecotourism*, 2(1), 33–53.

Garrod, B., & Wilson, J. (2003). Conclusion. In *Marine Ecotourism: Issues and Experiences* (B. Garrod, & J. Wilson, eds). Channel View Publications, Clevedon, UK, pp. 249–61.

Gelzen, P. (2002). Sagarmatha National Park. *The Rising Nepal Newspaper*, 28 June.

George, S. (2000) Sacred hunger: the story of surf exploration. *Surfer*, 41, 137–55.

Gergen, K.J. (2001) *Social Construction in Context*. Sage, London.

Gertsakis, J. (1995). Sustainable design for ecotourism deserves diversity. In *Ecotourism and Nature-Based Tourism* (H. Richins, J. Richardson, & A. Crabtree, eds). Ecotourism Association of Australia, Brisbane, Australia.

Getz, D., Carlsen, J., & Morrison, A. (eds) (2004) *The Family Business in Tourism and Hospitality*. CABI, Wallingford, UK.

Gilbert, D. (1984). *Tourist Product Differentiation*. Paper presented at Tourism: Managing for Results Conference, University of Surrey, UK.

Global Volunteers Network (2006). Mt Everest Trek. Retrieved 1 June, 2006, from, www.volunteer.org.nz/nepal/everest

Godbey, G., & Robinson, J. (1997) The increasing prospects for leisure. *Parks and Recreation*, 32(6), 75–82.

Godfrey-Smith, W. (1980, 19–23 July). *The Value of Wilderness: A Philosophical Approach*. Paper presented at Wilderness Management in Australia. Canberra College of Advanced Education, Canberra, Australia.

Gonsalves, P.S. (1984). Tourism in India: an overview and from leisure to learning: a strategy for India. In *Alternative Tourism: Report on the Workshop on Alternative Tourism with a Focus on Asia* (P. Holden, ed.). Ecumenical Coalition on Third World Tourism, Bangkok.

Goodman, R. (2002) Pastoral livelihoods in Tanzania: can the Maasai benefit from conservation? *Current Issues in Tourism*, 5(3), 280–6.

Goodwin, H. (2002) Local community involvement in tourism around national parks: opportunities and constraints. *Current Issues in Tourism*, 5(3), 338–60.

Gough, S., Scott, W., & Stables, A. (2000) Beyond O'Riordan: balancing anthropocentrism and ecocentrism. *International Research in Geographical and Environmental Education*, 9(1), 36–47.

Gould, K.A. (1999) *Evaluation of Three Market Based Strategies for Promoting Ecotourism in Peten, Guatemala: Green Certification, Private Reserves, and Collaborative Marketing*. Department of Forest Resources and Conservation, University of Florida, Gainesville, FL.

Graefe, A.R., Kuss, F.R., & Vaske, J.J. (1990) *Visitor Impact Management: The Planning Framework*, vol. 2. National Parks & Conservation Association, Washington, DC.

Graham, R. (1990). *Visitor Management and Canada's National Park*. Paper presented at First Canada/U.S. Workshop on Visitor Management in Parks and Protected Areas. Ontario, Tourism Research and Education Centre, University of Waterloo and Canadian Parks Service, Environment Canada, Waterloo, Canada.

Graham, R., Nilsen, P., & Payne, R.J. (1988) Visitor management in Canadian national parks. *Tourism Management*, 9(1), 44–62.

Gray, N.J., & Campbell, L.M. (2007) A decommodified experience? Exploring aesthetic, economic and ethical values for volunteer ecotourism in Costa Rica. *Journal of Sustainable Tourism*, 15(5), 463–82.

Great Barrier Reef Marine Park (2008a). Marine park zoning. Retrieved 15 July, 2008, from, www. gbrmpa.gov.au/corp_site/management/zoning.

Great Barrier Reef Marine Park (2008b). Great Barrier Reef Marine Park Zoning Plan 2003. Retrieved 15 July, 2008, from, www. gbrmpa.gov.au/__data/assets/pdf_file/0016/10591/Zoning_Plan.pdf.

Griffin, T., & Boele, N. (1993) Alternative paths to sustainable tourism. *Annual Review of Travel*, 15–23.

Grossberg, R., Treves, A., & Naughton-Treves, L. (2003) The incidental ecotourist: measuring visitor impacts on endangered howler monkeys at a Belizean archaeological site. *Environmental Conservation*, 30(1), 40–51.

Gunn, C.A. (1994) *Tourism Planning: Basics, Concepts, Cases*. Taylor & Francis, Washington, DC.

Hackett, M. (1992). Solving the ecotourism dilemma. In *Ecotourism Incorporating the Global Classroom* (B. Weiler, ed.). Bureau of Tourism Research, Canberra, Australia, pp. 207–11.

Hall, C.M. (1991) *Introduction to Tourism in Australia – Challenges and Opportunities*. Longman Cheshire, Melbourne.

Hall, C.M., & McArthur, S. (1996) *Heritage Management in Australia and New Zealand – The Human Dimension*, second ed. Oxford University Press, Oxford, UK.

Hall, C.M., & McArthur, S. (1998) *Integrated Heritage Management – Principles and Practice*. The Stationery Office, Norwich, UK.

Hall, C.M., McArthur, S., & Spoelder, P. (1991). Ecotourism in Antarctica and adjacent sub-Antarctic Islands. In *Ecotourism Incorporating the Global Classroom* (B. Weiler, ed.). Bureau of Tourism Research, Canberra, Australia.

Hall, C.M. (1994). Ecotourism in Australia, New Zealand and the South Pacific: appropriate tourism or new form of ecological imperialism? In *Ecotourism: A Sustainable Option* (E. Cater, & G. Lowman, eds). John Wiley & Sons, New York, pp. 137–55.

Hall, C. (2000) *Tourism Planning: Policies, Processes and Relationships*. Prentice Hall, Harlow, UK.

Hall, S. (1987) *The Fourth World: the Arctic and Its Heritage*. Hodder & Stoughton, London.

Ham, S.H. (1992) *Environmental Interpretation: A Practical Guide for People with Big Ideas and Small Budgets*. North American Press, Golden, CO.

Hammerscmidt, C. (2004) Sold to soul. *Inside Sport*, July, 50–7.

Hardin, G. (1968) Tragedy of the commons. *Science*, 162, 1243–8.

Hardin, G. (1993) *Living Within Limits: Ecology, Economics, and Population Taboos*. Oxford University Press, Oxford, UK.

Hardin, G. (1998) Extensions of the 'tragedy of the commons'. *Science*, 280, 682–3.

Harlow, S., & Pomfret, G. (2007) Evolving environmental tourism experiences in Zambia. *Journal of Ecotourism*, 6(3), 184–209.

Harrison, D. (1992) *Tourism and the Less Developed Countries*. Belhaven Press, London.

Harrison, D. (ed.) (2001) *Tourism and the Less Developed World: Issues and Case Studies*. CABI, Wallingford, UK.

Hawkins, R. (1995) An action plan for travel and tourism. *Environment and Development*, 5, 3–14.

Haywood, K.M. (1988) Responsible and responsive tourism planning in the community. *Tourism Management*, 9(2), 105–18.

Healy, R.G. (1989) *Economic Consideration in Nature-Oriented Tourism: The Case of Tropical Forest Tourism*. Southeastern Center for Forest Economic Research, Duke University, Durham, NC.

Hedstram, E. (1992) Preservation or profit? *National Parks*, 66 (1–2), 18–20.

Hendee, J., & Dawson, C. (2002) *Wilderness Management: Stewardship and Protection of Resources and Values*, third ed. Fulcrum Publishing, Golden, CO.

Henderson, M. (2005). Why the Sherpas of Nepal would leave our fittest soldiers standing. Retrieved 17 June, 2006, from, www.timesonline.co.uk.

Henion, K. (1975) *Ecological Marketing*. Grind Inc., Columbus, OH.

Henion, K., & Kinnear, T. (1976) *Ecological Marketing*. American Marketing Association, Chicago, IL.

Herath, G., & Kennedy, J. (2004) Estimating the economic value of Mount Buffalo National Park with the travel cost and contingent valuation models. *Tourism Economics*, 10(1), 63–78.

Higgins, B.R. (1996) The global structure of the nature tourism industry: ecotourists, tour operators, and local businesses. *Journal of Travel Research*, 35(2), 11–8.

Hill, D. (1992, 16–17 November). *Interpretation – A Manager's Perspective*. Papers presented at Inaugural Conference of the Interpretation Australia Association, Melbourne, Australia.

Hill, J., Woodland, W., & Gough, G. (2007) Can visitor satisfaction and knowledge about tropical rainforests be enhanced through biodiversity interpretation, and does this promote a positive attitude towards ecosystem conservation? *Journal of Ecotourism*, 6(1), 75–85.

Himalayan Rescue Association Nepal (2006). Himalayan safety training/workshop for mountain porters. Retrieved 1 June, 2006, from, www.himalayanrescue.org/hra.

Hjerpe, E.E., & Kim, Y.S. (2007) Regional economic impacts of Grand Canyon river runners. *Journal of Environmental Management*, 85(1), 137–49.

Holden, A. (2005) Achieving a sustainable relationship between common pool resources and tourism: the role of environmental ethics. *Journal of Sustainable Tourism*, 13(4), 339–52.

Holden, A. (2007) *Environment and Tourism*, second ed. Routledge, London.

Holden, A., & Mason, P. (2005) Editorial. *Journal of Sustainable Tourism*, 13(5), 421–3.

Holden, A., & Sparrowhawk, J. (2002) Understanding the motivations of ecotourists: the case of trekkers in Annapurna, Nepal. *International Journal of Tourism Research*, 4(6), 435–46.

Holden, P. (ed.). (1984) *Alternative Tourism: Report on the Workshop on Alternative Tourism with a Focus on Asia*. Ecumenical Coalition on Third World Tourism, Bangkok.

Honey, M. (1999) *Ecotourism and Sustainable Development: Who Owns Paradise?* Island Press, Washington, DC.

Honey, M. (2002) *Ecotourism and Certification: Setting Standards in Practice*. Island Press, Washington, DC.

Honey, M. (2007) *The Role of Certification and Accreditation in Ensuring Tourism Contributes to Conservation*. CAB International, Wallingford, UK.

Hore-Lacy, I. (1991) A mineral industry perspective on sustainable resource use. *The Australian Quarterly*, Summer.

Horn, C., & Simmons, D. (2002) Community adaptation to tourism: comparisons between Rotorura and Kaikoura, New Zealand. *Tourism Management*, 23, 133–43.

Howard, J.L. (1999) How do scuba diving operators in Vanuatu attempt to minimize their impact on the environment? *Pacific Tourism Review*, 3(1), 61–9.

Howitt, R. (2001) *Rethinking Resource Management: Justice, Sustainability and Indigenous Peoples*. Routledge, London.

Howitt, R. (2002) Social impact assessment as applied peoples' geography. *Australian Geographical Studies*, 31(2), 127–40.

Huang, Y., & Lo, S. (2005) Indicators of ecotourism opportunity spectrum. *Journal of Agriculture and Forestry*, 54(4), 283–96.

Hughes, M., & Saunders, A.M. (2005) Interpretation, activity participation, and environmental attitudes of visitors to Penguin Island, Western Australia. *Society and Natural Resources*, 18(7), 611–24.

Hultman, S.G. (1992). *Why Don't They Come? Guided Tours for Campers*. Paper presented at Proceedings of Heritage Interpretation International Global Congress, University of Hawaii Sea Grant College Program, Honolulu, HI.

Hummel, J. (2004). Pro-poor sustainable tourism: SNV Netherlands Development Organisation Nepal and Tourism Development for Poverty Reduction. In *Ferntourismus wohin? Der globale Tourismus erobert den Horizont* (K. Luger, & K.H. Wöhler, eds). StudienVerlag, Innsbruck, Austria.

Hunter, C. (1995) On the need to re-conceptualise sustainable tourism development. *Journal of Sustainable Tourism*, 3(3), 155–65.

Hunter, C. (2002). Aspects of the sustainable tourism debate from a natural resources perspective. In *Sustainable Tourism: A Global Perspective* (R. Harris, T. Griffin, & P. Williams, eds). Butterworth-Heinemann, Oxford, UK, pp. 3–24).

Huybers, T., & Bennett, J. (2002) *Environmental Management and the Competitiveness of Nature-Based Tourism Destinations*. Edward Elgar Publishing, Gloucestershire, UK.

Hvenegaard, L. (1994) Ecotourism: a status report and conceptual framework. *Journal of Tourism Studies*, 5(2), 24–34.

Inskeep, E. (1991) Environmental planning for tourism. *Annals of Tourism Research*, 14, 11–135.

Intathep, L. (2008). Island villagers switch to tourism after tsunami. *Bangkok Post Newspaper*, 22 March.

International Ecotourism Society (2008). Fact sheet: global ecotourism. Retrieved 1 January, 2008 from, www.ecotourism.org.

International Porter Protection Group (2003). Who are the Porters of Nepal? *IPPG Newsletter 2/2003*.

Interpretation Australia Association (2008). What is interpretation? & About us. Retrieved 22 February, 2008, from, www. interpretationaustralia.asn.au.

Ioannides, D., Apostolopoulos, Y., & Sonmez, S. (eds) (2001). *Mediterranean Islands and Sustainable Tourism Development*. Continuum Press, London.

IPSOS-Mori (2002) *Political Monitor: The Most Important Issues Facing the World Today*. IPSOS-Mori, London.

Isaacs, J.C. (2000) The limited potential of ecotourism to contribute to wildlife conservation. *Wildlife Society Bulletin*, 28(1), 61–9.

Iso-Ahola, S.E. (1983). *Towards a Social Psychology of Leisure and Recreation*. Wm. C. Brown, Dubuque, IA.

Ittelson, W.H., Proshansky, H.M., & Rivilin, L.G. (1974) *An Introduction to Environmental Psychology*. Holt, Rinehart & Winston, New York.

IUCN (International Union for the Conservation of Nature) (1992) *The Caracas Action Plan*. IUCN, Gland, Switzerland.

IUCN (International Union for the Conservation of Nature) (2004) *The Durban Action Plan*. IUCN, Gland, Switzerland.

IUCN (International Union for the Conservation of Nature) (2007). Protected area categories. Retrieved 10 December, 2007, from, www.iucn.org/themes/wcpa/theme/categories/what.

Jamal, T., Borges, M., & Stronza, A. (2006) The institutionalisation of ecotourism: certification, cultural equity and praxis. *Journal of Ecotourism*, 5(3), 145–75.

Jefferson, A., & Lickorish, L. (1988) *Marketing Tourism: A Practical Guide*. Longman, Harlow, UK.

Jenkins, J., & Wearing, S. (2003). Ecotourism and protected areas in Australia. In *Ecotourism Policy and Planning* (D.A. Fennell, & R.K. Dowling, eds). CABI, Wallingford, UK, pp. 205–34.

Jenkins, J.M., & Pigram, J.J. (2006). Outdoor recreation. In *A Handbook of Leisure Studies* (C. Rojek, S.M. Shaw, & A.J. Veal, eds). Palgrave MacMillan, Basingstoke, UK, pp. 363–85.

Jenkins, O., & McArthur, S. (1996) Marketing protected areas. *Australian Parks and Recreation*, 32(4), 10–5.

Jenner, P., & Smith, C. (1992). *The Tourism Industry and the Environment*. The Economist Intelligence Unit Special Report No. 2453, London.

Jennings, S. (2004) Landscape sensitivity and tourism development. *Journal of Sustainable Tourism*, 12(4), 271–88.

Jithendran, K.J., & Baum, T. (2000) Human resources development and sustainability – the case of Indian tourism. *International Journal of Tourism Research*, 2(6), 403–21.

Johnson, B. (1993) Breaking out of the tourist trap. *Cultural Survival Quarterly*, 14(1), 2–5.

Johnston, A.M. (2003). Self-determination: exercising indigenous rights in tourism. In *Tourism in Destination Communities* (S. Singh, D.J. Timothy, & R.K. Dowling, eds). CABI, Oxon, UK, pp. 115–32.

Jones, A. (1987) Green tourism. *Tourism Management*, 26, 354–6.

Joy, A., & Motzney, B. (1992). *Ecotourism and Ecotourists: Preliminary Thoughts on the New Leisure Traveller*. Paper presented at Seminar Proceedings of the American Marketing Association Winter Educator's Conference, Chicago, IL.

Kaczynski, A.T. (2008) A more tenable marketing for leisure services and studies. *Leisure Sciences*, 30(3), 253–72.

Kallen, C. (1990) *Tourism as a Conservation Tool* (working paper). World Resources Institute, Washington, DC.

Kamauro, O. (1996) *Ecotourism: Suicide or Development? Voices from Africa No. 6: Sustainable Development*. UN Non-Governmental Liaison Service, New York.

Kenchington, R.A. (1990). *Tourism in Coastal and Marine Settings: The Recreational Perspective*. Paper presented at 1990 Congress on Coastal and Marine Tourism – A Symposium and Workshop on Balancing Conservation and Economic Development. National Coastal Resources Research and Development Institute, Newport, OR.

Kerr, J. (1991, 25–27 September). Making Dollars and Sense Out of Ecotourism/Nature Tourism. Paper presented at First International Conference in Ecotourism, Brisbane, Australia.

Khan, M. (2003) ECOSERV: ecotourists quality expectations. *Annals of Tourism Research*, 30(1), 109–24.

Khan, S.A. (2002). Beyond the limits of sustainable growth: earth on the market. *Le Monde Diplomatique*, 8 December.

Klaushofer, A. (2007). Gap-year 'voluntourists' told not to bother. Retrieved 9 June, 2008, from, www.worldvolunteerweb.org.

Kollmuss, A., & Agyeman, J. (2002) Mind the gap: why do people act environmentally and what are the barriers to pro-environmental behavior? *Environmental Education Research*, 8(3), 239–60.

Koster, R., & Randall, J. (2005) Indicators of community economic development through mural-based tourism. *Canadian Geographer*, 49(1), 42–61.

Kotler, P., & Armstrong, G. (2004) *Principles of Marketing*, fourth ed. Prentice Hall, Englewood-Cliffs, NJ.

Kramer, R.A., Pattanayak, S., Sills, E., & Simanjuntak, S. (1997) *The Economics of the Siberut and Ruteng Protected Areas: Final Report*. Directorate General of Forest Protection and Nature Conservation, Government of Indonesia Biodiversity Conservation Project, Flores, Indonesia.

Krippendorf, J. (1982) Towards new tourism politics. *Tourism Management*, 3, 135–48.

Krippendorf, J. (1987) *The Holiday Makers*. Heinemann, London.

Krüger, O. (2005) The role of ecotourism in conservation: Panacea or Pandora's box? *Biodiversity and Conservation*, 14(3), 579–600.

Kumar, B., Adhikari, K., Subedi, G., & Gurung, Y. (2001). Nepal situation of child porters: a rapid assessment. International Labour Organization International Programme on the Elimination of Child Labour (IPEC). Retrieved 29 May, 2006, from, www.ilo.org/public/english/standards/ipec/simpoc/nepal/ra/porters.pdf.

Kusler, J. (n.d.) Protected areas approaches and ecotourism. Unpublished.

Kutay, K. (1990). Ecotourism: travel's new wave. *Vis a Vis*, July, 4–80.

Lao National Tourism Administration (2008). Ecotourism Laos. Retrieved 16 July, 2008, from, www. ecotourismlaos.com.

Lai, P.H., & Shafer, S. (2005) Marketing ecotourism through the Internet: an evaluation of selected ecolodges in Latin America and the Caribbean. *Journal of Ecotourism*, 4(3), 143–60.

Lanagan, D. (2002) Surfing in the third millennium: commodifying the visual argot. *The Australian Journal of Anthropology*, 13(3), 283–91.

Larrère, R., & Larrère, C. (2007) Should nature be respected? *Social Science Information*, 46(1), 9–34.

Lea, J.P. (1988) *Tourism and Development in the Third World*. Routledge, London.

Lea, J.P. (1993) Tourism development ethics in the third world. *Annals of Tourism Research*, 20, 701–15.

Leigh, A. (2008) *Public Opinion Towards Governance*. Australian National University, Canberra, Australia.

Leopold, A. (1966) *A Sand Country Almanac*. Ballantine, New York.

Lewis, W.S. (1980) *Interpreting for Park Visitors*. Eastern Acorn Press, Atlanta, GA.

Lillywhite, M. (1992, 28–31 August). *Low Impact Tourism: Sustaining Indigenous Natural Resource Management and Diversifying Economic Development*. Paper presented at 1991 World Conference on Adventure Travel and Ecotourism. Colorado Springs, CO.

Lillywhite, M., & Lillywhite, L. (1990). *Low Impact Tourism, Coupling Natural/ Cultural Resource Conservation Economic Development and the Tourism Industry*. Paper presented at Fifth Annual Travel Review Conference 1990, Washington, DC.

Lindberg, K. (1991) *Policies for Maximising Nature Tourism's Ecological and Economic Benefits* (International Conservation Financing Project Working Paper). World Resources Institute, New York.

Lindberg, K., Epler Wood, M., & Engeldrum, D. (1998) *Ecotourism: A Guide for Planners and Managers*, vol. 2. The Ecotourism Society, North Bennington, VT.

Lindberg, K. (2000). Economic impacts. In *The Encyclopedia of Ecotourism* (D.B. Weaver, ed.). CABI, Wallingford, UK, pp. 363–77.

Locke, J. (1841) *An Essay Concerning Human Understanding*. Dent, London.

Loker-Murphy, L. (1996) Backpackers in Australia: a motivational-based segmentation study. *Journal of Travel and Tourism Marketing*, 5(4), 23–44.

Lorimer, K. (2006) *Code Green: Experiences of a Lifetime*. Lonely Planet Publications, Footscray, Australia.

Lovelock, J. (1988) *The Ages of GAIA*. Oxford University Press, Oxford, UK.

Lovett, K. (1998) Custodians of the point. *The Surfers Journal*, 7, 84–119.

Lovett, K. (2005) Lowalani's kingdom. *Tracks*, 11, 92–104.

Lucas, R. (1984) The role of regulations in recreation management. *Western Wildlands*. 9(2), 6–10.

Lueras, L., & Lueras, L. (1997) *Surfing Indonesia: A Search for the World's Most Perfect Waves*. Periplus, Hong Kong.

Lutz Newton, J. (2006) *Aldo Leopold's Odyssey*. Island Press, Washington, DC.

MacCannell, D. (1976) *The Tourist: A New Theory of the Leisure Class*. Macmillan, London.

Machlis, G., & Field, D. (1992) *On Interpretation, Sociology for Interpreters of Natural and Cultural History*. Oregon State University Press, Corvallis, OR.

Machlis, G., & Tichnell, D. (1985) *The State of the World's Parks*. Westview Press, Boulder, CO.

Mackay, H. (1992) To tell a lie. *City Ethics*. 7, p. 3.

MacKinnon, J., MacKinnon, K., Child, G., & Thorsell, J. (1986) *Managing Protected Areas in the Tropics*. IUCN, Gland, Switzerland.

Mader, R. (1999) Ecotourism research and promotion on the web: experiences and insights. *International Journal of Contemporary Hospitality Management*, 11(2–3), 78–9.

Mader, R. (2002) Latin American ecotourism: what is it? *Current Issues in Tourism*, 5(3), 272–9.

Maguire, P. (1987) *Doing Participatory Research: A Feminist Approach*. The Centre for International Education, University of Massachusetts, Amherst, MA.

Mahapatra, S. (1998). Economic development, tourism and culture. In *Tourism and Development: Economic, Social, Political and Environmental Issues* (C.A. Tisdell, & K.C. Ray, eds). Nova Science Publishers, New York, pp. 21–36.

Manidis Roberts (1994) *An Investigation into a National Ecotourism Accreditation Scheme*. Commonwealth Department of Tourism, Canberra, Australia.

Manidis Roberts (1997) *Tourism Optimisation Management Model – Final Report*. Manidis Roberts Consultants, Sydney.

Manning, R.E., & Powers, L.A. (1984) Peak and off-peak use: redistributing the outdoor recreation/tourism load. *Journal of Travel Research*, 23(2), 25–31.

Marfut, E. (1999). Tourism in the third world: dream or nightmare? In *The Earthscan Reader in Sustainable Tourism* (L. France, ed.). Earthscan Publications, London, pp. 94–108.

Marion, J.L., & Reid, S.E. (2007) Minimising visitor impacts to protected areas: the efficacy of low impact education programmes. *Journal of Sustainable Tourism*, 15, 5–27.

Marriott, K. (1993) Pricing policy for user pays. *Australian Parks and Recreation*, 29(3), 42–5.

Marshall, G. (1994) *The Concise Oxford Dictionary of Sociology*. Oxford University Press, Oxford, UK.

Maslow, A. (1970) *Motivation and Personality*. Harper & Row, New York.

Mason, P. (1997) Tourism codes of conduct in the Arctic and sub-Arctic region. *Journal of Sustainable Development*, 5(2), 151–64.

Mason, P. (2005) Visitor management in protected areas: from 'hard' to 'soft' approaches? *Current Issues in Tourism*, 8(2/3), 181–94.

Masson, D. (1991). Holidays to help the planet. *The Australian Magazine*, 21 February.

Mastny, L. (2001) *Treading Lightly: New Paths for International Tourism.* Worldwatch Institute, Washington, DC, paper no. 159.

Mathews, F. (1987) Conservation and the politics of deep ecology. *Social Alternatives*, 6(4), 37–41.

Mathews, F. (1993) When the planet signs to us, Res Publica, 2(1), 9–14.

Mathieson, A., & Wall, G. (1982) *Tourism: Economic and Social Impacts.* Longman, London.

Mayes, G., Dyer, P., & Richins, H. (2004) Dolphin–human interaction: changing pro-environmental attitudes, beliefs, behaviours and intended actions of participants through management and interpretation programs. *Annals of Leisure Research*, 7(1), 34–53.

Mazibuko, S. (2007) Leakages and costs of eco-tourism: the case of AmaZizi in the northern Drakensberg. *Africa Insight*, 37(1), 150–68.

Mazimhaka, J. (2007) Diversifying Rwanda's tourism industry: a role for domestic tourism. *Development Southern Africa*, 24(3), 491–504.

Mbaiwa, J.E. (2004) The socio-cultural impacts of tourism development in the Okavango Delta, Botswana. *Journal of Tourism and Cultural Change*, 2(3), 163–84.

McArthur, S. (1996) Interpretation in Australia – is it running on borrowed time? *Australian Parks and Recreation*, 32(2), 33–6.

McArthur, S. (1997a) Introducing the national ecotourism accreditation program. *Australian Parks and Recreation*, 34(2), 11–3.

McArthur, S. (1997b). *Beyond the Limits of Acceptable Change – Introducing TOMM.* Paper presented at Tread Lightly World Conference, Coffs Harbour, Australia.

McArthur, S. (1997c). Growth and jobs in Australia's ecotourism industry. In *Australian Ecotourism Guide 1997/98*. Ecotourism Association of Australia, Brisbane, Australia, pp. 33–4.

McCool S.F. (1990). *Limits of Acceptable Change: Evolution and Future.* Paper presented at First Canada/U.S. Workshop on Visitor Management in Parks and Protected Areas. Tourism and Recreation Education Center, University of Waterloo, and Canadian Parks Service, Environment Canada, Waterloo, Ontario.

McCool, S.F., & Lime, D.W. (2001) Tourism carrying capacity: tempting fantasy or useful reality. *Journal of Sustainable Tourism*, 9(5), 372–88.

McCurdy, D. (1985) *Park Management.* Southern Illinois University Press, Carbondale, IL.

McDonald, M., Wearing, S., & Ponting, J. (in press). The nature of peak experience in wilderness. *The Humanistic Psychologist*

McGrath, G. (2007). Towards developing tour guides as interpreters of cultural heritage: the case of Cusco, Peru. In *Quality Assurance and Certification in Ecotourism* (R. Black, & A. Crabtree, eds). CABI, Wallingford, UK. pp. 364–94.

McGehee, N., & Andercek, K. (2008). "Pettin' the critters": exploring the complex relationship between volunteers and the volunteered in McDowell County, West Virginia, USA and Tijuana, Mexico. In *Journeys of Discovery in Volunteer Tourism: International Case Study Perspectives* (K.D. Lyons, & S. Wearing, eds). CABI, Wallingford, UK, pp. 12–24.

McGehee, N.G., Loker-Murphy, L., & Uysat M. (1996) The Australian international travel market: motivations from a gendered perspective. *Journal of Tourism Studies*, 7(1), 45–57.

McIntyre, G., Hetherington, A., & Inskeep, E. (1993) *Preparing Development Plans*. WTO Sustainable Tourism Development, Madrid.

McKercher, B. (1991a). The unrecognised threat to tourism: can tourism survive sustainability? In *Ecotourism Incorporating the Global Classroom* (B. Weiler, ed.). Bureau of Tourism Research, Canberra, Australia.

McKercher, B. (1991b). Understanding tourism's impacts: six truths about tourism. In *Benefits and Costs of Tourism* (P.J. Stanton, ed.). Institute of Industrial Economics, University of Newcastle, Newcastle, Australia, pp. 63–74.

McKinlay, D. (2003). The men who carry a country's economy on their backs. Retrieved 14 May, 2003, from, www.timesonline.co.uk

McLaren, D. (2003) *Rethinking Tourism and Ecotravel*, second ed. Kumarian Press, Bloomfield, NJ.

McNeely, J.A., & Thorsell, J. (1989) *Jungles, Mountains and Islands: How Tourism can Help Conserve Natural Heritage*. IUCN, Gland, Switzerland.

Mehmetoglu, M. (2007) Nature-based tourists: the relationship between their trip expenditures and activities. *Journal of Sustainable Tourism*, 15(2), 200–15.

Mercer, D. (1995) *A Question of Balance – Natural Resource Conflict Issues in Australia*. The Federation Press, Sydney.

Merino, S.E. (2006) Marine eco-tourism in Cape Verde: its potential for sustainable development and conservation of marine biodiversity. *Occasional Publication of the Irish Biogeographical Society*, 9, 199–206.

Merschen, A. (1992, 20–23 September). *Marketing Techniques and Critiques*. Paper presented at World Congress on Adventure Travel and Ecotourism, Vancouver, Canada.

Messer, J., & Mosley, G. (1980) *The Value of National Parks to the Community: Values and Ways of Improving the Contribution of Australian National Parks to the Community*. Australian Conservation Foundation, Melbourne, Australia.

Middleton, V. (1989) *Marketing in Travel and Tourism*. Heinemann, Oxford, UK.

Middleton, V., & Hawkins, R. (1998) *Sustainable Tourism: A Marketing Perspective*. Butterworth-Heinemann, Oxford, UK.

Mieczkowski, Z. (1995) *Environmental Issues of Tourism and Recreation*. University Press of America, Lanham, MD.

Miller, G., & Twining-Ward, L. (2005). Tourism optimization management model. In *Monitoring for a Sustainable Tourism Transition: The Challenge of Developing and Using Indicators* (G. Miller, & L. Twining-Ward, eds). CABI, Wallingford, UK, pp. 201–31.

Mitman Clarke, W. (1997). Insufficient funds. *National Parks*, July/August, pp. 26–9.

Morais, D.B., Cheng, Z., ErWei, D., & GuiHua, Y. (2006) Promoting sustainability through increased community involvement: the Shangri-La ecotourism demonstration project. *Tourism Review International*, 10(3), 131–40.

Mowforth, M., & Munt, I. (2008) *Tourism and Sustainability: Development, Globalization and New Tourism in the Third World*, third ed. Routledge, London.

Munn, C. (1991) *Macaw Biology and Ecotourism, or When a Bird in the Bush is Worth Two in the Hand*. Smithsonian Press, Washington, DC.

Musa, G. (2005). The importance of health as a factor in achieving sustainability in a high altitude destination in a less developed country: a case study of Sagarmatha National Park, Nepal. In *Nature-Based Tourism in Peripheral Areas: Development or Disaster?* (C.M.H.S. Boyd, ed.). Channel View Publications, Clevedon, UK, pp. 105–32.

Mustonen, P. (2005) Volunteer tourism: postmodern pilgrimage? *Journal of Tourism and Cultural Change*, 3(3), 160–77.

Murphy, P. (1985) *Tourism: A Community Approach*. Methuen, London.

Munro, J.K., Morrison-Saundersa, A., & Hughesb, M. (2008) Environmental interpretation evaluation in natural areas. *Journal of Ecotourism*, 7(1), 1–14.

Nash, R. (1989) *The Rights of Nature*. Primavera Press, Sydney.

Nash, R. (2001). *Wilderness and the American Mind*, fourth ed. Yale University Press, New Haven, CT.

National Park Service (1984) *Marketing Parks and Recreation*. Venture, State College, PA.

Nepal, S.K. (2002). Tourism as a key to sustainable mountain development: the Nepalese Himalayas in retrospect. Retrieved 23 March, 2004, from, www.fao.org.

Newsome, D., Moore, S.A., & Dowling, R.K. (2002) *Natural Area Tourism: Ecology, Impacts and Management*. Channel View Publications, Clevedon, UK.

Niefer, I.A., João, C.J., da Silva, G.L., & Amend, M. (2002) Analysis of the visitors of Superagüi National Park, Brazil. *Current Issues in Tourism*, 5(3), 208–21

Noam, M. (1999) *The Guide for Guides: A Tour Guide Manual*. Rafael Haim Cohen, Jerusalem.

Norris, R. (1994) Ecotourism in the national parks of Latin America. *National Parks*, 68 (1–2), 33–7.

Nowaczek, A.M., Moran-Cahusac, C., & Fennell, D.A. (2007). Against the current: striving for ethical ecotourism. In *Critical Issues in Ecotourism: Understanding a Complex Tourism Phenomenon* (J. Higham, ed.). Butterworth-Heinemann, Oxford, UK, pp. 136–57.

NZTIF (New Zealand Tourist Industry Federation) (1991) *Code of Environmental Principles for Tourism in New Zealand*. NZTIF, Wellington, New Zealand.

Okello, M.M. (2005) A survey of tourist expectations and economic potential for a proposed wildlife sanctuary in a Maasai Group Ranch near Amboseli, Kenya. *Journal of Sustainable Tourism*, 13(6), 566–89.

Olsen, K. (2006) Making differences in a changing world: the Norwegian Sámi in the tourist industry. *Scandinavian Journal of Hospitality and Tourism*, 6(1), 37–53.

O'Neill, M. (1991). Naturally attractive. *Pacific Monthly*, September, p. 25.

O'Riordan, T. (ed.) (1989) *The Challenge for Environmentalism*. Unwin Hyman, London.

Orams, M.B. (2001) Types of ecotourism. In *An Encyclopedia of Ecotourism* (D.B. Weaver, ed.). CABI, New York, pp. 23–36.

Orams, M.B. (2003). Marine ecotourism in New Zealand: an overview of the industry and its management. In *Marine Ecotourism: Issues and Experiences* (B. Garrod, & J.C. Wilson, eds). Channel View Publications, Clevedon, UK, pp. 213–48.

Owens, D., Patterson, C., & Owens, M. (2007) *The Business of Ecotourism*, third ed. Trafford Publishing, Victoria, Canada.

Page, S.J., & Dowling, R.K. (2002) *Ecotourism*. Prentice Hall, London.

Palacio, V., & McCool, S. (1997) Identifying ecotourists in Belize through benefit segmentation: a preliminary analysis. *Journal of Sustainable Development*, 5(3), 234–44.

Palmer, N.J. (2006) Economic transition and the struggle for local control in ecotourism development: the case of Kyrgyzstan. *Journal of Ecotourism*, 5(1–2), 40–61.

Parks Victoria (2008). Education. Retrieved 10 December, 2007 from, www.parkweb.vic.gov.au/education.

PATA (Pacific Asia Travel Association) (1992a) *Endemic Tourism: A Profitable Industry in a Sustainable Environment*. PATA, Sydney.

PATA (Pacific Asia Travel Association) (1992b) *Code for Environmentally Responsible Tourism*. PATA, San Francisco, CA.

Payne, R., & Graham, R. (1993). Visitor planning and management. In *Parks and Protected Areas in Canada: Planning and Management* (P. Dearden, & R. Rollins, eds). Oxford University Press, Toronto, Canada.

Pearce, F. (2006) One degree and we're done for. *New Scientist*, 30, 8–9.

Pearce, P. (1984) Tourist-guide interaction. *Annals of Tourism Research*, 11(1), 129–46.

Pearce, P. (1988) *The Ulysses Factor: Evaluating Visitors in Tourist Settings*. Springer-Verlag, New York.

Pearce, P. (1993). Fundamentals of tourist motivation. In *Tourism Research: Critiques and Challenges* (D. Pearce, & R. Butler, eds). Routledge, London, pp. 113–34.

Pearce, P.L., Moscardo, G.M., & Ross, G.F. (1996) *Tourism Community Relationships*. Pergamon, London.

Pearce, P.J. (2005) *Tourist Behaviour: Themes and Conceptual Schemes*. Channel View Publications, Clevedon, UK.

Peet, R. (1999) *Theories of Development*. Guilford Press, London.

Peng, M. (1992). Nero's children. *New Internationalist*, April, 24–7.

Pepper, D. (1996) *Modern Environmentalism: An Introduction*. Routledge, London.

Periera, E. (2005) How do tourist guides add value to an ecotour? Interpreting interpretation in the State of Amazonas, Brazil. *FIU Hospitality and Tourism Review*, 23(2), 1–8.

Persoon, G.A. (1997). Defining wildness and wilderness: Minangkabau images and actions on Siberut (West Sumatra). Retrieved 11 July, 1997, from, www.lucy.ukc.ac.uk/Rainforest/Workingpaperspublic/wpa3_1.html

Persoon, G.A. (2003) Conflicts over trees and waves on Siberut Island. *Geografiska Annaler*, 85 B(4), 253–64.

Persoon, G.A., & van Beek, H.H. (1998). Uninvited guests: tourists and environment on Siberut. In *Environmental Challenges in South-East Asia* (G.A. Persoon, H.H. van Beek, & V. King, eds). Nordic Institute of Asian Studies, Copenhagen, pp. 317–41.

Peterson, G.L., Driver, B.L., & Gregory, R. (eds) (1988) Amenity resource valuation: integrating economics with other disciplines, Venture: State College, PA.

Pigram, J.J., & Jenkins, J. (2005) *Outdoor Recreation Management*, second ed. Routledge, London.

Pinchot, G. (1910) *The Fight for Conservation*. Doubleday, New York.

Pflanz, M. (2007). Masai Mara tourist ban. *The Telegraph Newspaper*, 21 January.

Ponting, J. (2007). *The Endless Bummer: The Past, Present and Future of Surfing Tourism in the Pacific*. Paper presented at the CAUTHE Conference, Sydney.

Ponting, J. (2008) *Consuming Nirvana: An Exploration of Surfing Tourist Space*. Unpublished PhD thesis, University of Technology, Sydney.

Ponting, J. (in press). Projecting paradise: the surf media and the hermeneutic circle in surfing tourism. *Tourism Analysis*.

Ponting, J., McDonald, M., & Wearing, S. (2005) De-constructing wonderland: surfing tourism in the Mentawai Islands, Indonesia. *Society and Leisure*, 28(1), 141–62.

Pope, J., Annandale, D., & Morrison-Saunders, A. (2004) Conceptualising sustainability assessment. *Environmental Impact Assessment Review*, 24(6), 595–616.

Porteous, A. (2000) *Dictionary of Environmental Science and Technology*, third ed. Wiley Blackwell, New York.

Price, G.G. (2003) Ecotourism operators and environmental education: enhancing competitive advantage by advertising environmental learning experiences. *Tourism Analysis*, 8(2–4), 143–7.

Price, G.G. (2004). Ecotourists environmental learning opportunity as a source of competitive advantage: are ecotourism operators missing the boat with their advertising? In *Consumer Psychology of Tourism, Hospitality and Leisure* (G.I. Crouch, R.R. Perdue, H.J.P. Timmermans, & M. Uysal, eds). CABI, Wallingford, UK, pp. 65–73.

Prideaux, B., & Falco-Mammone, F. (2007) *Economic Values of the Tourism in the Wet Tropics World Heritage Area*. Cooperative Research Centre for Tropical Rainforest Ecology and Management, James Cook University, Cairns, Australia.

Priporas, C.V., & Kamenidou, I. (2003) Can alternative tourism be the way forward for the development of tourism in Northern Greece? *Tourism*, 51(1), 53–62.

Prosser, G. (1986) The limits of acceptable change: an introduction to a framework for natural area planning. *Australian Parks and Recreation*, 22(2), 5–10.

Pyo, S., Mihalik, B.J., & Uysal, M. (1989) Attraction attributes and motivations: a canonical correlation analysis. *Annals of Tourism Research*, 16(2), 277–82.

Reeves, G. (2000). The anthropology of the Mentawai Islands. Retrieved 14 August, 2000, from, www.asian.gu.edu.au/mentawai/index.html.

Reuters. (2007). Perfect wave reveals dark heart of surfing. *The Melbourne Age*, 25 April 2007. Retrieved 25 April, 2007, from, www.theage.com/au/news/travel/perfect-wave-reveals-dark-heart-of-surfing/2007/04/25/1177459760469html.

Richards, G., & Wilson, J. (eds) (2004) *The Global Nomad: Backpacker Travel in Theory and Practice*. Channel View Publications, Clevedon, UK.

Richardson, J. (1991). The case for an ecotourism association. In *Ecotourism Incorporating the Global Classroom* (B. Weiler, ed.). Bureau of Tourism Research, Canberra, Australia.

Richardson, J. (1995). Strategic alliances. In *Ecotourism and Nature-Based Tourism: Taking the Next Steps* (H. Richins, J. Richardson, & A. Crabtree, eds). Ecotourism Association of Australia, Brisbane, Australia.

Rinne, P., & Saastamoinen, O. (2005) Local economic role of nature-based tourism in Kuhmo municipality, eastern Finland. *Scandinavian Journal of Hospitality and Tourism*, 5(2), 89–101.

Robinson, G. (1988) *Crosscultural Understanding*. Prentice-Hall, Hempel Hempstead, UK.

Robinson, J. (2006). Paddy Pallin, personal communication, 1 June.

Robinson, M., & Boniface, P. (Eds). (1999) *Tourism and Cultural Conflicts*. CABI, Wallingford, UK.

Rodger, K., Moore, S.A., & Newsome, D. (2007) Wildlife tours in Australia: characteristics, the place of science and sustainable futures. *Journal of Sustainable Tourism*, 15(2), 160–79.

Roe, D., & Urquhart, P. (2001) *Pro-poor Tourism: Harnessing the World's Largest Industry for the World's Poor*. International Institute for Environment and Development, London.

Roggenbuck, J.W. (1987). *Park Interpretation as a Visitor Management Strategy*. Paper presented at 60th International Conference of the Royal Australian Institute of Parks and Recreation-Metropolitan Prospective in Parks and Recreation, Canberra, Australia.

Ross, S., & Wall, G. (1999) Ecotourism: towards congruence between theory and practice. *Tourism Management*, 20, 123–32.

Rouphael, A.B., & Hanafy, M. (2007) An alternative management framework to limit the impact of SCUBA divers on coral assemblages. *Journal of Sustainable Tourism*, 15(1), 91–103.

Runte, A. (1997) *National Parks: The American Experience*. University of Nebraska Press, Lincoln, NE.

Ruschano, R., & Yaotanee, K. (2007, 30 January–2 February). *Application of Geographical Information System to Recreation Opportunity Spectrum Zoning, Chiang Mai Province*. Paper presented at 44th Kasetsart University Annual Conference, Kasetsart University, Chalermphrakiat Sakon Nakhon Province Campus.

Saglio, C. (1979). Tourism for discovery: a project in Lower Casemance, Senegal. In *Tourism Passport to Development? Perspectives on the Social and Cultural Effects of Tourism in Developing Countries* (E. De Kadt, ed.). Oxford University Press, New York.

Samacharparta, N. (2002). Kavre's child soldiers. Retrieved 1 June, 2006, from, www.nepalitimes.com

Saveriades, A. (2000) Establishing the social tourism carrying capacity for the tourist resorts of the east coast of the Republic of Cyprus. *Tourism Management*, 21(2), 147–56.

Saville, N. (2001) *Practical Strategies for Pro-poor Tourism: Case Study of Pro-poor Tourism and SNV in Humla District, West Nepal (Pro-poor Tourism Report No 3)*. ODI, IIED & CRT, London.

Scarpaci, C., Nugegoda, D., & Corkeron, P.J. (2004) No detectable improvement in compliance to regulations by "swim-with-dolphin" operators in Port Phillip Bay, Victoria, Australia. *Tourism in Marine Environments*, 1(1), 41–8.

Scheyvens, R. (1999) Ecotourism and the empowerment of local communities. *Tourism Management* 20(2), 245–9.

Scheyvens, R. (2007). Ecotourism and gender issues. In *Critical Issues in Ecotourism: Understanding a Complex Tourism Phenomenon* (J. Higham, ed.). Elsevier, Amsterdam, Netherlands, pp. 185–213.

Schilcher, D. (2007). Growth versus equity: the continuum of pro-poor tourism and neoliberal governance. In *Pro-poor Tourism: Who Benefits? Perspectives on Tourism and Poverty Reduction* (C.M. Hall, ed.). Channel View Publications, Clevedon, UK, pp. 56–83.

Schott, C. (2006) Proactive crises management tools: ecolabel and Green Globe 21 experiences from New Zealand. *Tourism Review International*, 10(1–2), 81–90.

Scott, N.R. (1974) Toward a psychology of wilderness experience. *Natural Resource Journal*, 14, 231–7.

Semple, W. (2005) Traditional architecture in Tibet: linking issues of environmental and cultural sustainability. *Mountain Research and Development*, 25(1), 15–9.

Sills, E.O. (1998) *Ecotourism as an Integral Conservation and Development Strategy: Econometric Estimation of Demand by International Tourists and Impacts up Indigenous Households in Indonesia.* Unpublished PhD thesis, Duke University, Durham, NC.

Shackley, M. (1995) The future of gorilla tourism in Rwanda. *Journal of Sustainable Development*, 3(2), 61–72.

Sharpe, G.W. (1982) *Interpreting the Environment*. John Wiley, New York.

Sharpley, R. (2006) Ecotourism: a consumption perspective. *Journal of Ecotourism*, 5(1–2), 7–22.

Sharpley, R., & Telfer, D. (eds) (2002) *Tourism and Development: Concepts and Issues*. Channel View Publications, Clevedon, UK.

Sheppard, D. (1987) *Parks Are for the People – or Are They?* Unpublished paper. NSW National Parks and Wildlife Service, Sydney.

Shepherd, N. (2002) How ecotourism can go wrong: the cases of SeaCanoe and Siam Safari, Thailand. *Current Issues in Tourism*, 5(3), 309–18.

Shiva, V. (1989) *Staying Alive: Women Ecology and Development*. Zed Books, London.

Shrestha, M. (2001). Can trekkers help Manaslu? Retrieved 21 March, 2004, from, www.peolpleandplanet.net.

ShuYang, F., Freedman, B., & Cote, R. (2004) Principles and practice of ecological design. *Environmental Reviews*, 12(2), 97–112.

Silverberg, K.E., Backman, S.J., & Backman, K.F. (1996) *A Preliminary Investigation into the Psychographics of Nature-Based Travellers to the Southeastern United States*. Clemson University Press, Clemson, SC.

Simmons, M., & Harris. R. (1995). The great barrier marine park. In *Sustainable Tourism: An Australian Perspective* (R. Harris, & N. Leiper, eds). Butterworth-Heinemann, Melbourne, Australia, pp. 11–9.

Sirakaya, E. & Uysal M. (1997) Can sanctions and rewards explain conformance behaviour of tour operators with ecotourism guidelines? *Journal of Sustainable Tourism*, 5(4), 322–32.

Sithole, E. (2005) Trans-boundary environmental actors: the Zambezi Society's campaign for sustainable tourism development in the Zambezi Bioregion. *Journal of Sustainable Tourism*, 13(5), 486–503.

Slater, E. (2001). Ship of feuds. Retrieved 28 August, 2005, from, www.surfline. com.

Small, J. (1997) *A Simple Model of Tourist Motivation*. Unpublished research paper, School of Leisure and Tourism Studies, University of Technology, Sydney.

Smith, A.J., Lee, D., Newsome, D., & Stoeckl, N. (2006). Production and consumption of wildlife icons: dolphin tourism at Monkey Mia, Western Australia. In *Tourism Consumption and Representation: Narratives of Place and Self* (K. Meethan, A. Anderson, & S. Miles, eds). CABI, Wallingford, UK, pp. 113–39.

Smith, R. A. (2000). Tourism planning and development in Southeast and South Asia. In *Tourism in South and Southeast Asia: Issues and Cases* (C.M. Hall, & S. Page, eds). Butterworth-Heinemann, Oxford, UK, pp. 104–14.

Sofield, T.H.B. (1991) Sustainable ethnic tourism in the South Pacific: some principles. *Journal of Tourism Studies*, 2(1), 56–72.

Sofield, T.H.B. (2003) *Empowerment for Sustainable Tourism Development*. Pergamon, Amsterdam.

Spaltenberger, T. (2003). Tourism in the Himalaya. Retrieved 27 April, 2004, from, www.spaltenberger.de/usa/himalayantourism.pdf.

Speelman, N. (1996) The land of Smetana and Martinu. *World Leisure and Recreation*, 38(1), 15–21.

Stankey, G., & McCool, S. (eds) (1985) *Proceedings – Symposium on Recreation Choice Behaviour (United States Forest Service General Technical Report INT-184)*. United States Department of Agriculture, Ogden, UT.

Stankey, G.H. (1991). *Conservation, Recreation and Tourism: the Good, the Bad and the Ugly*. Paper presented at 1990 Congress on Coastal and Marine Tourism – A Symposium and Workshop on Balancing Conservation and Economic Development. National Coastal Resources Research and Development Institute, Newport, OR.

Stankey, G.H., Cole, D.N., Lucas, R.C., Peterson, M.E., & Frissell, S.S. (1985) *The Limits of Acceptable Change (LAC) System for Wilderness Planning*. United States Forest Service General Technical Report INT-176, Ogden, UT.

Stanton, M. (2003). Economics and tourism development on Easter Island. In *Pacific Island Tourism* (D. Harrison, ed.). Cognizant Communication Corporation, Elmsford, NY, pp. 110–24.

Stanton, W.J., Miller, K.E., & Layton R.A. (1992) *Fundamentals of Marketing*. McGraw-Hill, Sydney.

Stear, L., Buckley, G., & Stankey, G. (1988). Constructing a meaningful concept of 'tourism industry': some problems and implications for research and policy. In *Frontiers in Australian Tourism: The Search for New Perspectives in Policy Development and Research* (B. Faulkner, & M. Fagence, eds). Bureau of Tourism Research, Canberra, Australia.

Steele, P. (1995) Ecotourism: an economic analysis. *Journal of Sustainable Tourism*, 3(1), 29–44.

Strasdas, W., Corcoran, B., & Petermann, T. (2003). *Capacity-Building for Ecotourism: Training Programmes for Managers of Protected Areas*. Paper presented at the Tourism and Protected Areas: Benefits Beyond Boundaries. The Vth IUCN World Parks Congress, Durban, South Africa.

Stretton, H. (1976) *Capitalism, Socialism and the Environment*. Cambridge University Press, Cambridge, UK.

Strom, A. (1980). Impressions of a developing conservation ethic 1870–1930. In *100 years of parks*. Australian Conservation Foundation, Melbourne, Australia.

Subedi, S. (2000). Celebrating the porters. Retrieved 1 June, 2006, from, www.nepalitimes.com.

SurfAid International (2005) *Annual Report 2004*. SurfAid International, Encinitas, CA.

Surfline (2005). Forecast. Retrieved 22 August, 2005, from, www.surfline.com/surfology/surfology_forecast2.cfm.

Svoronou, E., & Holden, A. (2005) Ecotourism as a tool for nature conservation: the role of WWF Greece in the Dadia-Lefkimi-Soufli Forest Reserve in Greece. *Journal of Sustainable Tourism*, 13(5), 456–67.

Swain, M.B., & Swain, M.T.B. (2004) An ecofeminist approach to ecotourism development. *Tourism Recreation Research*, 29(3), 1–6.

Swanson, M.A. (1992, 10–12 February). *Ecotourism: Embracing the New Environmental Paradigm*. Paper presented at the International Union for Conservation of Nature and Natural Resources (IUCN) IVth World Congress on National Parks and Protected Areas, Caracas, Venezuela.

Swarbrooke, J. (1999) *Sustainable Tourism Management*. CABI, Wallingford, UK.

Taylor, G. (1990). *Planning and Managing Visitor Opportunities*. Paper presented at First Canada/US Workshop on Visitor Management in Parks and Protected Areas. Tourism Research and Education Centre, University of Waterloo and Canadian Parks Service, Environment Canada, Waterloo, Canada.

Taylor, J.E., Dyer, G.A., Stewart, M., Yunez-Naude, A., & Ardila, S. (2003) The economics of ecotourism: a Galapagos islands economy-wide perspective. *Economic Development and Cultural Change*, 51(4), 977–97.

Tourism Council Australia (1998) *Code of Sustainable Practice*. Tourism Council Australia, Sydney.

Teo, A. (1996) Managing Sakau Rainforest Lodge – Malaysia, British Airways Tourism for Tomorrow Awards 1996, Pacific Region (unpublished).

Telfer, D.J. (2002). Tourism and regional development issues. In *Tourism and Development: Concepts and Issues* (R. Sharpley, & D.J. Telfer, eds). Channel View Publications, Clevendon, UK, pp. 112–48.

Tepelus, C. (2008) Reviewing the IYE and WSSD processes and impacts on the tourism sustainability agenda. *Journal of Ecotourism*, 7(1), 77–86.

The Himalayan Trust UK (2006). Welcome. Retrieved 1 June, 2006, from, www.himalayantrust.co.uk.

The International Ecotourism Society (2007). Definition and principles. Retrieved 10 December, 2007, from, www.ecotourism.org/webmodules/webarticlesnet/templates/eco_template.aspx?articleid=95&zoneid=2.

The International Ecotourism Society (2008). Ecotourism facts and statistics. Retrieved 10 December, 2007, from, www.ecotourism.org/webmodules/webarticlesnet/templates/eco_template.aspx?articleid=15&zoneid=2.

Timothy, D.J. (2001). Gender relations in tourism: revisiting patriarchy and underdevelopment. In *Women as Producers and Consumers of Tourism in Developing Regions* (Y. Papostolopoulos, S. Sonmez, & D.J. Timothy, eds). Praeger, Westport, CT, pp. 235–48.

Timothy, D.J., & Tosun, C. (2003). Appropriate planning for tourism in destination communities: participation, incremental growth and collaboration. In *Tourism in Destination Communities* (S. Singh, D.J. Timothy, & R.K. Dowling, eds). CAB International, Oxon, UK, pp. 181–204.

Tilden, F. (1957) *Interpreting Our Heritage.* John Wiley, New York.

Tilden, J. (1977) *Interpreting Our Heritage*, third ed. University of North Carolina Press, Chapel Hill, NC.

Tisdell, C. (2004). Biodiversity conservation and globalisation: global economic failures with implications for developing countries. In *Economic Globalisation: Social Conflicts, Labour and Environmental Issues* (C. Tisdell, & R.K. Sen, eds). Edward Elgar Publishing, Cheltenham, UK, pp. 269–79.

Tisdell, C., & Wilson, C. (2005) Perceived impacts of ecotourism on environmental learning and conservation: turtle watching as a case study. *Environment, Development and Sustainability*, 7(3), 291–302.

Todd, G. (1989) Tourism and the environment. *Travel and Tourism Analyst (EIU)*, 5, 68–86.

Tokalau, F. (2005). The economic benefits of an ecotourism project in a regional economy: a case study of Namuamua Inland Tour, Namosi, Fiji Islands. In *Nature-Based Tourism in Peripheral Areas: Development or Disaster?* (C.M. Hall, & S. Boyd, eds). Channel View Publications, Clevedon, UK, pp. 173–87.

Tolhurst, C. (1994) Seeing red over green rulings 'with no teeth'. *Travel trade*, November, 16–29.

Tonge, R., & Myott, D. (1989) *How to Plan, Develop and Market Local and Regional Tourism*. Gull Publishing, Brisbane, Australia.

Tonnini, C.C., Lunardi, R., & Guido, L.A. (2006) Rural tourism: a way to quality of life. *Agrociencia*, 10(2), 39–44.

Tourism Concern (2002). Radical move by UK trek tour operators helps transform mountain porters' lives (press release November 26, 2002). Retrieved 19 June, 2003, from, www.tourismconcern.org.uk.

Tourism Concern (2008). Trekking wrongs: porter's rights. Retrieved 16 June, 2008, from, www.tourismconcern.org.uk.

Tourism Optimisation Management Model (2008). Background. Retrieved 16 June, 2008, from, www.tomm.info.

Travel Industry Association (TIA) 2004) *Executive Summaries – Travelers' Use of the Internet*. Travel Industry Association, Washington, DC.

Travel Industry Association (TIA) (2008). Volunteer vacations in the United States. Retrieved 6 June, 2008, from, www.tia.org.

Travis, A.S. (1985). *The Consequences of Growing Ecological Consciousness, and Changing Socio-Cultural Needs, on Tourism Policy*. Paper presented at Trends in Tourism Demand Conference, Bregenz, Austria.

Trip Consultants (2006). *Draft Papua New Guinea Tourism Sector Review and Master Plan 2007–2017: Growing Tourism as a Sustainable Industry*. PNG Tourism Promotion Authority & Independent Consumer and Competition Commission, Port Moresby, Papua New Guinea.

Tubb, K.N. (2003) An evaluation of the effectiveness of interpretation within Dartmoor National Park in reaching the goals of sustainable tourism development. *Journal of Sustainable Tourism*, 11(6), 476–98.

Tubb, P. (1997). Victoria, British Airways Tourism for Tomorrow Awards 1997, Pacific Region (unpublished).

United Nations Educational, Scientific and Cultural Organisations (UNESCO) (2001). Namha ecotourism project. Retrieved 12 December, 2007, from, www.unescobkk.org/index.php?id=486.

Valentine, P.S. (1991). Ecotourism and nature conservation: a definition with some recent developments in Micronesia. In *Ecotourism Incorporating the Global Classroom* (B. Weiler, ed.). Bureau of Tourism Research, Canberra, Australia.

Valentine, P.S. (1993) Ecotourism and nature conservation: a definition with some recent developments in Micronesia. *Tourism Management*, 14(2), 107–15.

Vanclay, F. (2003) International principles for social impact assessment. *Impact Assessment and Project Appraisal*, 21(1), 5–11.

van der Duim, R., Peters, K., & Wearing, S. (2005) Planning host and guest interactions: moving beyond the empty meeting ground in African encounters. *Current Issues in Tourism*, 8(1), 286–305.

van Klaveren, S. (2000). *Celebrate Your Porter! Research on the Structural Embeddedness of the Capitals that Porters Use in the Trekking Industry of Nepal*. Unpublished masters thesis, Catholic University, Nijmegen.

Vanuatu Cultural Centre (2008). Moratorium (ban) on commercial filming of Nagol (Pentecost island land dive). Retrieved 24 March, 2008, from, www.vanuatuculture.org.

van Veuren, E.J. (2003) Capitalising on indigenous cultures: cultural village tourism in South Africa. *Africa Insight*, 33(1–2), 69–77.

Vellas, F., & Becherel L. (1995) *International Tourism: An Economic Perspective*. MacMillan Business, London.

Verrender, J. (2000). The perfect break. *Sydney Morning Herald*, 28 October, p. 1.

Vickland, K. (1989) New tourists want new destinations. *Travel and Tourism Executive Report*, 9, 1–4.

Viñals, M.J., Morant, M., El-Ayadi, M., Teruel, L., Herrera, S., Flores, S., et al. (2003). A methodology for determining the recreational carrying capacity of wetlands. In *Marine Ecotourism: Issues and Experiences* (B. Garrod, & J.C. Wilson, eds). Channel View Publications, Clevedon, UK, pp. 79–99.

Vincent, V.C., & Thompson, W. (2002) Assessing community support and sustainability for ecotourism development. *Journal of Travel Research*, 41(2), 153–60.

Waayers, D., Newsome, D., & Lee, D. (2006) Observations of non-compliance behaviour by tourists to a voluntary code of conduct: a pilot study of turtle tourism in the Exmouth region, Western Australia. *Journal of Ecotourism*, 5(3), 211–22.

Wallace, G. (1992, 10–12 February). *Real Ecotourism: Assisting Protected Area Managers and Getting Benefits to Local People*. Paper presented at the International Union for Conservation of Nature and Natural Resources, IVth World Congress on National Parks and Protected Areas, Caracas, Venezuela.

Walpole, M.J., Goodwin, H.J., & Ward, K.G.R. (2001) Pricing policy for tourism in protected areas: lessons from Komodo National Park, Indonesia. *Conservation Biology*, 15, 218–227.

Warshaw, M. (2004) *The Encyclopaedia of Surfing*. Penguin Books, New York.

Watson, A.E. (1989, 13–14 January). *Wilderness Visitor Management Practices: A Benchmark and an Assessment of Progress*. Paper presented at National Outdoor Recreation Forum. Tampra, FL.

WaveHunters. (2005). Indonesia swell forecasting tools: Mentawai. Retrieved 22 August, 2005, from, www.wavehunters.com/mentawais/indo_swell.asp.

WCPA (World Commission on Protected Areas) (2007). Best practice guidelines. Retrieved 12 December, from, www.iucn.org/themes/wcpa/pubs/guidelines.htm#national.

Wearing, S. (2001) *Volunteer Tourism: Experiences that Make a Difference*. CABI, Wallingford, UK.

Wearing, S., & Chatterton, P. (2007). *The Practice of Community Based Tourism: Developing Ecotrekking for the Kokoda Track, Papua New Guinea*. Paper presented at the 17th CAUTHE 2007 Conference, Tourism: Past Achievements, Future Challenges.

Wearing, S., Cynn, S., Ponting, J., & McDonald, M. (2002) Converting environmental concern into ecotourism purchases: a qualitative evaluation of international backpackers in Australia. *Journal of Ecotourism*, 1(2/3), 133–48.

Wearing, S., & Deane, B. (2003) Seeking self: leisure and tourism on common ground. *World Leisure Journal*, 45(1), 4–12.

Wearing, S., & Gardiner, M. (1994). *Outdoor Adventure Programs as a Form of Nature* Interpretation. Unpublished Report, University of Technology Sydney, School of Leisure and Tourism.

Wearing, S., & McDonald, M. (2002) The development of community-based tourism: re-thinking the relationship between tour operators and development agents as intermediaries in rural and isolated area communities. *Journal of Sustainable Tourism*, 10(3), 191–206.

Wearing, S., McDonald, M., & Ponting, J. (2005). Building a decommodified research paradigm in tourism: the contribution of NGOs. *Journal of Sustainable Tourism*, 13(5), 424–39.

Wearing, S., & Wearing, M. (1999) Decommodifying ecotourism: rethinking global–local interactions with host communities. *Losire et Societe/Society and Leisure*, 22(1), 39–70.

Wearing, S., & Wearing, M. (2006) Rereading the subjugating tourist in neoliberalism: postcolonial otherness and the tourist experience. *Tourism Analysis*, 11(2), 145–63.

Weaver, D. (1998) *Ecotourism in the Less Developed World*. CAB International, Wallingford, UK.

Weaver, D. (2001a) *Ecotourism*. John Wiley & Sons, Brisbane, Australia.

Weaver, D. (2001b) Ecotourism as mass tourism: contradiction or reality? *Cornell Hotel and Restaurant Administration Quarterly*, 42(2), 104–12.

Weaver, D.B. (2002) Hard-core ecotourists in Lamington National Park, Australia. *Journal of Ecotourism*, 1(1), 19–35.

Weaver, D. (2006) *Sustainable Tourism: Theory and Practice*. Elsevier, Butterworth-Heinemann, Amsterdam.

Weiler, B., & Hall, C. (eds) (1992) *Special Interest Tourism*. Belhaven Press, London.

Weiler, B., & Johnson, T. (1991, 3–4 October). *Nature Based Tour Operators: Are They Environmentally Friendly or Are They Faking It?* Paper presented at National Tourism Research Conference. Nelson Bay, Australia.

Weiler, B., & Ham, S.H. (2001). Tour guides and interpretation. In *The Encyclopedia of Ecotourism* (D.B. Weaver, ed.). CABI, Wallingford, UK, pp. 549–63.

WenJun, L., XiaoDong, G., & ChunYan, L. (2005) Hiking trails and tourism impact assessment in protected area: Jiuzhaigou Biosphere Reserve, China. *Environmental Monitoring and Assessment*, 108(1–3), 279–93.

Wescott, G. (1993) Loving our parks to death. *Habitat Australia*, 21(1), 12–19.

West, P.C., & Brechin S.R. (eds) (1991) *Resident Peoples and National Parks: Social Dilemmas and Strategies in International Conservation*. University of Arizona Press, Tucson, AZ.

Western, D., & Wright, M.R. (eds) (1994) *Natural Connections: Perspectives in Community-Based Conservation*. Island Press, Washington, DC.

Westwood, N.J., & Boyd, S. (2005). Mountain scenic flights: a low risk, low impact ecotourism experience within South Island, New Zealand. In *Nature-Based Tourism in Peripheral Areas: Development or Disaster?* (C.M. Hall, & S. Boyd, eds). Channel View Publications, Clevedon UK, pp. 50–63.

White, L. (1967) The historical roots of our ecologic crisis. *Science*, 155.

Wight, P. (1993) Ecotourism: ethics or eco-sell? *Journal of Travel Research*, 31(3), 4–14.

Wight, P. (1994). Environmentally responsible marketing of tourism. In *Ecotourism: A Sustainable Option?* (E. Carter, & G. Lowman, eds). John Wiley & Sons, New York, pp. 39–55.

Wight, P. (1996a) North American ecotourists: market profile and trip characteristics. *Journal of Travel Research*, 34(4), 2–10.

Wight, P.A. (1996b) North American ecotourism markets: motivations, preferences, and destinations. *Journal of Travel Research*, 35(1), 3–10.

Wight, P.A. (1997) Ecotourism accommodation spectrum: does supply match demand? *Tourism Management*, 18(4), 209–20.

Wight, P.A. (2000). Ecotourists: not a homogeneous market segment. In *The Encyclopaedia of Ecotourism* (D.B. Weaver, ed.). CAB International, Wallingford, UK, pp. 37–62.

Wight, P.A. (2001). Environmental management tools in Canada: ecolabelling and best practice benchmarking. In *Tourism Ecolabelling: Certification and Promotion of Sustainable Management* (X. Font, & R.C. Buckley, eds). CABI, Wallingford, UK, pp. 141–64.

Wight, P.A. (2002) Ecotourism in the Americas in the international year of ecotourism. *Téoros, Revue de Recherche en Tourisme*, 21(3), 28–37.

Wild, C. (1994). Issues in ecotourism. In *Progress in Tourism, Recreation and Hospitality Management* (C.P. Cooper, & A. Lockwood, eds). JohnWiley & Sons, New York.

Williams, P. (1990). *Ecotourism Management Challenges*. Paper presented at Fifth Annual Travel Review Conference Proceedings 1990: A Year of Transition. Washington, DC.

Wink, R. (2005) Eco-tourism and collective learning: an institutional perspective. *International Journal of Environment and Sustainable Development*, 4(1), 2–16.

Worrall, B. (2005). Himalaya sherpas get falls creek gear. *The Border Mail Newspaper*, 12 May.

Worboys, G., Lockwood, M., & De Lacy, T. (2005) *Protected Area Management: Principles and Practice*, second revised ed. Oxford University Press, Oxford, UK.

World Bank (1992) *The World Bank and the Environment*. World Bank, Washington, DC.

WTO (World Tourism Organization) (1990) *Tourism to the Year 2000*. World Tourism Organization, Madrid.

WTO (World Tourism Organization) (2002) *Tourism and Poverty Alleviation*. World Tourism Organization, Madrid.

WTO (World Tourism Organization). (2004). Sustainable development of tourism: conceptual definition. Retrieved 6 December, 2007, from www.world-tourism.org/sustainable/concepts.htm.

WTO (World Tourism Organization) (2007). Facts and figures. Retrieved 23 June, 2007, from www.unwto.org.

WTO (World Tourism Organization) (2008). Global code of ethics in tourism. Retrieved 5 June, 2008, from, www.world-tourism.org/code_ethics/eng/global.htm.

World Wide Fund for Nature (WWF) (1992) *Beyond the Green Horizon: a Discussion Paper on Principles for Sustainable Tourism*. WWF, Surrey, UK.

World Wide Fund for Nature (WWF) (2001) *Tourism and Climate Change: A WWF Tourism Issue Paper*. WWF, Surrey, UK.

WTTC (World Travel and Tourism Council) (1994) *Travel and Tourism: A New Economic Perspective*. WTTC, Madrid.

WTTC (World Travel and Tourism Council) (2006) *WTTC Progress and Priorities: Travel and Tourism*. WTTC, Madrid.

Yamaki, K., Hirota, J., Ono, S., Shoji, Y., Tsuchiya, T., & Yamaguchi, K. (2003) A method for classifying recreation areas in an alpine natural park using recreation opportunity spectrum. *Journal of the Japanese Forestry Society*, 85(1), 55–62.

Young, J. (1990) *Post Environmentalism*. Belhaven Press, London.

Yum, S.M. (1984). Case report on attempts at alternative tourism, Hong Kong. In *Alternative Tourism: Report on the Workshop on Alternative Tourism with a Focus on Asia* (P. Holden, ed.). Ecumenical Coalition on Third World Tourism, Bangkok.

Żarska, B. (2006) Sustainable tourism in natural protected areas: the concept of the set of general planning principles. *Horticulture and Landscape Architecture*, 27, 123–31.

Zheng, G. (2000) Strategies for minimising tourism leakages in Indo-Chinese development countries. *Asia Pacific Journal of Tourism Research*, 5(2), 11–20.

3 Sisters Adventure Trekking (2006). Empowering the women of Nepal: adventure tourism training centre. Retrieved 1 June, 2006, from, www.3sistersadventure.com.

Index

A

Alaska Native Brotherhood, 135
Alternative tourism (AT), 1, 4
  definition of, 2
  features of, 5
American Birds, 5
American Society of Travel
    Agents, 49
Antarctic marine ecosystem, 23
Anthropocentric ethic, 21
Anthropocentric morality, and
    ethics of use, 18

B

Biocentric ethics, 21
Biodiversity, 21
Biosphere, 21
Biotic community, 23

C

Caracas Action Plan, 64
Carrying Capacity, 76–79
Case studies
  Amboseli National Park, 70–71
  Anangu and Tiwi Island, 124
  Australian government policy, 42
  Belize, Central American, 191
  Bhutan, 41
  Canadian tourism industry, 57
  Cape Otway Centre for
    Conservation Ecology, 100
  Catlins Wildlife trackers, New
    Zealand, 175–176
  codes of conduct in the Arctic, 50
  Cradle Mountain Huts, 172
  Dancing and The Fire Devil, 101
  diversification of ecotourism
    products, Rawanda, 58–59
  Dolphin Discovery Tours, 113
  ecotourism after Indian Ocean
    earthquake and tsunami,
    120

  ecotourism in
    Ecuador, 210
    Laos, 39
  funding for US National Parks,
    67
  Galapagos Islands, Ecuador,
    35–36
  Global Code of Ethics in
    Tourism, 118
  Great Barrier Marine Park
    Zoning Plan 2003, 60
  Great Barrier Reef, Australia, 54
  Gulf Savannah of Northern
    Australia, 111–112
  heritage trails in New Zealand,
    98
  Kangaroo Island in South
    Australia, 85
  Kingfisher Bay, Fraser Island,
    Australia, 48
  Kokoda Track, Papua New
    Guinea, 137–139
    history of, 139
    planning for trekking
      development in,
      144–146
    strategy for trekking,
      142–144
    tourism, 140–141
    trekking and involvement
      of host community,
      141–142
    trekking strategy, 142–144
  Kruger National Park, 172
  Maasai Mara, Kenya, 44
  National Geographic Traveller,
    103
  Nepalese Himalayas, 29
  Papua New Guinea, 127
  partnership between Sitka
    National Historical Park
    and native people,
    134–135

  Pentecost Land Dive, Vanuatu,
    131
  porters and the trekking industry
    of Nepal, 146–147
    implications for ecotourism
      on, 150
    Nepalese porters, 147–148
    representations in tourism
      marketing, 148–150
  pro-poor tourism (PPT) and
    World Tourism
    Organization, 125
  role of government in planning
    for sustainable
    tourism, 45
  Sakau Rainforest Lodge, Borneo,
    129
  surfing tourism in Indonesia's
    Mentawai Islands,
    156–159
  UNESCO-MAB and Costa
    Rica National Park project,
    132
Chernobyl disaster, 20
Climate care, 224
Climate change, and ecotourism,
    223–225
Code of conduct, for tourists and
    tour operators, 46–50
  areas of concern, 50
Codes of Ethics, 178
CO_2 gas emissions, reduction of,
    16
Community-based conservation
    (CBC), 218
Community-based tourism (CBT),
    2
Community-focused institutes,
    156
Conservation. *See* Nature
Conventional mass tourism
    (CMT), 2
Cultural tourism, 3

D

Deep ecology
    and influence of human beings,
        25
    principles of, 22
    and relation with nature, 22
Doldrums, 160
Durban Action Plan, 64

E

Ecocentric management, 30
Ecocentrism, 20
    perspectives of, 21
Ecological conscience, 23
Ecological economics, concept of,
        73
Ecologically Sustainable
        Development Steering
        Committee (ESDSC), 57
Ecological marketing
    definition of, 176
    issue of relationship between
        demand and supply, 176
Ecological sustainable
        development, 25
Ecosphere, human-centered value
        system, 20
Ecosystem
    and economic values, 24
    factors influencing stability of, 23
    sustainable development of
        shared, 30
Ecotourism
    alternatives of, 2–6
    approaches for developing, 48
    benefits and development of
        partnership in, 218–222
    and benefits for biodiversity
        conservation, 222
    benefits to local communities,
        34, 115
    climate change and, 223–225
    as community-based
        conservation (CBC), 218
    and community development,
        218
    cooperative government and
        industry initiatives for
        developing, 54–55
    best practice for, 56–59
    zoning, 59–61
    decision-making relating to, 121

development strategies for, 33
economic benefits of, 71
environmental and social effects
        of, 34
evolution of, 1
factors influencing planning for,
        43
forms of, 6
as funding source for conserving
        biodiversity, 227
and host–community
        interactions, 220
impacts on natural ecosystems, 1
implications for, 150
    complexities of development
        and, 151–152
    complexities of local
        economies and, 152–153
industry-led planning and
        policy for
    accreditation, 52–54
    compliance schemes, 51–52
    development of code of
        practice for tourists, 46–50
and integrated rural development
        projects, 35
interdependence on social and
        physical environment, 117
international conservation
        guidelines for, 219
international industry for, 220
interpretive techniques utilized
        by, 96–97
and local communities
    employment, 126–130
    issues and problems,
        121–125
    local planning and
        development, 130–135
marketing of, 173, 176
    opportunities in, 183–184
    strengths in, 181
    threats in, 181–183
    weaknesses in, 184–194
and natural environment, 6
nature of, 6–8
and nature-oriented tourism, 63
negative effects of, 37
place in tourism industry,
        171–172
planning and management, 223
planning and policy frameworks
        for developing

government-led planning and
        policy initiatives for,
        38–42
integrated policy and
        planning for, 42–45
as potential in generating foreign
        exchange, 33
and protected areas, 65–66
short-term, 74
supply-led approach and its
        impact on, 37
and sustainable development,
        9, 36–37
sustainable models and,
        222–223
unsustainable, 37
volunteering and, 225–227
Ecotourism Accreditation
        Committee, Australia,
        53
'Ecotourism and Small Business in
        the Pacific' conference,
        174
Ecotourism Opportunity
        Spectrum, 184
Ecotourists
    classification of, 21
    factors for motivating, 200
    model for motivating, 199
    primary groups of characteristics
        of, 196
    profile of, 196–199
    push/pull model for identifying
        desire for pleasure of, 200
    social interactions influencing,
        203–209
Ecumenical Coalition of Third
        World Tourism
        (ECTWT), 3
Energy supply, renewable forms of,
        224
'Environmental best practice,'
        concept of, 56
Environmental conservation, and
        principles of
        sustainability, 104
Environmental degradation,
        levels of, 87
Environmentalism, ecocentricity/
        anthropocentricity, 19
Environmental Management
        Industry Association of
        Australia (EMIAA), 174

Environment, quality of, 20
Ethic of nature. *See* Ecocentrism
Exxon Valdez disaster, 20

F

The Fight for Conservation, 26

G

GAIA hypothesis, 22
Global warming, 26, 178, 213, 224–225
Green Globe Programme (GGP), 51
'Greening' market, 177–180
Greenpeace, 178
Gross Domestic Product (GDP), 33
Gross National Product (GNP), 174

H

Himalayan Environmental Trust Code of Conduct, 49
The Historical Roots of Our Ecologic Crisis, 20
Human–nature relationship, 16
  ethic of use and, 17
  influence of values on, 17

I

'Industry Quality Continuum,' as guide to self-regulation, 46–47
Integrated rural development projects, 35
Intergenerational equity, 25
Intergovernmental Panel on Climate Change, 20
International Ecotourism Society, 11
International Porter Protection Group (IPPG), 147
International Union of the Conservation of Nature, 65
Interpretation
  benefits of
    as conservation management tool, 108–109
    economic, 109–110
    educational, 107–108
    problems limiting, 111–114

promotional, 104–105
recreational, 106–107
definition of, 96–97
and measurement of behavioral change, 98
principles for successful, 103–104
services of Canadian National Parks, 104
techniques
  displays and exhibits, 100
  education centers, 100
  guided tours, 102
  publications, websites and DVDs, 101
  self-guided trails, 101–102
  visitor centers, 99–100
Interpretation Australia Association, 97
Inter Tropical Convergence Zone (ITCZ), 160

L

Land ethic, evolution of, 23
Land use
  planning in developed countries, 72
  zoning, 59
Limits of Acceptable Change (LAC), 55, 76, 80–82
Low Impact Tourism (LIT), 7, 220
  characteristics of, 8

M

Mass tourism (MT), 1, 4
  concerns of, 215
Modern Environmentalism: An Introduction, 20

N

National Ecotourism Accreditation Programme, 53
National Ecotourism Accreditation scheme, 53
National park, 91
National Strategies for Ecologically Sustainable Development, 40
National Sustainable Tourism Policy, 40

Natural sciences, 26
Nature
  conservation
    of biodiversity, 63
    public support for, 63
  deep ecology and relationship with, 22
  humanities and, 22
  preservation and conservation of, 18
  tourism, 31
Non-Government Organizations (NGOs), 141

P

Participatory Rural Appraisal (PRA), 144
Pro-poor tourism (PPT), principle of, 125
Protected areas
  benefits to society, 70
  and capitalist realism, 67–70
  categories of, 66
  definition of, 65–66
  interpretation, benefits of, 109
  management of, 76
  and sustainable management strategies, 76–77
  carrying capacity, 77–79
  education, 90–92
  limits of acceptable change (LAC), 80–82
  managing visitor use, 84–85
  recreation opportunity spectrum (ROS), 79–80
  tourism optimization management model (TOMM), 84
  trial system design, 89–90
  use limitation, 85–88
  user fees and charges, 92–93
  visitor activity management process (VAMP), 83–84
  visitor impact management (VIM), 82–83
  zoning, 88
  tourism and, 65–66

Q

Queensland National Parks and Wildlife Service, 97

R

Recreational use management, 59
Recreation Opportunity
          Spectrum (ROS), 76,
          79–80, 184
Resource conservation, 26, 73
Resource management, 26
    ethics of, 28–31
Restrained development. *See*
          Resource conservation
Royal National Park, 65

S

Shangri-La Ecotourism
          Demonstration Project
          (SLED), 40
Silent Spring, 20
Social marketing, definition of,
          177
Strengths, weaknesses,
          opportunities and threats
          (SWOT) analysis, 180
Surfing tourism, sustainable
          management of, 168
Sustainability, concept of, 24
Sustainable development
    in relation to ecotourism, 37,
          222–223
    of shared ecosystems, 30
    of tourism industry, 40
Sustainable management
    models for, 55
    of surfing tourism, 168
    techniques for, 74–76
Sustainable tourism, 8–11, 38, 44
    development, 36–37
    industry planning and policy
          initiatives for, 46
    stakeholder involvement in, 54

T

Technocentrism, 20
    principles of, 21
Technological environmentalism.
          See Technocentrism
Terai Arc Landscape, 71
Tourism
    carrying capacity, elements of, 78
    destination product life cycle,
          207
    expenditure, 34
    industry, ecotourism's place in,
          171–172
    low impact, 31
    management, concept of, 77
    marketing, 175
    nature, 31
    sustainable, 25, 31
Tourism Ecodollars, 174
Tourism optimization
          management model
          (TOMM), 84
Tourist motivation
    based on Maslow's hierarchy
          of needs, 201
    'push' and 'pull' factors
          influencing, 202
Tourists. *See* Ecotourists
Tourists and tour operators, codes
          of practice for, 46–50
Tragedy of the Commons, 26
Transpersonal sense of ecological
          self, 23
Turisimo ecologico, 5

U

UNESCO-LNTA Nam Ha
          Ecotourism Project, 39

United Nations Capital
          Development Fund
          (UNCDF), 133
United Nations Climate Change
          Conference, 16, 222
United Nation's Development
          Programme (UNDP), 39
United States Aid Programme
          (USAID), 220

V

Visitor Activity Management
          Process (VAMP), 76,
          83–84
Visitor Impact Management
          (VIM), 76, 82–83
Visitor Impact Management
          Model (VIMM), 55
Volunteer tourism, 225

W

Wilderness Society in Australia,
          178
Wildlife reserve, 219
World Commission on Protected
          Areas Best Practice, 56
World Congress on National Parks
          and Protected Areas, 64
World Tourism Organization
          (WTO), 10, 218
World Travel and Tourism Council
          (WTTC), 51
World Wide Fund for Nature
          (WWF), 141, 178, 219

Y

Yellowstone National Park, 65